625.

3/71

O+B

GREAT NORTHERN STEAM

Great Northern Steam

W. A. TUPLIN
DSc, MIMechE, AILocoE

LONDON

IAN ALLAN

First published 1971

SBN 7110 0179 0

Published by Ian Allan Ltd, Shepperton, Surrey and printed in the
United Kingdom by A. Wheaton & Co., Exeter

CONTENTS

PREFACE

MALCOLM MUGGERIDGE discovered, on taking over the editorship of *Punch* in 1953, that readers complained more about the introduction of a new joke than the repetition of an old one. The editor of *The New Yorker*, he assumed, had to cater for the American passion for novelty, but the editor of *Punch* for his readers' deep and passionate conservatism. The big hand in an English music hall was always for the joke everyone knew.

I had discerned, some thirty years earlier, the same circumstance in respect of the literature of the steam locomotive. Anything that disagreed with old myths and pontifications, right or wrong, was deeply resented, and this reaction is not dead yet. Its existence comforts any author worried because he can find (for example) neither a new way of stating that the first GN Atlantic was numbered 990, nor evidence that it wasn't. But although he may be convinced that some readers would resent anything new, no writer has any easy means of finding how numerous they are; he therefore tends to take the safe and easy way of assuming them to be in the majority. This is no doubt why many interesting things have been left unpublished, so that there can be reasons for writing, even now, about Great Northern steam.

Muggeridge remarked that the funniest documents that came to him as editor of *Punch* were communications from irate readers. Editors of the popular railway journals must have had the same experience and perhaps wished that there could have been more of such stimulating complaints. Their work brought little other fun.

Every author is wise to remember that railway enthusiasts have not been encouraged to countenance humour. The subject is serious and frivolity about it is out of place. Now and again a writer might be moved to hilarity by a misprint in Bradshaw, but he won no applause by it; he had gone too far.

If you saw an engine driver open the regulator in response to the guard's green flag, only to find that the engine was not coupled to the train, you took care not to smile. A resentful frown was the right response and not a word to anyone. Study of railway working was to be conducted in solemn awe, and the constant fear of all writers about railways is that they may inadvertently let slip something that is either gay or light on unction. Some indeed are moved to read what they have written before it goes for printing, but even so, blemishes of this kind occasionally get through.

When lecturing, one is reminded by glacial facial response to any hint of levity that some of those present have not come to be amused, and one returns at once to the beaten track, but anything like a joke in print about railways remains as perpetual evidence that here the writer had let his mind wander from his job. So caution is as important in writing on railways as it is in running trains on them.

This book takes a look at generally recognised facts of Great Northern Railway history, at others firmly established in my mind because I saw for myself and at still others credibly reported by eye-witnesses. It attempts to present a coherent picture of what the engines were like and of how some of them did their work.

I gratefully acknowledge the work of the numerous earlier writers in this field, and specially that of F. A. S. Brown for what he has told of Great Northern Locomotive Engineers.

I have made many references to G. F. Bird's classic *Locomotives of the Great Northern Railway*, notable for its very numerous reproductions of careful line drawings, and also to the *Railway Magazine*, the *Locomotive*, *The Engineer*, *Engineering*, and so on.

I am specially indebted for photographic illustrations in this book to T. G. Hepburn, to Kenneth Leech, to R. A. H. Weight and to British Rail.

A common type of comment on books on railway subjects prompts me to remark that in writing this one, I was compelled by limitations of space to reject about 93 per cent of the information that I might have used in it.

Although a great deal of time and effort have been expended in determining and checking the numerous figures in this book, I do not believe that they are all right. (A youthful ambition to write the first book with no numerical error was abandoned after a little experience.) One does one's best with all available help, but can only apologise for the errors that are sure to have got through. There could be about ten in this book.

NOTATION

IN THIS BOOK the Whyte convention is used for defining the wheel arrangement of a locomotive, eg 4-4-0 except that, to save space in tables, the dashes are omitted so that 4-4-0 becomes 440. The letter T signifies a side-tank engine, ST a saddle-tank engine and WT a well-tank engine.

Except where the locomotive has two inside cylinders and no others, the Whyte designation is preceded by a figure equal to the number of cylinders and by the letter C if the engine used compound expansion.

Thus the standard Ivatt Atlantics are classified as 2/4-4-2 and the compound Atlantics are 4C/4-4-2.

For convenience in locating any class of locomotive in Table 5, it is identified by its reference-number in the first line of that table. Thus n35 implies a large Atlantic and n38 the Vulcan compound Atlantic.

GENERAL BACKGROUND

THE GREAT NORTHERN RAILWAY began operations in 1848 and ended in 1922 because it was then merged into the group called the London & North Eastern Railway. The three largest railways of Britain before the grouping of 1923 were the Great Western Railway, the London & North Western Railway and the Midland Railway.

The Great Northern was roughly half the size of the average of these and approximate figures relating to it in 1922 are:

Total route length	700 miles
Running powers over	250 miles
Number of locomotives	1360
Number of passenger vehicles and others of similar style	3500
Number of goods vehicles	38000

The main locomotive "districts", each including a number of running-sheds, were 1 Doncaster, 2 Peterborough, 3 London, 4 Nottingham, 5 Leeds, 6 Bradford, 7 Grantham, 8 Lincoln, 9 Retford, 10 York GN, 11 Manchester GN.

In each district the head man at the main shed was responsible for a number of sub-sheds. In the ordinary way each locomotive in service carried at the back of the cab-roof a disc embossed with the number of the district that included the running shed to which the locomotive "belonged" at the time.

Great Northern engines normally worked as far north as York and Harrogate, as far east as Hull, Grimsby, Skegness and Cambridge, as far west as Stafford. The southern limit was London, a rather vague description that might include sub-Thames journeys with goods trains to such places as New Cross and Hither Green.

There was great variety in the geographical nature of Great Northern routes between the flatness near The Wash and the mountainous gradients, curves and tunnels on the route from Keighley to Halifax, between the sulphur of the Metropolitan tunnels and the wind-swept purity of the rural height at Stoke Summit. But there was no special deployment of locomotives to cope with this variety except that singles were kept out of the West Riding, apart from their use on the main line from Doncaster to Leeds, and that only engines with condensers were allowed to go down on to the Metropolitan line from Kings Cross.

Till 1853 the locomotive repair works of the GN were at Boston. In that year the works on an 11½-acre site at Doncaster began repairing GN locomotives. It was not until 1867 that a locomotive (0-4-2) No 18 (n23) was built there and as late as 1921 the GN was still buying locomotives from private firms in Great

Britain even though the Doncaster Works had expanded on to 200 acres and employed about 4500 people.

All matters concerning the acquisition, design and running of GN locomotives were under the control of:

Archibald Sturrock	1850–1866
Patrick Stirling	1866–1895
H. A. Ivatt	1895–1911
H. N. Gresley	1911–1923

The basic colour of GN engines was green but before 1866, goods engines were black, and after 1916 they began to get painted grey.

Round about 1880 a change was made to a darker green. Smokeboxes were black and the outer surfaces of frames were reddish brown; the inner surfaces were bright red. Lagging bands and panel lines were white-edged black.

Each engine was numbered and lettered in dignified style by transfers. The initials GNR were displayed on tender or tank; the running number was displayed on each side and also on the front buffer beam and on the rear buffer beam or the rear of the bunker. Each engine had at least one "works plate" identifying its origin in time and space.

This book does not concern itself with details of the very earliest locomotives on the GNR. It begins with the appointment of Sturrock in 1850. Of the locomotives then running on the GN, the most notable were a set of 50 small 2-2-2s known as "Little Sharps", the proper noun being derived from the name (Sharp Bros & Co) of the builder and the adjective a reference to their size. Comparable in style and dimensions, but less numerous, were the 20 "Small Hawthorns" built by R. & W. Hawthorn between 1847 and 1851 and numbered 51-70. Their general design was quite similar to what Sturrock had become used to on the Great Western Railway and he was probably glad to find himself at home in at least one part of his new job. He felt no compulsion to introduce immediately to the existing staff any revolutionary ideas about building or running engines. That might come later, but at the start it was satisfactory to be able to follow already accepted practices.

MAIN LINE GRADIENTS

THE GN MAIN LINE was less mountainous than is suggested by the gradient profile on p. 12. The vertical distances on that diagram are 264 times as great as the real heights in relation to the horizontal distances. This makes them catch the eye. Fine detail has not been attempted in drawing this diagram; its purpose is to give a general picture of the grades to be surmounted.

The number associated with each place-name in the diagram is the height (in feet) of the track at that point above Ordnance Survey datum. Height differences over a few miles may not be very reliable; for any distance greater than 20 miles they are good enough to serve as a basis for estimating power exerted in overcoming gravity. The upper edge of the thick line represents the average gradient between the points at the ends of any straight parts of it.

Some published gradient profiles are wrong in showing a level start out of Kings Cross. It is very distinctly downhill (at about 1 in 100) from the platform-end and although the fall extends only to the mouth of the tunnel, it is a great help in getting a train on the move. From the tunnel-end there is a good mile up 1 in 107. This makes for a slow start, but offered no real difficulty to steam engines provided that the sanding gear was working properly; if it was not, slippery rails could mean real trouble.

Out in the country the steepest gradient is that of 3 miles at 1 in 178 from Corby (97 miles) to the summit at Stoke box. Then there is nothing worse than 2 or 3 miles up 1 in 200 here and there on the way to Doncaster.

Beyond Doncaster there is no gradient worth mentioning right on to York and the net rise is only 25 ft in 32 miles. The only serious speed-restrictions on the York run were at Peterborough and Selby.

Notable is the near coincidence in height of the three summits at Stoke, Woolmer Green and Potters Bar. At Stoke, in the parish of Bitchfield and Bassingthorpe, the scene is still as rural as it was in the days of Stirling, but changes have occurred at the other two places.

Gradients as steep as 1 in 150 occur between Doncaster and Wakefield; between there and Leeds are stretches of a few miles at 1 in 100. To get out of Bradford means climbing 1 in 50.

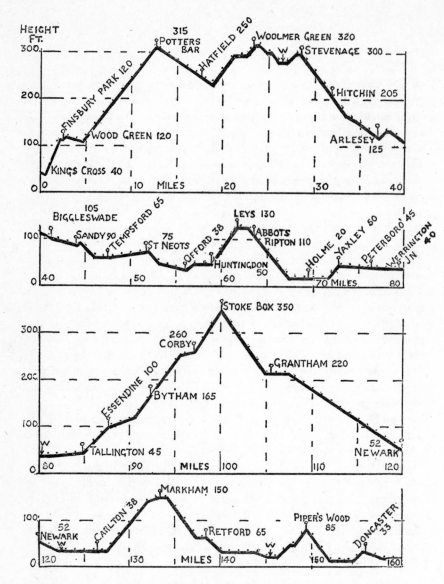

FIG. 1. Gradient profile, Kings Cross to Doncaster.

CHAPTER ONE

Introductory

THE VERY NAME "Great Northern" with its hard "th" gave the impression that this was a tough aggressive customer fit to cope with the rigours of the far north. One retains vague memories of pictures of fire-spitting locomotives tearing through the night and casting a ruddy glow on their steam clouds in a colourful race to the north. When one heard the official statement that "the Great Northern Railway ended in a ploughed field four miles north of Doncaster" one was a little surprised, but this was at a time of life when one found many things surprising. It seemed odd to be running trains with such splendid energy only to end in a ploughed field. One wondered whether it was not so much the railway as the trains themselves that ended in ploughed fields because they went so fast that the track would not hold them. It was naughty, although dramatic, to mention the ploughed field without adding that another railway, heading south, ended by a valuable coincidence in that same ploughed field and that the rails of the two lines were laid, in fact, in the same furrows.

And with the Great Northern was that most famous train-name in British railway history, the "Flying Scotsman". As the Kings Cross station clock struck ten in the morning, a high-stepping single-wheeler scrabbled the "Flying Scotsman" out of the station, down into the tunnel and then up and away to the north. Daylight was less romantic than darkness and the day-Scotsman did not fly so excitingly over the metals as the "Tourist Express" did on certain occasions in the summer of 1895.

It was mildly disappointing to learn that Great Northern engines were painted (even the goods engines) in a lightish shade of green. One had expected black (like on the North Western) or perhaps battleship grey as befitted a hurrying fighter; green seemed too restful a colour for a renowned go-getter.

Before the writer had seen any GN locomotives he had been delighted to examine official postcards depicting the more notable classes in vivid (though factual) colour. He was impressed most of all by a sturdy-looking single-wheeler No 267 and perhaps the more so because in those early days it was possible to buy a readily recognisable pressed-tin replica of No 267 about 3 in long. Not only was the locomotive replicated in "tin" but so also was a very solid plume of black smoke obviously pressed backwards by a high relative wind in spite of vigorous vertical projection from the chimney.

Moreover this was a running model. The wheels of the engine and the axle-boxes of the tender were reproduced on a flat tin surface that just cleared the surface of a floor when the engine was set down on it, because the weight was taken by four tin discs mounted on two axles and hidden within the space enclosed by the united right-hand and left-hand pressings.

Furthermore this was a working model. In the tender a lead flywheel was carried on a spindle that rested on the rear wheels within the constraint imposed by extension of the spindle through a vertical slot on each side-sheet of the tender. By rotating the flywheel one could wrap a fair length of strong thread on the spindle. An upward pull on the thread would life the spindle clear of the wheels and spin the flywheel before it dropped, on complete unwrapping of the thread, on to the rear wheels whereupon the engine would move forward or backward (one could with a little care and thought predict which) until friction had dissipated the kinetic energy of the flywheel.

This model was too lightly made to stand up for long to children's hands and so fatal damage usually came early. There was never any question of repair because a brand-new replacement was obtainable for the sum of one penny. Repeated requests for "a penny black-smoke engine" emphasised the writer's earliest acquaintance with anything positively associated with GN steam.

The reading-matter on the Great Northern postcards indicated that Doncaster was no mere Roman camp site. It included a works where they built GN locomotives; nothing else they did in the town could be so interesting to an engine-enthusiast as was that activity. Butterscotch they might make and horse-racing they might tolerate but engine-building was a rare speciality. This was a place to visit some time.

Before the railway came, Doncaster was a small market town on the Great North Road, a little to the south of its bridge over the River Don. Between the town and the bridge, the Road and the GNR intersected in what was a level crossing till well into the 1900s, and the establishment of the locomotive works to the west of the station in 1867 made an increasingly big difference to the town. It was never so completely a "railway town" as was Crewe nor did the activity in Doncaster station compare in volume with that at Crewe, but it had more varied interest for the observer in that locomotives of six railways in four colours were to be seen regularly and that many trains ran through it at speed.

The office block of the Locomotive Works and Carriage works hid them from any observation from the station and the engine shed ("Carr Loco") was a mile away to the south east abreast of extensive sidings on a flat area of marshy land. In that region, signal box names like Childers Drain and Decoy hinted at its nature and the wild fowl that had been one of its attractions for some people.

To the north of the station the main line threw out on the west a branch to Wakefield and Leeds and on the east one to Hull and Cleethorpes. To the south a westward line ran to Sheffield and Manchester. At Black Carr Junction $2\frac{1}{2}$ miles to the south east, diverged the Lincoln line.

Doncaster was thus a bottle-neck into which three northbound routes converged and immediately diverged. This main line layout was very simple compared with the complex of auxiliary lines normally used only for goods and mineral traffic in the neighbourhood of Doncaster. For much of every day the station was a scene of great activity, on summer Saturdays it was feverish and on the three St Leger days in September it was fantastic. At the headquarters of Great Northern steam, manual labour, manual dexterity and manual signalling handled trains at a rate beyond the credulity of those who have known only the sophistication of long-range electrical signalling in its more serene sites. Liverpool Street at a rush hour is one of the few comparable cases in the 1970s.

Although the "Flying Scotsman" tradition is firmly attached to the GNR and although that railway was long and rightly associated in many minds with railway speed, the fastest GN trains were not (usually) trains running between London and Scotland. It was competition with the Midland Railway for traffic from London to Sheffield and the West Riding of Yorkshire that inspired the liveliest regular efforts of Great Northern steam. Even with World War I well on the way one could travel from Leeds to London in 3 hr 25 min, with time to stop at Wakefield to pick up coaches from Halifax and Huddersfield. The latter linked that town with London in 4 hr 2 min but World War I did "kill" this connection. It never reappeared and its time was never beaten on any route in the "up" direction. Let's see what it was like.

The first stages of the journey were deceptively deliberate. The London coach, at the rear of a Lancashire & Yorkshire three-coach set, left Huddersfield 3 min after a London & North Western train booked to stop at Bradley and Mirfield and therefore bound to delay the London coach before it reached Mirfield. There it was backed into an east-facing bay, the coaches in front of it were taken away and it awaited the arrival of a GN train that had left Halifax at 1.15 pm and had come rather sharply down the Calder Valley, although calling at all stations. This train was backed onto the coach from Huddersfield and proceeded further down the valley calling at Thornhill and Horbury to reach Wakefield (West-gate) at 2.01 pm. An engine attached at the rear then took the London coaches up the curving rise to Wakefield (Westgate) and through the station, backed them alongside the up platform and pulled them ahead again to lie in a loop alongside the incoming line from Leeds until the main train rolled in at 2.17 pm behind a big green engine, a GN large Atlantic No 1426. Green engines were never seen at Huddersfield and so now we were quite clearly in new country.

Still another reversal in direction of movement brought the Halifax coach up against the train from Leeds and the Huddersfield coach was the last of six in a non-stop train to London. We were ready for "off" at 2.20 pm, 57 min after leaving Huddersfield about 15 miles away by rail. It was clear that things would have to get moving soon and so they did.

With six vehicles weighing about 220 tons, a downhill start at 1 in 100, a nicely warmed up large Atlantic and a driver going home, we left Westgate with what seemed like electric train acceleration after what we had suffered earlier. We passed Sandal (1.7 miles) in just over 3 min and touched almost 60

mph in the dip beyond. We were in the country by then, running between fields
as green as the engine under bright sun in a late spring. Before us lay a hundred-
and-seventy-odd miles of moving pictures of a strange land. The prospect left
us with envy for no one, but we would do a bit of timing whilst watching what
went by.

Four miles up at 1 in 150 pulled our speed down to 50 mph. Then, diving for
Doncaster we passed Hemsworth at 61 mph, South Elmsall at 75, Hampole at
78 and Carcroft at 79 after which steam seemed to be shut off and speed gradually
fell as we ran past Castle Hills towards the junction with the GN main line where
the brakes went severely "on", and we ran cautiously on to the station. Signals
were evidently adverse and we almost stopped on the through line abreast of the
station, in 19 min 55 sec after leaving Wakefield.

After this furious start the rest of the running seemed sedate. There was time
to look around and for a stranger to the route there was much to see. One would
have liked a longer look at the engines ranged outside Carr Loco, one noted
saddle tanks and 0-6-0s moving or brooding among the coal wagons near
Decoy on the right, a line rising on the left to coil round and pass overhead,
Black Carr signal box and the flying junction with the Great Eastern line and
the convergence of goods lines right and left. With the train up at the mile-a-
minute rate that should suffice to get it on time into Kings Cross, one saw
Rossington Church, the plantation associated with Rossington Hall and the
signal box called Piper's Wood at the top of the rise. Then down through a
cutting, round a bend past a water-softening tower and along a viaduct with a
high-level view of red-roofed Bawtry. We touch 70 as we skim the Scrooby
water-trough and keep going at that rate or a little less to Retford where we
note the sensational curvature of the line to Sheffield, and the sharp tattoo of the
wheels over the level crossing with the Great Central line from Worksop to
Gainsborough. You can't see much of Retford from the railway but Ordsall
Church shows prominently on the right before the train runs under the Great
North Road and begins to climb to Markham. This is a nuisance to the driver of
a heavy train that has started from Retford but a large Atlantic that has passed at
speed with only "six on" hardly feels it. The scenery in every direction is easy
on the eye, the mile-posts are on the right if you want their aid in timing the
train and the rail-joints are below if you don't.

After Askham Tunnel the view opens out on the left and a little search reveals
Lincoln Cathedral about 20 miles away. But now we are tearing down past
Tuxford with a glimpse of an engine shed belonging to the Lancashire, Derby-
shire & East Coast Railway and we pass under the main line at the interchange
station of Dukeries Junction. A few fast miles down 1 in 200 follow before the
train crosses the Great North Road on the level at Crow Park where it is useful
to note the time as the next station, Carlton, is just a mile away. It takes 49 sec
to cover the distance, corresponding to 73·5 mph in fair accordance with the
rail joint estimate of 74 just before we reached the crossing. The country is very

flat round here and at Muskham one forms the impression that the GN had decided to get another water-trough in while it lasted. Speed falls a little (after all we don't *need* to do seventy all the way) but we boom briskly through the great bridge over the Trent, do a very quick rat-tat-tat over the Midland line to Lincoln and the fireman resigns himself to an almost continuous rise of 20 miles from Newark to Stoke Summit beyond Grantham. It calls for no undue exertion on this train but if the engine had "fifteen on" it would be a different matter, 660 tons to lift instead of 330. But there's no real hurry. We passed Newark at 3.20 pm and even if we were to take half an hour over these next 20 miles we should still have 95 min left for 100 miles to Kings Cross and the first 20 of them very fast and easy. But things are nothing like so "tight" as that. We are doing a mile a minute as we pass Balderton signal box and the driver could afford to let speed drop gradually to 40 mph at Stoke without having anything to bother about. These are our reflections as we examine the striking spire of Claypole Church and look ahead at the hill barrier about seven miles away. Nothing steeper than 1 in 200 has to be climbed but after two miles of it past Barkston Junction we have come down to 50 mph at the entrance to Peascliffe Tunnel. We come out onto a level stretch through pleasant parkland, pass over the Great North Road again, spare a glance for Barrowby Road Junction where an Atlantic (No 276) was disastrously derailed in 1906, and another for the engines outside Grantham shed. We pass at 3.38 pm at about 55 mph, run under the Great North Road and begin the five miles at 1 in 200 to Stoke box through some of the pleasantest country on the whole trip. It is partly in cutting but through the breaks are wide views on the right and the sight of the Somerset-style church tower at Great Ponton is breath-catching. We hear a little more than heretofore of the Atlantic's chimney chatter especially as she takes us into Stoke Tunnel. We make a check and find her to be doing 45 mph just before passing Stoke box, the highest point between York and London. It's 3.45 pm and so we have 100 min for the last 100 miles. Even allowing for severe speed restriction through Peterborough and slow running over the last two miles into Kings Cross, a little over a mile-a-minute will do the trick.

Before us stretches Essendine Bank, ten miles averaging 1 in 300 down followed by ten miles still favourable and no curve to call for speed restriction. Ninety miles an hour has been touched on this length. Shall we do it today? It's not likely! There is no need for it as there is no justification for haste. But we must look out for the top speed usually just after Little Bytham or after Essendine. So we gaze about at the billowing countryside as the engine picks up speed on this fine bit of road. The train glides smoothly through the quiet fields and copses seemingly remote and timeless and the fleeting glimpse of Corby station hardly spoils the illusion. We reflect on this for a minute or so and then we catch sight of two magnificent farm houses in old grey stone and of an architectural style that brings us back to earth and what part of earth? The Cotswolds! Where on earth are we going? The Cotswolds? How?

No! we're going from Yorkshire to London by a direct route but this part of the world is geologically identical with the Cotswolds and it is geology that decides what the country looks like and what can be done with it. But here is Little Bytham and it's time to see how fast we're going. From rail-joints beats we find we're doing eighty or perhaps a little more. We try again and get eighty-two. A third trial shows eighty-two or perhaps eighty-three. This seems to be the limit. Essendine Junction flashes by and yet another trial shows about eighty. Speed then drops slowly off as we continue to roll smoothly through parkland past Tallington station, past Lolham box with a lovely old road-bridge over a stream nearby (there is actually one such bridge on each side of the railway) and soon after a railway runs towards us from the right. On it, as we get together, is Helpston station with the village church tower not far away. Thence the (Midland) line lies close to the GN main line right into Peterborough. Then suddenly the brakes go rather sharply "on" and the engine tender skims the top layer of water from a trough just before we reach Werrington Junction. Eighty miles to Kings Cross and no more troughs.

We are getting far from home now as the unfamiliar names on coal wagons in station sidings have told us. Coote & Warren is a combination unknown in Yorkshire and so also is Gilstrap Earp on a malthouse just before we come to the engine shed and large area of railway sidings at New England. We had picked up some speed after picking up water, but we soon begin to slow down again. Indeed brakes now go on pretty hard and we seem not to be greatly exceeding walking pace as we take a sharpish left bend to run under the station roof at Peterborough. We note the time is 4.05 pm and are delighted to see on the right a 4-4-0 painted in a fabulous yellow-brown colour. It has a Midland outline and belongs in fact to the Midland & Great Northern Joint Railway extending from here to Yarmouth.

We cross the River Nene and pick up speed smartly before passing Fletton Junction signal box and rows of tall brickworks chimneys sometimes called "the Peterborough poplars". Fletton bricks have a high reputation and this is where they are made. Deep pits show the origin of the raw material and large double-bogie wagons in sidings are to convey bricks in quantities to London. We soon pass this small industrial area, the only one we have noticed since clearing Doncaster, and we are down onto a fen. The land has drains rather than roads but we do cross a road at Holme station and at Connington start to rise from the plain on an embankment that leads into a cutting containing Abbots Ripton station. A little further on we evidently pass over a crest and then make a dive for Huntingdon. We dash through at 70 or so, fly over the Ouse and then for a mile or two keep within sight of its winding banks. For 20 miles from Huntingdon we run at about 65 mph over undulations averaging level and then adverse 1 in 200 faces us.

We pass the tree-decked platforms at Sandy and the sandy hill that must have inspired the name and we note the North Western branch to Cambridge bearing away to the east. After the oddly-named station of Three Counties we start a climb passing the Cambridge-line junction just short of Hitchin where GN engines lie by the shed alongside the station.

Chiltern-style scenery makes this stage of the journey as attractive as any and softens the feeling, three and a half hours after leaving Huddersfield, that it is about time we were getting there. Are enginemen affected by environment after running a long way without a stop? Does a careful driver see much more than the track ahead of him at any time?

In principle he ought never to look anywhere but ahead except when necessary to help the fireman to cope with the difficulties that occasionally arise in keeping the boiler well supplied with water and coal. After finding none but favourable signals all the way for 150 miles is a driver likely to get into a frame of mind that disinclines him to believe that there might be an unfavourable one just ahead? While we browse over speculations of this kind the train is still covering 25 yd a second and one hopes that drivers' minds don't wander even when they are getting a bit jaded. A short downhill beyond Stevenage raises the speed but then we go up again past Knebworth and after Woolmer Green box we plunge into a couple of tunnels in quick succession. We dash through Welwyn station and onto a high viaduct. We are picking up speed all the time and touch 75 before Hatfield where once again the grade is against us and our tireless Atlantic has another pull up to Potters Bar.

How are we doing? It's 5.09 pm, 16 min left, with 12½ miles to go. No need to rush. The driver keeps her pulling till she's through the first tunnel and doing about 65. He then shuts off steam and without losing speed the train runs through a quick succession of tunnels and stations with no help but from gravity.

Among the fields in sight of the train there are signs of suburbia and by the time we pass Wood Green it seems certain that London is not far away. This is confirmed by the extensive sidings and engine shed at Hornsey and by Harringay the houses are closing in. Finsbury Park is a large junction station, multiple tracks join us now, carriage sidings follow and as the train goes down into grimy cuttings with brakes tentatively "on" we are nearly there. We pass through a tunnel, come out for a "breather", pass more slowly through a second tunnel and come out cautiously onto the fan of lines leading to Kings Cross platforms, with trains headed by engines keyed up to retrace our steps, slower still we run and at length come very gently to rest at 5.23 pm, four hours to the minute since we left Huddersfield. We get out and as we walk along the platform we look at the engine and have a feeling that we ought to say, "Fancy meeting you here! You were in Wakefield when I saw you last." The enginemen have already got her set for backing out of the station and the driver has started to go round her feeling wheel-bosses and axleboxes with the back of his hand. He may well find everything "quite cool" as he says, but the average man-in-the-street should be cautious about touching anything so described by such a man.

So this is Kings Cross, as reached by Great Northern steam! There is no better way but we feel glad that we don't have to start back on the 5.45 pm out even though we might thus be in Huddersfield again by 9.59 pm only 8 hr 37 min after we left.

We go to the outer end of Platform 10 however to see trains leave at 5.30 pm for Newcastle (through coaches to Middlesbrough and Saltburn), 5.45 pm for Leeds and Bradford (through coaches to Halifax and Huddersfield) and 6.05 pm for Hull with coaches for Sheffield and Manchester.

During this time GN tank engines leave with suburban trains and if we like to remain till 6.15 pm we may expect the up "Scotsman" which left Edinburgh at 10 am and runs up non-stop from Grantham in just over 2 hr.

The afternoon and evening have shown some variety in the application of Great Northern steam but it is hardly a representative picture. To obtain that we should need to spend some time on main line stopping trains, on branch line stopping trains, on night trains and on excursion trains. Even this would leave goods train working untouched and of course it always was untouchable by a non-railwayman apart from very special permission and promises not to tell anyone. It is some solace to reflect that what the amateur enthusiast was not normally allowed to see would probably have been less interesting to him than what he could see or could learn from magazines and books.

But those hidden things were vital. If a heavily-laden goods engine failed to struggle from Grantham up to Stoke and get onto the relief line in the time allowed, it could derange the GNR right back to Doncaster and Nottingham. It could stop southbound "flyers" as effectively as could their vacuum brakes. So goods engines had to be kept in good running order by men at the running-sheds whose insides might have inspired the description "dark, satanic mills". There, regular maintenance and running repairs had to be carried out in very uncomfortable circumstances. There the sleekest flyer and the humblest shunter were pulled apart, probed and restored against time in darkness and dirt. Ardent admirers of the steam locomotive may prefer not to know about this, but the full picture must pay tribute to the men who did such work and to the cleaners who turned engines out again looking as if nothing had happened.

Steam on the Great Northern Railway (as on any other) is thus a wide subject. Here we shall try to find a middle course between beaming on the exalted ancestry of chief mechanical engineers and tut-tutting four-letter words from men excruciated by the worst jobs in keeping the engines in order. We shall look at the Stirling singles that did their share in the 1895 Railway Race, at the Ivatt Atlantics that beat their fastest efforts with far heavier loads and at the Gresley 2-6-0s that could cope with coal-trains or with top-rank main line passengers, but we shall try to remember that such engines were far outnumbered by very ordinary six-wheelers that did most of the work and brought in most of the money. We shall certainly remember the Gresley Pacifics, born at the last Great Northern minute to dominate running on the East Coast route for a quarter-century and more.

CHAPTER TWO

Four Engineers

STURROCK (1850-1866)

I DON'T KNOW whether you've noticed, but the first thing a bright boy does when he gets a very good job is to appoint an assistant to do the work, so that he himself can concentrate on holding the job. This is how Archibald Sturrock came to become, at the age of 24, Assistant Locomotive Superintendent of the Great Western Railway. Daniel Gooch had been appointed Locomotive Superintendent at the age of 21 (!) and rather naturally thought that he could do with someone a bit older to do the real work. So he "sent for" (to use the managerial verb) his friend Sturrock who had served an apprenticeship in the East Foundry at Dundee where he learned how to make molten metal behave.

So Sturrock went to the Great Western in 1840 and took charge of the newly built Swindon Works in 1843. Under his supervision the 2-2-2 type of locomotive was built for passenger trains but fractures of leading axles led to the substitution of the 4-2-2 wheel-arrangement, not with any leading bogie but with all eight axleboxes taking load from the main frame. As this general design persisted in GWR broad-gauge locomotives for over forty years it was evidently well on top of requirements in the 1840s and 1850s.

Sturrock had thus had ten years of most valuable experience when he joined the GNR in 1850. His headquarters were at first at Boston, but not long afterwards he took charge of the new GN works at Doncaster. The main activity there was originally the repair of locomotives and it was not until 1867 that Doncaster built a new locomotive.

In his early days on the GWR, Sturrock had become used to the practice of ordering private builders to supply locomotives to GW designs. He used this method in building up a reliable stock of locomotives for the GNR. He laid down main principles and principal dimensions, but builders were allowed latitude in details. Consequently there was fair variety in the 400 locomotives supplied by some 15 different manufacturers to the GNR between 1851 and 1866. General characteristics of the Sturrock designs were outside frames (which were common enough in Great Britain at the time) and boiler pressures up to 150 lb/sq in which was unusually high. Well over 60 per cent of these locomotives were of the 0-6-0 tender type that has always dominated the British railway scene. Of the remainder about a quarter were 2-2-2 engines and about a sixth were 2-4-0s.

Right outside the general run were two outside-cylinder 2/0-8-0 tank engines built by the Avonside Engine Company for the purpose of bringing GN goods trains from the vicinity of Blackfriars through the Metropolitan Railway tunnels with gradients as steep as 1 in 35 in climbing into the comparatively fresh air at Kings Cross. These engines were similar to two others previously supplied by Avonside to the Vale of Neath Railway. They might well have been specially designed for this special job on the GN, and indeed they remained on it for 14 years, but no similar engine was ever used for that service. Like many of the "special" engines, these were good enough to keep but not to multiply.

They had condensers in their side-tanks, to accord with Metropolitan requirements for working in tunnels; what coal they could carry had to be stacked somewhere on the side-tanks, as there was neither a bunker nor space for any.

Sturrock's other "specials" were the famous 4-2-2 No 215 and the "steam tenders" noted separately on p. 97.

Many people may well regard Sturrock as one of the most "successful" men who ever lived. He was in industrial employment from the age of 16 for 34 years and then began a new life of 43 years in luxurious retirement. This cost money, of course, and an old legend is that Sturrock secured it by a lucrative marriage. F. A. S. Brown has established, however, that whatever happened it did not include marriage. But such obligations as Sturrock accepted, left him with leisure to pursue an active country life in which he did his bit in the local control of nature by shooting birds, catching fish and encouraging dogs to mangle foxes. Not everyone will find envy uppermost in his reactions to contemplation of this part of Sturrock's life but many would be prepared to risk it. Sturrock himself might have chosen differently had his relations with the GN in 1866 been happier. His steam tenders, he had to admit, could not be justified and the GN could not afford expensive failures. He may have been asked to submit his resignation but even if the atmosphere was not so highly charged as all that, he could discern that the likelihood of his receiving a "golden handshake" from the company on retirement was much too weak to justify him in ignoring a guaranteed equivalent from without.

His retirement from his position with the GN did not sever his connections with Doncaster Works and there is a well-known photograph of him and Ivatt posed before a "Long Tom" 0-8-0 in 1907. The intermediate incumbent, Stirling, had died some 12 years earlier.

On January 1, 1909 Sturrock died in his 93rd year at his home in Cadogan Place where he had been roughing it since 1889, when the more robustious sides of his rural life were becoming a bit too much even for him.

STIRLING (1866-1895)

It may have been mere coincidence that Patrick Stirling, Sturrock's successor as head of Great Northern steam, had also served his apprenticeship at a foundry in Dundee. On the other hand it is possible that the GN directors, seeking a successor to Sturrock, had considered that as he was, apart from a tendency to expensive experiment, a very good man for the job, they might do well to get someone else from the same stable and to impress on him that there was no money for building anything that might not earn its keep.

Apart from any consideration of this kind, Stirling had an admirable background of experience. After 1843 he had had jobs with the Vulcan Foundry, Warrington, with Neilson & Company, Glasgow, with R. & W. Hawthorn, Newcastle, had been locomotive engineer with the small Bowling & Ballock Railway and had been for 13 years Locomotive Superintendent of the Glasgow & South Western Railway. Obviously he would have no difficulty in filling the position left by Sturrock at the head of a department developed with great competence over a period of 16 years. It was not a job that demanded any exceptional imagination or unorthodox technical skill; the need was for more locomotives, and perhaps bigger locomotives and, as usual, means of reducing running costs.

During the 30 years of his reign at Doncaster, Stirling was responsible for the building of about 850 new locomotives. Of these, 210 were tank engines of wheel-arrangements (0-4-4T and 0-6-0ST) not used by Sturrock, but Stirling's 194 0-6-0s were less numerous than the 0-6-0s bought for the GN by Sturrock. Stirling built 88 singles, more than twice as many as those ordered by Sturrock during his 16 years with the GN.

Patrick Stirling's brother James and his son Matthew were also locomotive superintendents in Great Britain and they were united in their preference for domeless locomotive boilers. Blood is thicker than water and they were satisfied that they (or at least the men who had to run their engines) could keep the mastery over boiler-water without using steam-domes. Sturrock had also come from a domeless school but, having got away, adopted the dome as a standard component of every locomotive.

Domelessness, a rigorously smooth external style, and single frames distinguished the general run of Stirling locomotives from those of Sturrock. Double frames were used by Stirling only for 2-4-0s and 2-2-2s and the outside frames had no axlebox for any driving axle. Outside cylinders were limited to 53 locomotives of the 4-2-2 wheel arrangement and these were consequently marked departures from the general Stirling style.

People have waxed almost lyrical about the beauty of the Stirling singles and if they had confined themselves to the Stirling 2-2-2s the writer would have been well disposed to agree. But he cannot evade the impression of primitive crudity conveyed by the sight of an outside cylinder driving a single wheel. It calls to mind the elemental working "model" steam locomotives that were sold in shops in the reign of Victoria and that would no doubt command very high prices in an age when £500 is quoted for a discarded nameplate. It calls to mind Stephenson's *Rocket* and the very few of his other engines with that layout. It seems to be an appalling anachronism or at least an incongruity in a locomotive that is otherwise a neat example of Victorian practice. To the writer's eye the Stirling 2-2-2s were incomparably superior and he felt happily justified in that opinion when he first learned that they were in fact better engines in that they could do, at lower cost, anything that the 4-2-2s could do.

But the name of Stirling has long been associated with "8 ft single" and will no doubt continue to be so associated even though engines of that description were not his most useful product.

Concentration of figures for dimensions of locomotives into columns in chronological order makes it very easy to discern trends and changes with time. The impression one gains in this way about the 30 years of Stirling's superintendence at Doncaster is that there was no marked trend or change at all. The most important class of locomotive, the 0-6-0s built in 1896, were pretty much the same as those of 1866, apart from being heavier because of strengthening to take higher steam pressure. There were however many variations in detail and one perceives a marked difference from what was done at Crewe Works, which over 50 years or so turned out over 900 0-6-0s of one class and 500 of another and 310 of yet another.

Similarly the Stirling 2-4-0s built in 1895 differed in little but boiler pressure from those introduced in 1867.

An odd thing about Doncaster Works practice under Stirling was that they were usually building locomotives of different classes slowly and simultaneously whereas concentration on one class at a time might seem more economical.

What enlargement there may have been of GN motive power requirements over 30 years could evidently be covered by building more locomotives rather than different ones and so the technical side of Stirling's job demanded no special brilliance. Over the years it got easier because of advances in metallurgy; steel became cheaper than wrought iron and far more reliable. Experience developed skills in manufacturing operations; fewer jobs would go wrong. One feels that Stirling's position was hardly more stressful than that of Sturrock in his retirement and Stirling may well have thought for a long time that there was no point in retiring.

But things do change eventually, and the GN got caught up in some of them. There was, for instance, rivalry between the East Coast and West Coast railway routes from London to Scotland. For years it set no special problem to the motive power departments but the "race to Scotland" in 1888 made a flurry and that of 1895 produced a frenzy. The aftermath was a truce on speed but competition in provision of amenities. This meant heavier trains and therefore engines that were stronger without necessarily being faster and this suggested a possible need to abandon a cardinal feature of Stirling's design policy. He insisted that no express passenger train on the GN should have more than one engine and that that engine be limited to a single pair of driving wheels. To maintain this he had increased driving axle loads on his singles to nearly 20 tons and rails were beginning to break under them. He began to see, and so did others, that singles were soon going to be overmastered by the train-loads and so his 29-year old policy would have to go. At the age of 75 he could not easily cope with a situation of this sort and it may not have been pure coincidence that he died a few months after the "Railway Race" of 1895.

The legendary prowess of the Stirling singles has led writers to pay humble homage to the memory of Patrick Stirling and his portrait has been published in many books. It is that of a benign old gentleman with a nose a shade too aquiline to be entirely handsome, but it suggests nothing out of keeping with what one expects of the son of a clergyman. But F. A. S. Brown's account of Stirling, not an 8-footer but certainly 6 ft 4 in by 2 ft by 1 ft 3 in, reproving an ungrateful workman with a neat kick where it would do least harm, gives a different impression of this renowned Scot. It suggests a surprising incongruity between the man and his engines which, in appearance at least, were plain and demure rather than huskily aggressive.

IVATT (1895–1911)

The coming of H. A. Ivatt to the Great Northern was dramatic. Without even showing the loaded revolver that tended to be his constant companion in Ireland he fixed his own salary. Soon after he moved in, he walked over the GN main line between Doncaster and London and told the GN Chairman that if he had known that the track was in such a mess he would not have taken the job on. Soothing words and track improvements soon followed.

One's first thought about Ivatt's inspection of 150 miles of track is that it was a personal affront to the Civil Engineer as it implied refusal to accept an official statement on the subject. Reflection, however, suggests a quite different and more probable alternative. The Civil Engineer must have known that the track was defective and having unsuccessfully applied for expenditure to put it right probably used the newly-arrived Ivatt to repeat his own complaints far more forcefully than he himself dared to do. As it was in Ivatt's own interest that something should be done, and quickly, he would naturally use his temporarily unique position to underline what was probably a long-standing complaint by the Civil Engineer. An immediate protest from a new recruit gets far more attention that it would if he delayed it for six months.

It is interesting to speculate about the details of Ivatt's long walk and to wonder whether he took his revolver with him. There are some lonely stretches on the GN main line and rural suspicion of strangers extended well into the 20th century.

As Stirling's final headache had been the failing ability of his singles to cope with the heaviest express trains, one would have thought that Ivatt's first care on taking charge at Doncaster would be to produce a four-coupled engine with a boiler not smaller than that of the latest Stirling singles. He certainly produced a 4-4-0, No 400 (n20) in 1896 but its boiler was no larger than that of the Stirling 2-4-0s and indeed Ivatt also applied it in ten 2-4-0s that he himself built in 1897.

Ivatt saw no harm in domes and they soon became an identification mark, on the GN, of Ivatt locomotives.

Ivatt's first advance on the Stirling singles was seen in No 990 (n34), turned out of Doncaster Works in the middle of 1898. This engine was the first Atlantic in Britain and that was its one and only distinction. The design was simply a rational reinforcement of the Stirling 8 ft single. The urgent need was for greater adhesion weight and so a second pair of large wheels was inserted in front of the driving wheels and coupling rods divided the driving effort between them. Although the coupled wheels were 16 in smaller in diameter than the driving wheels of the 8 ft singles the overall length of No 990 was much greater than that of No 1 even after the wheels had been packed closely together.

No 990 was followed, within a year, by the first Lancashire & Yorkshire 4-4-2 No 1400. This engine was identical with No 990 in wheel arrangement but differed markedly in practically everything else except height and width.

No 990 remained the sole engine of her class for some two years during which she worked some of the principal main line passenger trains on the GN. She was by no means universally welcomed by enginemen or by the operating department. Stirling's remark that a coupled-wheel engine in motion was like "a laddie running wi' his breeks doon" had impressed some professional engineers almost as deeply as it was bound to impress amateurs. Ivatt learned that during a period of his absence from GN territory, No 990 had remained idle in Grantham shed because the man in charge didn't like coupled engines on fast passenger trains. For deliberately keeping the engine out of traffic to which she was well suited, at a time when it was important to find how she reacted to service conditions, the official was "demoted" by Ivatt from Grantham to York.

Ivatt's most dramatic contribution to the development of British locomotive design was the large Atlantic No 251 (n35) produced in 1902. It had the same wheelbase as No 990 but a much larger boiler with a wide firebox extended laterally over the rear part of the frame to obtain a grate area of 31 sq ft, a figure not surpassed by any extensively multiplied design of British locomotive till the first Gresley Pacific (n69) appeared in 1922.

Because the firebox was wide, even this large grate area was accommodated in less than the usual length of firebox and so the side view of the engine gave no hint of it. As it was, No 251 looked large to the astonished observers in 1902 but she was in fact larger still in the origin of her power. These Atlantics were never extended to their limit until the 1930s and the very lateness of their full flowering seemed to some observers to imply a touch of mysticism in their conception and subsequent modifications.

On the freight side, Ivatt's 0-8-0 (n71) was a conventional enlargement of the elemental 0-6-0. It did its job, it was multiplied, which showed that it was not bad, but there was no means of deciding whether it was better or worse than the average British eight-coupled goods engine.

The 0-8-0 design was extended to produce a 0-8-2 tank engine (n74) intended to revolutionise the handling of Kings Cross suburban passenger trains by replacing the 4-4-2 tank engines and 0-4-4 tank engines that were dealing with it. But the 79-ton weight of the newcomer was found to be unacceptable by the Metropolitan Railways so that it could not take trains between Kings Cross and Moorgate. So it was lightened by shortening the side tanks and ten similar engines were built in 1904. Thirty more came in the next two years.

In 1906 Ivatt made another stab at the Kings Cross suburban job by trying a new 0-6-2T (n61). This also turned out to be too long in the tank to comply with Metropolitan weight restrictions but when this had been altered there remained an engine that could beat the 4-4-2Ts; a total of 56 were built.

Long before he came to the GN, Ivatt had tried compounding in a 4-4-0 built at Inchicore in 1895. He found, as everyone in Britain found, that compounding could not be relied upon to show any worthwhile advantage in ordinary service. Nevertheless when the short fashion for compounding struck Great Britain after the GW had bought a compound from France, Ivatt complied with it to the extent of building two 4-cylinder compound Atlantics and ordering another from the Vulcan Foundry. There is more than a hint that this was done more as an assurance to the GN directors that Ivatt was "on the job" than as a serious experiment. An alternative possibility is that he was instructed to try compounding on the GN in spite of his conviction that it was worthless. The cylinder dimensions he chose for the first GN compound (n37) were such as to ensure that compounding was not going to be any good in this particular engine.

Ivatt tried superheating in a small Atlantic from the middle of 1909 and was sufficiently impressed to order the building of ten large Atlantics with superheaters. These were completed in 1910 to bring the class to a total of 91.

These were the engines on which Ivatt's fame was based and by which it was extended after his retirement in 1910 and indeed after his death in 1923. They are among the most notable British locomotives of all time.

Ivatt was a down-to-earth engineer, not easily persuaded from practical commonsense by any apparently contradictory consideration that anyone might falsely deduce from natural laws. He once remarked that "A loco fitted with complicated gear which produces (indicator) diagrams with beautiful square corners is, I believe, no better in practice than one with the old link-motion which, very possibly, turns out a diagram shaped like a leg of mutton."

This expresses great truth, with an appropriate hint of levity conveyed by the reference to a leg of mutton. In actual fact, there was no special virtue or beauty in square corners and no real object in attaining them. An ideal indicator diagram might look as much like a leg of mutton as any other kind of leg.

GRESLEY (1911-1923)

The resignation or retirement of the head of a department in any large organisation leaves a vacancy that is preferably filled by promotion of a member of the
organisation, unless indeed a better man can be found outside it. This, of course,
is often difficult to judge but the appointment of a successor to Ivatt on the Great
Northern had been made easier than it might have been by the character of
H. N. Gresley, the Carriage and Wagon Superintendent at Doncaster. Ivatt
had placed Gresley in that position in 1905; his previous experience was in
similar work on the Lancashire & Yorkshire Railway after five years on locomotive work at Crewe, and three more at Horwich. He had impressed Ivatt
with his energy and progressive outlook, and it would have been hard to find
anywhere a better man for control of the GN locomotive, carriage and wagon
work. So Gresley was appointed in succession to Ivatt in 1911. To be given such
a position at the age of 35 was unusual in the 1900s; things had altered a great
deal since Gooch took charge of Great Western locomotives at the age of 21!
Gresley's appointment over the heads of older GN men who may well have
been quite worthy candidates must have disappointed them, but nothing in
Gresley's subsequent career suggested that the GN might have done better to
appoint anyone else to the top job at Doncaster.

The first locomotives built at Doncaster after Gresley took charge were 0-6-0s
(you couldn't go wrong in building 0-6-0s for any British railway) with 68 in
wheels that suggested "mixed traffic" rather than ordinary goods work. By this
time Churchward on the GW had produced his first 2/2-6-0s with 68 in wheels
for mixed traffic and it was easy to see the advantage of this type of engine over
a 0-6-0. All such engines tended to be heavy at the front end. The addition of a
pony-truck relieved the leading coupled wheels from some weight and some
flange-load in curving and made outside cylinders practicable. In turn these
eliminated need for crank axle and offered the possibility of bringing driving
mechanism and valve gear out into the open. But the way the crossheads
(unless of the three-bar type) on a 2-6-0 obstruct access to the leading crank-
pins in nearly every angular setting of the driving wheels is maddening.

In his first 2/2-6-0s (n66) Gresley improved on the Churchward design by
placing the valve gear outside and this was less startling at Doncaster than it
might have been as at least four GN engines had previously been fitted with
outside Walschaerts valve gear. Gresley tried ten of these 2/2-6-0s for a couple of
years and then began a series of similar engines (n67) (later LNER Class K2)
generally similar but with large boilers.

In the meantime he had made an analogous development of the 0-8-0 by
building some 2/2-8-0s (n76) with Walschaerts valve gear.

For the first time in GN history some 0-6-0 side-tank engines (n63) were built
and were shedded at Ardsley, between Wakefield and Leeds, for short distance
running with goods trains in that district.

Gresley's rebuilding of Ivatt Atlantic No 279 (n41) with four cylinders and Walschaerts valve gear complicated the engine without any benefit that justified any similar rebuilding. Ivatt Atlantics were improved by piston valves and superheating but no other change ever did any good that was worth the expense.

Ivatt was convinced that there was no point in building a locomotive with more than two cylinders unless there was no alternative, but by 1914 everyone knew that some British locomotives with four cylinders were doing very well indeed. Moreover it was easy to see that a locomotive of maximum power within the British loading gauge would need to have more than two cylinders unless its boiler pressure were much higher than the average of about 175 lb/sq in in 1914. The North Eastern had adopted the three-cylinder principle rather widely by this time and it was reasonable to reflect that if you must have more than two cylinders, three were possibly better than four.

Gresley tried three-cylinder propulsion in a 2-8-0 (n77) built in 1918 and in it used a mechanism whereby the valve for the inside cylinder was driven by combining the motions of the other two valves, operated by outside Walchaerts valve gear in the usual way. The mechanism was criticised in the columns of *The Engineer* and no doubt elsewhere. It was not repeated, for within two years Gresley adopted a very much superior mechanism devised by H. Holcroft, and used it afterwards as a standard component in hundreds of locomotives. (Such "conjugating mechanisms" were not new in 1920; David Joy had produced one as far back as 1882.)

GN 3/2-6-0 No 1000 (n68), built in 1920, was the first locomotive to have the Holcroft/Gresley conjugating mechanism. It was the largest 2-6-0 ever used in Britain and after the initial batch of ten, the LNE built or bought 183 more of them.

Kings Cross suburban traffic always wanted stronger engines. Ivatt's 0-6-2 tanks did quite well whereas his 0-8-2 tank had not met requirements at all. So Gresley built, primarily for this service, enlarged and superheated versions (n62) of the Ivatt 0-6-2 tank and these were so good that 60 were eventually built for GN needs.

Ivatt Atlantics could make good time with heavy passenger trains, but were slow in getting them off the mark. So uncertain were they in covering the first mile out of Kings Cross with a big train that during the coal-strike period of 1921, when heavy trains were being run to minimise engine-mileage, an engine was attached in front of the Atlantic to help in making a quick start and in climbing to Potters Bar, where it was detached. To meet probable requirements in a year or two, the top GN passenger train locomotive was going to need six-coupled wheels for reliable starting and this, in conjunction with the wide firebox that was such a valued feature of the Atlantics, would demand either a 2-6-2 or a 4-6-2.

Gresley had considered the former in some detail, and experience with his 2-6-0s at high speeds tended to show that a leading pony-truck could well be satisfactory. Nevertheless a 4-6-2 could be expected to be safer in this respect and in 1922 Gresley produced one (n69).

No 1470 was not just an enlarged and extended Ivatt Atlantic; it was also a "modernised" one. The wide firebox had a forward extension into the large end of the boiler barrel, which was coned from a record-breaking 6 ft 5 in diameter at the back end to 5 ft 6 in (equal to the Atlantic) at the front. The barrel ended just ahead of the coupled wheels so that the tubes were less than 20 ft long. The front of the smokebox was only just ahead of the bogie centre and so it looked a little "pushed back".

An eight-wheel tender was long enough and high enough to match the generous proportions of the engine, which seemed to promise that here was something that would set up new standards of performance on the GN main line. So it did and in the course of time and with detail improvements the Gresley Pacific established itself as one of the most notable designs in the history of the steam locomotive in Britain. One may feel glad to be old enough to have been able to greet it with critical interest when it first appeared.

A second identical Pacific was also completed at Doncaster in 1922 and this brings to an end the story of Great Northern steam proper. It came only at the start of Gresley's great work on the LNE although the creation of his first Pacific was perhaps a longer stride than any other he ever made. The term "Gresley Pacific" gradually became as significant as "Flying Scotsman" associated since the 1860s with the GNR.

CHAPTER THREE

Six-coupled Six Wheelers

(AND 0–6–2TS)

RAILWAYS WERE ORIGINALLY MADE as a means of transporting minerals, goods and merchandise economically, which meant not specially fast, and over the history of steam as the tractive agent on railways it was the non-passenger trains that brought in the bulk of the revenue. For the large part, six-coupled six wheel engines did the work; it may well be that they were the only engines that earned more than they cost. They were so numerous and, on any one railway, so similar that they were less attractive to the average railway enthusiast than were the passenger-train "flyers". Moreover he was not able to record their normal work in such detail, or with such possibility of assessment, as was the case with the passenger engines, and so he could only guess whether this or that goods engine was a "good" one or not.

0–6–0s

For 50 years or more the GN 0–6–0 classes altered little in main dimensions. The trend was upwards in size and power but it was barely perceptible. Indeed many of the goods engines remained at work for 40 or 50 years with only small modifications, if any, to the original design.

Sturrock, Stirling and Ivatt each left his mark on GN 0–6–0s. Sturrock used outside frames and domes, but no cab. Stirling used inside frames, no domes and not much cab. Ivatt retained inside frames but reverted to domes, added something like a roof to the Stirling cab, and fattened the boilers a bit. When Gresley took charge he built more of the biggest Ivatt 0–6–0s but did not produce his own design with that wheel arrangement until the LNE had got into its swing.

Stirling rebuilt some Sturrock 0–6–0s with domeless boilers. Ivatt rebuilt Stirling 0–6–0s with domed boilers. Gresley reboilered many Stirling 0–6–0s and Ivatt 0–6–0s.

The vast majority of GN 0–6–0s had Stephenson link-motion working flat valves between the cylinders. Some of the later 0–6–0s had rocking levers whereby the link-motion worked flat valves above the cylinders. The GN 0–6–0s with superheaters had piston valves above the cylinders.

Wheel-diameter was generally either 55 or 62 in (as wear in service reduces the diameter by anything up to 3 in, there is no point in quoting half-inches for this dimension). When, in 1908, Ivatt went up to 68 in, he probably felt that as the engine was at the top of its class in this respect it might properly have the same number (1) as was given to the first GN 8 ft single 38 years earlier. That engine had been happily preserved and when, 30 years after the appearance of 0-6-0 No 1, the old single ran again on the old GN line, the goods engine had been renumbered 3001 by the LNER and so there was no chance for anyone to cry "Snap!"

An outstanding item (n49) in Table 5 is the GN Class I of six engines, built between 1871 and 1874. They were big engines in that their grate area of 18·4 sq ft was not matched by any later GN 0-6-0 until 1908 and very few British locomotives have ever had 28 in piston-stroke in inside cylinders. There is a tradition that a crank-axle with 14 in throw cannot be made strong enough and if there is any truth in this, it might help to explain why GN Class I was never expanded. It has also been suggested that the reason for this was that the engines were found to be "too big" (or perhaps "unnecessarily big") for their work, but this might have been recognised without actually building one.

The 19 in cylinders of Class I were just too fat to admit valves between them. So the valves were placed below the cylinders and in fact below the leading axle. They were worked by the usual link-motion, rocking shafts and links lying below the axle. So that the distance between the cylinders and the valves could be minimised the crossheads were guided by single slide-bars above them.

The size of the Class I locomotives and their screw reverse (which is slow and laborious when shunting) suggests that they were intended for heavy main line goods trains rather than for the general run-of-mine work done by the average 0-6-0.

It happened that a particular geographical condition prohibited these bigger 0-6-0s from taking the heavier loads that they were able to handle. This was the spacing of level crossings on the GN main line through the city of Lincoln. Because of complaints that stationary goods trains were blocking the streets for unconscionable periods, it was decided that no train that was to go through Lincoln should be longer than the minimum distance between successive crossings, lest a delay on the railway should block two streets at once: Sturrock's "steam tenders" could take trains longer than the sidings; Stirling's intended substitute could take trains too long for Lincoln. So only six were built.

The later GN 0-6-0s did a fair amount of passenger train working and so far as wheel-diameter is a factor, the 68 in wheel 0-6-0s were the most suitable for the job. It has been said, however, that the higher pitch of their boilers made them less happy at speed than were the other 0-6-0s which were preferred by the enginemen. Whether the preference really arose out of the character of the riding is something that cannot now be established. Enginemen could base dislikes on matters too trivial for the authorities to consider, and would therefore complain on some other ground more likely to be taken seriously.

0-6-0STs (n55 to n60)

Until the year 1913, 0-6-0 tank engines on the GN had saddle-tanks, and Stirling produced the first GN locomotive of this description in 1868. Table 5 shows the increase in dimensions of successive classes till 1897.

Class J4, introduced in 1890, is distinctive because the four engines were built to run to Thames Wharf and their maximum height above rail level was restricted to 10 ft 10 in because of a low bridge on the way. Perhaps to diminish the risk of damage to enginemen's heads by this bridge, "all over" cabs were provided for the first time on GN 0-6-0 saddle-tank engines and on all subsequent locomotives of that description. Earlier ones had longer cab roofs than those of Stirling tender-engines and the "cutaway" was similar in shape to that of the old hansom horse-cabs.

But some enginemen complained that the all-over cabs were too hot at times and so 20 of the largest GN saddle-tanks, built in 1901-02, were given roof-ventilation through a 6 in high gap between the edges of a large rectangular hole in the roof and a slightly larger rectangular plate above it. Whoever made the drawing for this departure from the existing standard probably wondered why anybody had ever started putting all-over cabs on the GN saddle-tank engines.

For working on the Metropolitan line a few of Class M4 were fitted with condensing apparatus which included a cylindrical projection above the saddle-tank. Some observers regarded this as a cautious move by Stirling towards the use of domed boilers but that was not the case. Indeed even the first five members of Class M6 had Stirling chimneys, domeless boilers and brass safety-valve covers, but all subsequent 0-6-0 saddle-tank engines had built-up chimneys, domes and Ivatt cast-iron covers to Ramsbottom safety-valves.

Most of these engines had ejectors and vacuum pipes so that they were not debarred from handling passenger trains in emergency. More importantly, they could work empty coaching-stock trains and act as passenger-station shunting engines. Most importantly they shunted in goods yards and ran short trips with goods trains.

0-6-0Ts (n63 and n64)

The first GN 0-6-0T was No 167 produced by Gresley in 1913 and it was notable in several ways.

It had a superheater that was large in relation to the boiler and that was removed after a few years' service. The other nine engines in the first batch had no superheater nor had any of 30 similar GN engines or of 48 others built between 1923 and 1931 by the LNE. This is in accordance with the general opinion that a superheater is of little used in a shunting-engine as its periods of hard work are normally so short that the fire never gets hot enough for the superheater to make much difference to the temperature of the steam that passes through it.

The most striking external feature of these engines was extension of the side tanks to the front of the smokebox, the large cutaway in them to give access to the motion, their great width and the bevelling of the front of their top surface to improve the view through the front look-outs of any low vehicle that the engine approached.

The bunker had eight coal-rails spread vertically to cab roof height and "stepped" so as to leave a clear view through the back look-outs even with the bunker packed to the limit with coal.

This feature was not included in a modified version of the design, first produced in 1922, but the frame was lengthened to increase the capacity of the coal-bunker from 2 tons to $3\frac{1}{2}$ tons. Even at the originally quoted total weight of 57 tons these were strong six-wheel shunting engines.

These GN engines were among the heaviest six-wheel locomotives ever to run in Great Britain. LNE versions of the class were quoted as weighing over 58 tons even though they had boilers smaller than that of No 167 and similar in main dimensions to those first applied by Stirling to 2-2-2s in 1870. But even at 58 tons they barely matched the weight of the 1500 Class 2/0-6-0PT produced by the Western Region of BR in 1949.

Because these engines were originally allocated to Ardsley shed they were, in their later days, identified as "Ardsley tanks". Until well after the grouping of 1923 they were virtually confined to the West Riding of Yorkshire but the later engines built by the LNE had a wider territory. They were not normally used on passenger trains and there has been no hint that they could safely match the mile-a-minute gait of GWR standard pannier tank engines.

GN 0-6-2Ts (n61 and n62)

In an attempt to deal decisively with the Kings Cross suburban/Metropolitan problem, Ivatt stepped from 4-4-2Ts to 0-8-2Ts but was no doubt disappointed to find that the big engines were no marked improvement on the little ones. Work was therefore found elsewhere for the big ones and the problem was re-examined with the reflection that as the bold masterful stroke had not succeeded, perhaps something more modest should be tried. Accepting this, a six-coupled engine was the obvious choice and practice elsewhere suggested that a 0-6-2T was the thing to try.

So a good solid 0-6-2 condensing tank engine No 190 was built in 1906, and as usual, the Metropolitan Railway engineer found it to be too heavy. So, as in the case of 0-8-2T No 116, the tanks were shortened and the weight was then accepted.

The celerity with which this was done rather suggests that Ivatt believed that whatever was built, the Metropolitan would find it to be too heavy. They had probably come to regard this as a right that they would not lightly relinquish. So the thing for the GN to do was to build an engine heavier than what was deemed to be necessary in order that it could be lightened in polite deference to the Metropolitan's wishes and then be just right for the job. This supposition matches known events exactly and the 190 class (n61) was the best that the GN had placed on Metropolitan metals up to that time. There were later detail alterations such as the one that enabled the men to get into the cab without "ducking" under the entrance-arch.

Engines of this type, without condensing gear, also did well on local passenger trains over the steep GN grades in the West Riding, and a total of 56 were built before 1913. Some of them were later fitted with superheaters and were distinguishable by two small snifting valves just behind the chimney.

After World War I, Gresley looked at the Kings Cross suburban scene and found that whilst the 0-6-2Ts were satisfactory there was room for a little "pepping-up". Piston valves plus a bigger superheater make a good recipe for this operation and that is how the Gresley 0-6-2T No 1606 (n62) came into being.

Piston valves above the cylinders caused the boiler to be raised by 7 in, and the dome and chimney to be cut down by the same amount. The change in appearance was very noticeable. In place of a demure creature looking afraid to hurry, came an aggressive go-getter straining to show what she could shift and then proclaiming that she was shifting it in a voice of crisp decision such as was never matched at Kings Cross till *Pendennis Castle* turned up in 1925. The similarity of the chimney-height of No 1606 and No 1000 caused some observers to believe that the new tank engines also had 6 ft boilers, but that was not so. The actual diameter (56 in) and the other major dimensions of the boiler were the same as those of the boilers in the Ivatt 0-6-2Ts.

For feeding the boiler with tank-water heated by condensed steam, the Gresley engines each had a Westinghouse water-pump attached to the front of the right hand tank. Ordinary injectors will not pick up warm water and earlier GN condensing tank engines each had a crosshead-driven pump for feeding the boiler with water from warm tanks.

In later years an injector was developed to handle hot water and when an engine was fitted with these, the Westinghouse water-pump was removed.

Ten of the Gresley 0-6-2Ts were built at Doncaster and 50 by the North British Locomotive Co. Between 1924 and 1930 53 generally similar locomotives were built for the LNER.

CHAPTER FOUR

Single-wheelers

A LOCOMOTIVE with a single driving axle used to be called a single-wheeler or a single. The former word is used as the title of this section, in spite of its suggestion of a monorail, as the latter is hardly sufficiently descriptive.

Single-wheelers did a great deal of the express passenger train work in Victorian times and this, in conjunction with the (usually) large diameter of their driving wheels tended to associate them with speed.

Patrick Stirling was strongly opposed to coupled-wheel engines for fast running and he was equally opposed to using more than one engine on any one train. He was on the point of abandoning these oppositions when he died; GN requirements were tending to overmaster single-wheelers and to cope with the most difficult jobs, assisting engines were becoming necessary. Ivatt came at the right time to save the situation with four-coupled engines. When he retired, the need for six-coupled engines was just emerging.

But through nearly all the Stirling period the maximum pull thar any passenger train demanded lay below the maximum that could be exerted through the friction of a single pair of wheels carrying 19 tons on clean dry rails

GN 4-2-2 NO 215 (n4)

Under the superintendence of Gooch on the Great Western, Sturrock had expanded the original 2-2-2 locomotive design into the 4-2-2 that dominated the locomotive landscape of the GW throughout the life of the broad gauge right down to 1892. With something rather better "up his sleeve" Sturrock left the GW to join the GN in 1850 and after producing designs to cover basic needs, he built No 215, which was a standard-gauge version of the sandwich-frame broad gauge single in more elegant-looking form in that the wheelbase was longer. But this caused derailment on sharp curves and so something different was needed.

It is surprising to learn that at one time bogies were considered to be unsafe at high speed. This was, however, when many of the bogies used had only a short wheelbase. It is not hard to believe that a bogie with wheelbase not much greater than the distance between the rails could be liable to run in a skewed position with flanges grinding on the rails, or could suffer violent rotational oscillation about its vertical axis. Sturrock knew all this and, realising that a leading bogie is basically advantageous, placed one with 7 ft 2 in wheelbase under the front end of No 215. But some of the clearances were so fine as to vanish when frames were deformed by the action of moisture on the wooden centres of the sandwiches. The bogie was then reluctant to swivel and derailments recurred. There was, however, no difficulty in putting matters right by enlarging clearances.

Equalising levers between the two rear axles and equalising levers between the bogie axles gave the bulk of No 215 the desirable "3-point support", two at the rear and one in the middle of the bogie. The driving wheels were flangeless and so the engine had 2-point lateral location on the track.

No 215 was about 40 per cent bigger than was necessary for any job on the GN at the time and no similar engine was ever built. Sturrock seems to have produced her to show the directors that he was a really live man able to give them what they would want if the East Coast group (Great Northern, North Eastern and North British Railways) should decide to run trains from Kings Cross to Edinburgh in 8 hr. This had evidently been mooted as far back as 1852, but some 80 years had to elapse before that time was achieved by regular trains.

So there was never any need for 215 to prove that she could do what Sturrock had promised. She remained as a Triton among minnows that did all that the GN needed for the next 15 years or so. By that time Sturrock had been succeeded by Stirling who scrapped No 215 when heavy repairs became necessary but used the driving wheels in a Stirling 2-2-2 No 92.

To give an idea of the "advanced" character of No 215 it may be mentioned that on the GNR, apart from what Sturrock himself did, her boiler diameter and grate area were not surpassed for over 40 years. One may regret that, so far as is known, No 215 made no "demonstration run" by which her powers may be assessed. The absence of any notable performance by a rather special engine produced for a specific purpose may make one wonder whether she was so good as her dimensions suggest she could have been. She may well have had defects that were not worth correcting because, in spite of them, she could meet current GN requirements. This kind of thing happened half a century later in respect of the GWR's *The Great Bear* Pacific.

In accordance with common British practice at the time, there was no roof over the footplate of No 215. The men had no protection against the weather-elements except that when the engine was running forward a low weatherboard above the firebox might deflect some of the relative wind over their heads. In addition there was another "windbreak" in the form of a plate about 3 ft ahead of the weatherboard and this was probably quite a comfort to the enginemen at speed.

In accordance with GW practice at the time (Sturrock kept interest in what Gooch did) No 215 had no brakes. Normally braking effort was obtained from handbrakes on the wheels of the tender. Great Western tenders had brake blocks on only three of the six wheels; whether No 215 was better provided in this respect is not made clear in recorded history. But her tender did have the GW "iron coffin" from which a man could keep watch over the train.

An odd feature of No 215 is that the sandboxes were ahead of the smokebox and the sand pipes were attached to the guard-irons at the very front of the engine. By ensuring that no sand could be dropped through the pipes on to the rails whilst the engine was running round a curve this must have caused crews to curse. If the sand-pipes had been flexible, and attached at their lower ends to brackets fixed to the bogie frame, the sand might have been directed onto the rails in all circumstances. This was done, 80 or 90 years after the building of No 215, on Chapelon four-cylinder compound 4-8-0s in France.

GN 2-2-2s (n1 TO n8A)

Just as the simplest practicable all-adhesion locomotive is a 0-6-0, the simplest practicable single is a 2-2-2. The GN used this wheel arrangement before adopting the 2/4-2-2. The last 2-2-2 (n8A) was built 24 years later, the last 2/4-2-2 (n11) following within a year. So the longer class did not supersede the shorter one and it may be doubted whether there was justification for building it at all. Although the last half dozen 2/4-2-2s, built in 1894/5, were distinctly larger engines than the largest 2-2-2s they do not seem to have done any better work on the road.

The earliest 2-2-2 (n1) produced by Sturrock was an extensive rebuild in 1851 of a 4-2-0 of a group of "Cramptons" ordered from Longridge & Co before his appointment. One of these engines took the first Kings Cross-York train (October 1852) on the first stage of its journey but the class as a whole were unsatisfactory. Sturrock's first rebuilds of them were known as "converted Cramptons". They were very successful and ran what were at that time some of the fastest trains in Britain. These were scheduled to run from Kings Cross to a stop at Hitchin, 32 miles in 38 min at an average of 50½ mph with a steep start, 8 miles climbing at 1 in 200, and average adverse gradient from end to end of 1 in 1000. Even though the coach-load did not exceed 100 tons, this was good going for an engine weighing less than 30 tons. Present-day dwellers in Hitchin may well wonder by what artifice their predecessors persuaded the GN to provide a 38 min train from Kings Cross in 1857. (In 1938, certain trains ran from Hitchin to Kings Cross in 37 min with a stop at Welwyn Garden City. In 1970 the best time was 35 min, representing an average gain of just over 1½ sec per year.)

The twelve "Large Hawthorns" (n3) of 1851 were given that name to distinguish them from the ten "Small Hawthorns" (1848) and they were in fact of about the same size as the "converted Cramptons" (n1). They were 2-2-2s with outside frames; some had domes, but none had a cab. They had overhung springs, with equalising levers between the leading axle and the driving axle. No 210 of this class figures in a remarkable story related by Michael Reynolds who used to insist that engine-driving was not just driving an engine. The story (as relayed by G. F. Bird) runs:

"The down Scotch express was going down Retford Bank, signals all clear, when Oliver Hindley saw a train going east from Sheffield to Lincoln, which would meet him on the level crossing. He could not stop, and with that clear mind which is so marked in Englishmen in time of danger, he put on full steam and sent Mr Sturrock's beautiful express engine clean through the goods train, scattering the trucks like match splinters, and carrying all safe. When asked about the matter, Hindley said he could not keep clear, so he would clear away his obstruction. There is no doubt that, had he hesitated or feared, many lives would have been sacrificed. No 210 engine carried the dents and scars like an old warrior, and looked handsomer than ever for this brush with the enemy of express trains."

This was perhaps an acceptable story in Victorian days, but more knowledgeable readers in the 20th century will discern that it is not complete. Quite clearly the guard of the goods train must have been no less alert than Hindley. He saw that whilst No 210 might well pass between two wagons of the goods train, those to the west of the main line would continue to move to the east, and so derail the passenger train unless he did something about it. So, quick as thought, he slammed on his brake to stop the rear part of his train very quickly and in the right way to break a coupling so that the forward part of his train could continue in motion while the other part stopped clear of the down main line. He did this so successfully that No 210 and her train got through with hardly a scratch. Thus a desperate situation was saved by one man's swift perception, lightning decision and action applied with such precision as to suggest that he must have had a lot of practice. And then somebody else got the credit!

Stirling's first 2-2-2s (n6) built in 1868 were in main dimensions similar to Sturrock's 229 class (n5). They had double frames; the driving axle boxes were in the inside frames and the other axleboxes were in the outside frames. This feature persisted in all the GN 2-2-2s and 2-4-0s.

In the writer's view the appearance of the early Stirling 2-2-2s was spoiled by the built-up chimney and the sector-shaped slots in the driving wheel splashers. Stirling seems to have formed a similar opinion during the 15 years following the completion of Class B, for Class Q (n7) of 1885 had smooth chimneys and plain splashers.

A year later an enlarged version (n8) of Class Q appeared and this was (with n8A), to the writer's eye, Patrick Stirling's most distinguished design. To contemporary eyes the tender may have looked colossal, its uppermost coal-rail overtopping the boiler. The heaviest tender used later was indeed heavier than the engine in working order and very few British locomotive designs have had this feature.

One may admire the neatness of the Stirling 2-2-2s but one's attitude may change on realising that neatness was achieved partly by hiding things that ought to be easily visible for maintenance purposes. Laminated springs, for example, rarely suffer sudden complete failure; that happens only when the number of broken plates in a spring has become so great as to make it unable to carry the load. Plate-breakage of exposed springs is easily noticed by anyone working round the engine. The front and rear springs of a Stirling 2-2-2 could not be properly inspected without lifting the engine off its wheels. To the writer's eye the engine would have looked better with exposed springs matching those under the tender. In some Ivatt rebuilds of these engines, the springing was altered in this way.

The axleboxes on the front and rear axles of the 2-2-2s had a small amount of side-play so that the engine could get round sharp curves at low speed, but there was no centralising mechanism, and so the 2-2-2s swayed when running on the straight. There was no particular danger about this in moderation if the track were strong and true, and the enginemen soon got used to it.

STIRLING 8 FT SINGLES (n9 n10 n11)

However much one may admire the Stirling 8 ft singles for their looks or for their abilities, one has to admit that it is hard to find a real reason for introducing the design. On the other hand there might have been a reason for building no more 2/4-2-2s after the first dozen or so. At no time did they show themselves to be stronger or faster than the Stirling 2-2-2s which Stirling himself declared to be less expensive to build and to run. If that had been proved it would have been a reason for ending production of 2/4-2-2s but it was something that would be very hard to prove and indeed impossible to prove in only a few years.

The 8-footers seem however to have won popular admiration and one wonders whether some of it affected Stirling's normally austere and practical judgment. Did "8 ft single" seem to the amateur much better than "seven-foot-six single"? For over a century there has persisted the belief that big wheels, and only big wheels, can be fast and so the bigger the better.

Stirling believed that the bigger the wheel the higher the coefficient of friction between tyre and rail. General knowledge of friction does nothing to encourage that belief and even if there were anything in it, a change of 6 per cent in diameter would be unlikely to have any marked effect.

A positive advantage of a change from inside cylinders to outside cylinders was the elimination of the crank-axle, always an expensive item and in those days not a very reliable one; Stirling said that any crank-axle would break eventually. Another point was that absence of inside cranks enabled the boiler to be set lower than was otherwise possible with any given wheel-diameter, provided of course that the barrel was slim enough to be placed between the wheels.

The bogie under an 8 ft single pivoted horizontally about a pin situated a few inches behind the bogie centre but no side-play was deliberately provided. The bogie "nudged" the front end of the engine slightly more gently into a curve than did the front wheels of a 2-2-2 and although the difference cannot have been great, it was at least in the right direction.

Stirling did not adopt the 2/4-2-2 with any precipitate enthusiasm. Only five such engines were built in the first three years and only four in the succeeding two years. Even after initial imperfections had been identified and corrected, the production rate was not markedly increased; the building of 47 engines was spread over 23 years.

The wide span of building dates suggests the reverse of mass-production methods at Doncaster and the possibility of differences between nominally identical engines. The 8-footers did indeed differ because of modifications in design as time went on, especially in the early years. The first engine, No 1, for example was said to be a "poor steamer" and no doubt everyone knew that if no more sophisticated remedy occurred to anyone, a smaller blastpipe orifice would put matters right. But perhaps it was the poor steaming that led Stirling to include in each of the fireboxes of the next two 8-footers a feature mischievously called a "mid-feather".

This was in fact a "water-arch" instead of the usual brick arch. It was a complicating deformation of the normal firebox adopted in defiance (or ignorance?) of the fact that the incandescence of a brick arch in normal running conditions is an important factor in reducing smoke. No other Stirling engine had a water-arch and the two that were made did not last long.

Stirling's insistence on the rule "one train, one engine" was not regarded by all GN men as being entirely sensible and Stirling sought to apply some enforcement of it in respect of 8 ft singles by fitting no brake pipe at the front of any of them. The idea was that no helper-engine could be attached in front of an 8 ft single on a passenger train without infringing the rule that the driver of the leading engine must take charge of the brakes. Whether the rule always remained unbroken cannot now be ascertained, but in the 1890s it became clear that the 4-2-2s were uncertain in handling the heaviest loads that were becoming common. Stirling had to discontinue his "No double-heading" rule and front brake-pipes were added to all passenger train engines that had lacked them. Moreover he built six enlarged 8-footers rather hurriedly in 1894/95 in an effort to show that the design was not really outclassed.

These engines (n11 in Table 5) were distinctly larger in firebox and grate than their predecessors and even more markedly so (23 per cent) in nominal tractive effort. The increase in cylinder volume was accompanied by a slight reduction in heating surface of the tubes and many amateur commentators thought this to be very shocking. They imagined that the big cylinders would "empty the boiler" because they relied on the tacit assumption that evaporative power was measured by heating surface and on another that boiler steam filled each cylinder twice in each revolution of the driving wheels.

These final big 8-footers may well have been better engines than their pre-decessors, especially for the heavier trains, but they had little chance to show it as Stirling died before the end of 1895 and within a year his successor Ivatt was building four-coupled engines for fast passenger trains.

He also fitted some of the later 8-footers with domed boilers that had bigger grate area than before and it seems likely that, on dry rails at least, these engines could have been made to develop a good deal more power than they are known to have done.

An extraordinary step taken by Ivatt in designing these boilers was to adopt a width of $1\frac{3}{4}$ in for the water-spaces round the firebox. This was in strange con-trast to Stirling's standard 3 in which, in later days at least, was regarded as the minimum desirable value of this dimension. Ivatt soon became convinced of this.

In 1905 the *Railway Magazine* recorded that 8-footer No 93 (then having a domed boiler) included in her regular duties the haulage, from Kings Cross to Peterborough, of the 5.30 pm Glasgow "express goods" train loading up to 24 piped vehicles aggregating 340 tons. This practice hardly suggests anxiety about inadequate adhesion weight.

In the *Railway Magazine* for July 1915, E. L. Ahrons recalled that in 1896-98 the 5.45 pm dining-car express from Kings Cross to Leeds loaded up to 17 vehicles (270 tons) and was normally worked by an 8 ft or a 7 ft 6 in single with no help except over the length of the Kings Cross platform by the engine that had brought in the empty stock. He went on to say that "the way the singles . . . dealt with the trains up to Potters Bar was wonderful." He went further, very regrettably, to say that "One could prove mathematically that they could never do it"! He might have added that one can "prove" mathematically that 1 equals 2, but in the absence of any such corrective note, enraptured enthusiasts no doubt accepted his remark as "proving" that Stirling singles were super-natural.

When the Stirling singles were handling all the main line expresses on the GNR it had the reputation of being a fast line. How fast could the Stirling singles go? Deliberate urging to the utmost down Essendine Bank gave an answer in the region of 85 mph. As it happened, that was also an "ordinary" maximum anywhere on the GN right until it lost its identity at the end of 1922. Maxima up to 90 mph were not unknown in the vicinity of Essendine but anything over 85 was rare.

IVATT SINGLES (n12 n12A)

The weak point in a single is the low adhesion weight. Stirling had been rather naughty in loading the driving wheels of his later singles more heavily than the civil engineer knew until a couple of rail breakages by Stirling singles after his death brought the matter sharply to Ivatt's notice. He had the axleloads adjusted to the nominal limit of 18 tons and emphasised the need for better track on the GN main line. Yet after all this he introduced an inside-cylinder 4-2-2 in 1898 and built eleven generally similar ones in 1900-1901.

As Ivatt had intermediately built ten Atlantics, it is clear that he did not intend the 4-2-2s to be used for the heaviest trains but for some specifically fast, but lighter, ones. The Ivatt 4-2-2s were distinctly larger in the firebox (but not in nominal tractive effort) than the Stirling singles that preceded them and with adhesion weight restricted to 18 tons they were no better in getting away from rest. There is in fact no evidence that the Ivatt singles beat the best Stirling singles in any way.

When in later years competition with the Great Central and the Midland induced the GN to run some fast light trains from Kings Cross to Sheffield and to Leeds, the work was shared between Ivatt singles and—not 8-footers—but Stirling 2-2-2s rebuilt with domed boilers by Ivatt. The Ivatt 4-2-2s did not distinguish themselves in any comparison made in respect of these services nor, so far as published records go, in any other. They were the last singles to be built for any British railway and their history suggests that they came a little too late to find any job for which they were peculiarly suitable. Work for singles on the GN was gradually diminishing and the Stirling singles were well able to cope with it.

The later Ivatt singles differed from the pioneer No 266 of 1898 in greater depth of frame between the cylinders and the driving axleboxes, and in having cylinders sufficiently large in diameter to make it more convenient to have the valves above them and this required rocking-shafts in the motion. Flat valves were used with Richardson strips and exhaust straight up through the valve to the blast pipe.

These singles had larger grate area than the contemporary Ivatt 4-4-0s and so, like the Stirling singles 20 years earlier, they might well be more powerful at speed than were the four-coupled engines.

The story of these engines is rather melancholy, but they were good to see as their "lines" were elegant and their light green and brown paint did nothing to detract from them. But in 1918 Gresley withdrew them all in one swoop and had them photographed in a disconsolate line on the scrap-road in Doncaster Works.

CHAPTER FIVE

Four-coupled Engines

0-4-2 ENGINES (n23 n24 n25)

THE EARLIEST GN 0-4-2s were four outside frame engines built by Tayleur & Co and bought second-hand in 1849-50. Their performance was evidently not so distinguished as to persuade Sturrock to try the 0-4-2 wheel arrangement. Stirling had used it on the Glasgow & South Western with such success that he adopted it whole-heartedly on the GN.

A sound reason for coupling all the wheels of a six-wheel engine is that it enables the total weight of the locomotive to be used to get a frictional grip on the rails. One can see a reason for coupling none of the wheels. It simplifies the engine, minimises friction in the mechanism and has no disadvantage provided that the driving wheels carry enough weight for friction with the rails to be able to transmit the desired maximum tractive effort to the rails. If this condition cannot be realised, then the driving axle must be coupled to one of the other axles. Coupling to the rear axle was common enough. For what reason might coupling to the leading axle be preferable?

Steam locomotives tend to be heavy at the front rather than at the back because of the weight of the cylinder block. So for any particular combination of boiler, cylinders and wheels a 0-4-2 is likely to have a greater nominal adhesion weight than a 2-4-0.

For fast running, the leading wheels should preferably have some controlled side-play and should be small rather than large because that makes the leading wheel-flanges less likely to "climb" the outer rail on a sharp curve.

So for a service in which pulling rather than high speed is important the 0-4-2 has the advantage of greater adhesion weight. The Stirling Class A 0-4-2 of 1867 (n23), for example, had 12 tons on the leading axle and only 6 tons on the trailing axle. A 2-4-0 with the same weight distribution would therefore have had about 6 tons less adhesion weight. The difference would in fact have been less than this because the difference in weight of the wheels and axles themselves would have to be deducted. Against 26 tons adhesion weight on the 0-4-2, the 2-4-0 would have had about 21 tons.

This, however, is in the condition of repose. When the engine was pulling hard the backward pull of the tender at about $3\frac{1}{2}$ ft above the rails would transfer about $1\frac{1}{2}$ tons of axle load from the front axle to the rear axle. Hence the effective adhesion weights when the engine was pulling hard (which is when adhesion weight really matters) would be about 24½ tons for the 0-4-2 and 22½ tons for the 2-4-0. The former would have roughly 10 per cent advantage.

This could be held to justify the building of 0-4-2s as against 2-4-0s for "mixed traffic" which meant the slower passenger trains and the faster goods trains. It might be asked, however, whether there would have been any harm in coupling the rear wheels as well and thus to make a 0-6-0 with larger wheels than usual. Most British railways seem to have looked at the matter in this way as the 0-4-2 was not much used in Britain between the Thames and the Tweed, but Stirling built 0-4-2 engines as late as 1895.

The Stirling 0-4-2s were of two main classes, differing in little but external appearance and boiler pressure. The first class, with built-up chimneys and cut-away splashers, numbered 121 engines built between 1866 and 1880. The other class, with smooth chimneys and plain splashers, was of 33 engines built between 1881 and 1896.

By far the most impressive-looking 0-4-2s on the GN were Nos 67 and 70 (n25). They had outside frames, 6 ft driving wheels and the Stirling smooth chimney. They were nominally "rebuilds" of "Small Hawthorn" 2-2-2 engines, and among the very few re-used pieces were the cut-away splashers. These were "rebuilt" to the extent of having half-moon shaped backing plates added to blank-off the cut-away whilst leaving evidence of its earlier existence.

GN 2-4-0 LOCOMOTIVES (n13 to n19)

The 2-4-0 wheel arrangement had a great vogue in Britain during the 19th century. It was, in effect, the universal 0-6-0 modified to cope rather better with high speeds by trains not heavy enough to require six-coupled wheels to get them on the move.

Sturrock bought some 40 2-4-0s of three general designs from five engine builders.

Stirling was so convinced of the value of 2-4-0s that he gave himself as his first GN job the production of a 2-4-0 design and its application to orders for 20 engines from outside builders. This was in 1867. Twenty-eight years later Doncaster Works completed an order for 56 virtually identical engines and, two years later, an order by Ivatt for ten only slightly larger 2-4-0s with domed boilers and with the springs over the leading axle exposed instead of hidden.

The GN 2-4-0s were passenger-train engines but they did not normally work the principal express trains. During most of Stirling's period of office those trains were not heavy enough to demand more adhesion weight than that of the singles and as the bigger wheels of those engines made them faster than the 2-4-0s with similar cylinders and valves, the four-coupled engines were naturally used on passenger services for which reliability in getting away from rest was more important than comfortable attainment of high speed.

The building of virtually identical 2-4-0s over 30 years suggests that for that period the demands of certain classes of service did not alter very much and indeed 2-4-0s were widely used in Great Britain at least until World War I. After the 1895 Race to Scotland, agreement on Anglo-Scottish speed tended to divert competition between railways to the provision of more comfortable accommodation for passengers and therefore heavier trains. The principal passenger-train engines had therefore to be more powerful than before. The demands of the secondary services did not alter much and 2-4-0s tended to have long useful lives.

It happened that in 1895 the North Western 2-4-0s were faster engines than the "top link" compounds on that railway and so they were used between Crewe and Carlisle in the "race" of that year. The fastest running of the whole race was achieved by North Western 2-4-0 No 790 at a level unapproached by any other 2-4-0. Whether any other 2-4-0 could have approached it will never be known now, but the Stirling 2-4-0s were never even given any chance of showing how fast they could go for 140 miles. None of them ever headed a train on which a really "hot" run could have been justified.

Stirling himself seems to have been content, or satisfied, or perhaps even glad to be convinced that his 2-4-0s were not so good as his singles. He may even have been sure that the extra friction in coupling rods inevitably made coupled engines inferior to singles. At all events he built more than enough singles to handle all the principal passenger trains and so the 2-4-0s never had any chance of suggesting by their performance in service that the superiority of the singles was not proven.

So no Stirling 2-4-0 is known to have approached the best efforts of North Western 2-4-0s nor, for that matter, did any Stirling single do so.

The later lots of Stirling 2-4-0s were handsome engines, being close analogues of the later Stirling 2-2-2s. Members of both classes were rebuilt by Ivatt with domed boilers and small-cased Ramsbottom safety-valves. It would not be outrageous to suggest that perhaps they looked better like that (see pp. 51–52).

GN 4-4-0s (n20 n21 n22)

It was not surprising that one of Ivatt's earliest moves on the GN was to produce a few 4-4-0s. He had used this wheel-arrangement in Ireland, it was obviously "coming in" in England and the GN had no such engine. The first Doncaster 4-4-0 was, as nearly as possible, a modification of the Stirling 2-4-0 limited to inside frames. It had less boiler power than the Stirling singles and so it was clearly not intended for running principal main line passenger trains. Its production was an unadventurous move and Ivatt's subsequent production of ten 2-4-0s suggests him to have been doubtful as to whether it was a sensible one.

In a couple of years he evidently decided that there could be GN use for some rather bigger 4-4-0s than the first lot. In 1898 Doncaster turned out 4-4-0 No

1321 and in the following year a total of 70 similar engines had been built. (This was for Doncaster Works a "high production" effort.)

An early application of this class was to express trains between Doncaster and Leeds. Between Wakefield and Leeds are gradients on which singles could never be very reliable in bad rail conditions. As it was common to "change engines" of Kings Cross-Leeds trains at Doncaster it was sensible to use coupled engines for running into Leeds (or more especially out of Leeds) even though singles could cope with conditions on the GN main line.

A departure made in the later 4-4-os from detail design of the earlier ones was the raising of the running board in the vicinity of the splashers so that the oil-boxes on the coupling rods were readily accessible in all angular positions of the coupled wheels. In the original design the running-board was continuous and auxiliary "splashers" arranged to clear the oil-boxes in their highest positions effectually hid them in those positions.

The most notable published record of work by any of the Class D2 4-4-os was taken by Cecil J. Allen when No 41 worked a train of 425 tons from Grantham to York 82·7 miles in 10 sec less than the booked time of 97 min. With an average of 51·7 mph on a generally favourable road, this was not a hard run for a large Atlantic of which the GN had plenty at that time, but the mere thought of hitching a small 4-4-0 onto 425 tons would have produced heart-failure on one railway in close competition with the GN.

But the driver of No 41 thought it worthwhile at least to "have a go". They touched 69 mph near Claypole and averaged 65 over 6½ nearly level miles from Newark to Carlton. The minimum at Markham summit was 37 mph but 64 was touched before Retford. On to Bawtry the average was 59 mph and thence to Doncaster over Piper's Wood "knob" it was 52½. Here the train was nearly a minute earlier than the scheduled time of 58 min and so there was hope of keeping time to York although the big train would hamper recovery of speed after the restriction over the swing-bridge at Selby. So they kept at it, but the average over the 18·4 level miles from Doncaster to Selby was little higher than the 51·2 mph booked for the whole journey and so there was clearly not much to spare. After Selby the gradient profile is finely saw-toothed with an average rise of 1 in 1800 but No 41 stopped in York just on the right side of "time".

In similar circumstances No 58, a 4-4-0 of the larger Class D1 with 410 tons passed Doncaster in 55 min but was very badly delayed by signal checks from there on to York. Further details of these runs are given in Table 2, p. 197.

GN FOUR-COUPLED TANK ENGINES (n26 to n33)

The first GN tank engines (n26) for handling passenger trains in the tunnels of the Metropolitan Railway were outside-frame 0-4-2 well-tank engines, of which 15 were built in 1865-6 by Avonside and five by Neilson. The latter were somewhat longer than the others and had deeper frame plates, but the main dimensions were common to all. They had raised fireboxes with rather steeply sloping grates and each boiler had a dome on the middle of the barrel. A single bent sheet formed a cab-roof and two weatherboards. Exhaust steam could be condensed by directing it through a pipe in the well-tank until the water there became too hot when there would be considerable escape of steam from the end of a vertical pipe close to the back of the cab. Apart from dome and cab-roof these engines were in the usual Sturrock style and did their work well.

In 1868-71 Stirling built 13 locomotives (n27) that were enlarged versions of the Sturrock engines except that they had no dome and that the coupled-wheel axleboxes were between the wheels.

In 1876-78 Stirling built half a dozen 0-4-2 saddle-tank engines (n28) with inside frames and no condenser. On two of these, particularly, the tall brass safety-valve cover towered markedly above a rather low bent-iron cab-roof. This class of engine was used for a long time on the Stamford branch from Essendine Junction.

In 1872 Stirling adopted the 0-4-4 wheel arrangement in well-tank engines (n29) and 48 of them were built between 1871 and 1882. In main dimensions these were no larger than the Sturrock 0-4-2WT engines but the bogie and the longer frame enabled the water capacity to be increased to 1000 gal with $1\frac{1}{2}$ tons of coal. Some were built with condensers and cut-down chimneys for working on the Metropolitan line.

By the time the last of the 48 was built, there was a need for something bigger and in the succeeding four years Stirling built some 16 side-tank engines (n30) with the 0-4-4 wheel arrangement. These made the 0-4-4WTs look rather primitive. The cab-roof and the side-sheets of side-tanks and bunker were (to the observer's eye) formed out of a single sheet of metal, bent to a generous arc in each transition from vertical to horizontal. The earlier engines were built to run short-distance passenger trains in the West Riding, and were normally stationed at Bradford. Some, however, were adapted to Metropolitan line working by being fitted with condensers and having chimney and safety-valve casing appropriately reduced in height.

As on the 8ft singles a wavy splasher-trough lay over the bogie wheels of the Stirling tank engines.

In 1889 came the first of Class R 0-4-4Ts, (n31) similar to Class O but having larger cylinders besides some detail differences that made the later engines a few tons heavier. They were cut down to Metropolitan height and were, to the writer's eye, the most impressive-looking tank engines on the GN in the 19th century, although they might have looked better still with domes. A detail of these and all later condensing engines on the GN was that each tank vent-pipe had a flange geometrically similar to that on the smooth Stirling chimney.

The four engines (n32) of Class R2 were generally similar to Class R but the side-tanks were shorter, a well-tank was provided to offset the loss of water capacity, and the bunker was lengthened. The shortening of the tanks spoiled

No 6 (n6) Stirling single (1868) with port-hole boarded up. Note lever connected by rope to communication cord in train and double vacuum ejector (for 'straight' vacuum brake) alongside smokebox.

No 1 (n9) at Grantham in 1938. Wavy splashers over bogie wheels and concealed springs over tender axleboxes.
[T. G. Hepburn.

No 876 (n8A) Stirling single (1894). Concealed springs over leading and trailing axles. Helical springs under driving axle.

No 267 (n12A) Ivatt single (1900) with very deep frame-plate and small safety-valves.

No 258 (n15) Sturrock 2-4-0 (1866) rebuilt by Stirling. All springs are easily visible. Single vacuum ejector.

No 709 (n18) Stirling 2-4-0 (1874) built by Kitson & Co. Widely slotted coupling-rod splashers.

No 1066 (n19) Ivatt 2-4-0 (1897) with Stirling-type safety-valve cover.

No 4070 (n19) Ivatt 2-4-0 (No 1070, 1897) reboilered with extended smokebox. Acquired by LNER.   [T. G. Hepburn.

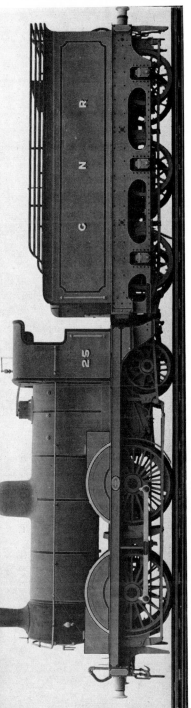

No 25 (n23) Stirling 0-4-2 (1870) with Ivatt boiler.

No 28 (n23) Stirling 0-4-2 (1875) with slotted splashers and communication-cord lever.

No 248 (n29) Stirling 0-4-4WT (1880) with train of four-wheel coaches climbing 1 in 61 near Crouch End.

No 766 (n31) Stirling 0-4-4T (1889). Steam-pipe to condenser lies underneath the mechanism.

No 1077 (n20) Ivatt 4-4-0 (1897) with Stirling-type safety-valve cover.

No 1072 (n20) Ivatt 4-4-0 (1897) reboilered with extended smokebox and Ramsbottom safety-valves.

No 1373 (n21) Ivatt 4-4-0 (1900) ready to go. Note 3-link coupling and safety-chains.

No 65 (n22) Ivatt/Gresley 4-4-0 (1911) with superheater and piston-valves. Lever on smokebox works the superheater damper. Tender with unequal axle-spacing.

No 990 (n34) Ivatt 2/4-4-2 (1898). Lever on smokebox controls
a variable blastpipe.

No 987 (n34) Ivatt 2/4-4-2 (1900) rebuilt with superheater and
extended smokebox.

No 271 (n36) Ivatt 4/4-4-2 (1902) as originally built.

No 271 (n36). This is (n 36) rebuilt (1904) with different cylinders, four valves and Walschaerts valve-gear for outside valves.

No 271 (n40). This is (n36) rebuilt (1911) with superheater, piston valves and no outside cylinder.

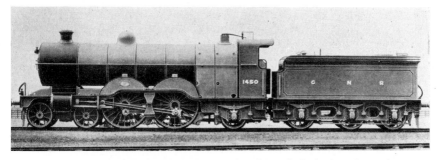

No 1450 (n35) Ivatt large Atlantic (1908), nearly the last one to be built without a superheater.

No 1421 (n35) rebuild of (n39) to the standard superheated large Atlantic design.

No 4431 (ex.-1431) (n35) superheated large Atlantic on **LNER** train climbing from Grantham to Stoke Summit.

[T. G. Hepburn.

No 292 (n37) Ivatt 4C/4-4-2 (1905).

No 1300 (n38) Vulcan 4C/4-4-2 (1907).

No 1421 (n39) Ivatt 4C/4-4-2 (1907).

No 279 (n41) Gresley 4/4-4-2 rebuild (1915) of (n35).

Sturrock outside-frame 0-6-0 (n47) of 1865 with steam-tender (number unknown).

No 367 (n46) Sturrock outside-frame 0-6-0 (Vulcan 1854) rebuilt by Stirling.

No 365 (n50) Stirling 0-6-0 (1875).

No 73 (n54) Ivatt 0-6-0 (1912) with superheater, piston-valves, two sniffing valves and pyrometer.

the appearance of the engines (in the writer's view) but gave much easier access to the top side of the mechanism behind the cylinders.

The cab was altered so that there was nothing for an engineman to rest on when leaning out and looking forward. This disadvantage was intensified by the omission of side-doors whereas Classes O and R had them.

The cab was extended forward so as to enclose more of the boiler than was the case in Class R. This might have been better for the enginemen in cold weather but not in any other conditions.

The changes from Class R design removed nearly 3 tons of water and steel from the middle of the engine and placed it over the bogie. This reduced the load on the driving axle and perhaps the Metropolitan people had asked for some alleviation here. But it also reduced the adhesion weight and this was disadvantageous to an engine engaged on start-and-stop work. At the age of 75, Stirling may have been past his best.

Ivatt lost no time in producing a locomotive to do the jobs of the 0-4-4 tank engines with more boiler power but with hardly any more adhesion weight. This was a 4-4-2 tank engine (n33) that was evidently useful in several sections of GN locomotive work as 60 examples of it were built in ten years. (In the meantime, however, six-coupled tank engines began to take some of the Kings Cross suburban work and even some eight-coupled ones were tried.) The 4-4-2T had too many non-driving wheels to be able to make good use of its weight in starting from rest and therefore seems far from ideal for start-and-stop work. General British practice does not conflict with this thought but nevertheless the 4-4-2T survived well on the GN.

The first ten engines of the class had domed boilers with Ramsbottom-type safety-valves, but tall Stirling chimneys. Side-doors reappeared, and the side-tanks were convenient for leaning on when leaning out. After that came engines cut down and condenser-fitted for Metropolitan work and this remained the pattern for the rest of the number. In this form they had built-up chimneys and this style was used in replacements of the Stirling chimneys of the earlier engines.

On the Stirling 0-4-4Ts built before 1895, exhaust steam to be condensed in the tanks was conveyed to them from the cylinders by pipes lying under the coupled axles. (Extra things to be removed whenever you had to get coupled wheels out!) Two slide valves with spindles connected by a rocking lever directed exhaust steam either to the blastpipe or to the tanks.

On the later engines, Nos 931 to 944, directional control of exhaust-flow was by a flap valve worked by a lever on a spindle projecting from the lower half of the right hand side of the smokebox. Steam to be condensed passed from the smokebox to the tops of the tanks by prominent pipes. This arrangement was also used by Ivatt and Gresley as many as 30 years later, but the older engines retained the original layout.

CHAPTER SIX

Atlantics

SMALL ATLANTICS (n34)

There is no evidence that Ivatt 2/4-4-2 No 990 was the product of any inspiration higher than a desire to beat the Lancashire & Yorkshire Railway in producing the first British 4-4-2. No 990 was the sort of thing that Stirling might have developed out of his 8-footer when reluctantly convinced that in order to cope with dining cars, sleeping cars and other heavy vehicles, engines were simply going to have to have a few legs tied together. No 990 represented the very minimum useful departure from the Stirling 8-footer style. The 8 ft wheels had to be abandoned if only to minimise the wheel base of the Atlantic and Ivatt chose 80 in instead. Moreover, he packed the coupled wheels so closely together that a sixpence could touch two flanges at once. This looked so absurd that he hid it from normal view by hanging a plate abreast of it and using this as a support for two steps, although it was quite a wrong place for steps.

Two years' running of No 990 convinced Ivatt that there was scope for this class of engine and so in 1900 he produced ten almost identical engines. The only external change was not conspicuous but rather surprising. It was movement of the front sanding pipes from the leading coupled wheels to the driving wheels. This meant that on really slippery rails the engine was no more effective than a Stirling single, and now and again this was made painfully clear. The main advantage to be expected from the Atlantic was nullified by absence of means of sanding the rails ahead of the leading coupled wheels!

One may surmise that the reason for this change from No 990 was a spot of bother caused by dropping sand in front of only two out of four slipping wheels; this can overload the coupling rods to the point of buckling them. But the remedy was not to deprive the engine of half its effective adhesion weight, but to provide sand for both pairs of wheels and to strengthen the coupling rods. The last change is easy to make. Use a plain rectangular section instead of laboriously milling it down to I-section. Because coupling rods fail (when they *do* fail) by lateral buckling, the rectangular section strengthens them very considerably. It also makes then heavier but as their motion is purely circular, the rotary unbalance can be accurately neutralised by appropriate addition to the existing balance weights.

As it was, the later small Atlantics had better sanding for backward running

than for forward running, but the occasions on which this could be useful must
have been few.

A curious feature of the GN Atlantic (small and large) was that whilst the
big ends of the connecting rods moved on 24 in circles, the coupling rods followed 23 in circles. No valid reason was ever advanced for this harmless eccentricity,
but the Lancashire & Yorkshire Railway and the North Western copied it,
perhaps in the hope of discovering by trial in service what secret had inspired
Doncaster to adopt it.

In relation to the length of the engine, the short smokebox of a small Atlantic
made it look weak and undistinguished. It was not that the smokebox was
functionally short as in fact the front tube plate was set back in the boiler barrel
to about 12 in behind the rear edge of the wrapper plate. Nevertheless when in
later years superheaters were applied to these engines, the smokeboxes were
extended ahead of the chimney and the appearance of the engine was transformed. Instead of a poor wilting little bird, appeared one that stuck her chest out in
a way that suggested eagerness to get on with something. It is unlikely that the
change made any real difference to the working of the engine, but it was heart-
warming in its hint that there was someone at Doncaster with aesthetic perception.

No 990 was too long for the turntable at Kings Cross. Every time she went
there she had to travel four miles out to Hornsey to be turned on a triangle of
track and four miles back to pick up a train. Repeatedly GN locomotive engineers proclaimed that they were ahead of the traffic department by producing an
engine that was so strong or so long or so heavy as to be a nuisance.

The differences between the small Atlantics and the large Atlantics that
appeared after 1901 were almost confined to the boiler, and when the marked
superiority of the large Atlantics had been proved, it was stated that the small
engines would eventually be fitted with big boilers, but that was never done.

THE LARGE ATLANTICS

The fame of the Ivatt large Atlantics, their late-in-life achievements, the homage
that has been paid to them and the emotionally sycophantic statements that have
been made about them, ensure that any realistic comment is sure to offend
someone.

Ivatt had stretched Stirling's "8 ft single" into an "80 in Atlantic" in a fairly
obvious manner to produce No 990 and her sisters. After a year or two of
experience in running these engines he realised that within the same length and
width he could mount a much bigger boiler if he adopted a wide firebox with
the grate extended laterally over the rear-wheels. He might have done this by
"reboilering" an existing Atlantic but in fact he built an entirely new engine, No
251. This was naturally regarded as a large Atlantic, and the earlier ones ("long-
necked" someone called them) came to be small Atlantics.

In making the change the diameter of the boiler barrel was increased from 56 in to 66 in, a rise of 18 per cent. The height of the chimney was reduced from 35 in to 20 in and this drop of 43 per cent made the big engine appear to have an even greater advantage in power than it really had. On the GN, the move into the 20th century was dramatically emphasised by No 251. She looked not only bigger than the 990s but also more elegant and this was (partly) because her smokebox was markedly extended ahead of the chimney. This, of course, is only the writer's opinion and others no doubt think differently. There are those who like flat-chestedness, others who prefer some development, others who have no preference in the matter and others who can't see any difference. It is possible that Ivatt adopted the extended smokebox with the hope of reducing spark-throwing by providing plenty of opportunities for live cinders to be retained in the smokebox instead of being shot out of the chimney. Whether he had any aesthetic consideration in mind will probably never be known.

No 251 ran for some time with a plain stovepipe chimney suggesting that Ivatt was either toying with the idea of adding this second feature of American practice to his use of the wide firebox or had not decided exactly what embellishment to apply to the essential simplicity of this prominent feature of a locomotive. In the event the standard adopted for the large Atlantics was, very largely, a version, necessarily shortened, of the Stirling built-up (or apparently built-up) chimney.

The large Atlantics were magnificent engines that excited widespread admiration but they were built with no sand pipe in front of the leading coupled wheels and as axleload was limited to 18 tons they could pull no harder on slippery rails than could a Stirling single! Ivatt would hardly have dared to present the enginemen with such an anomaly had they not had two years in which to become inured to it in the small Atlantics.

By 1915 at least the nuisance had been diminished by fitting pipes from which sand was blown by steam under the leading coupled wheels but the pipes had each a long length only slightly inclined to the horizontal and feed of sand was consequently quite unreliable.

Acquaintance of designers with the tenacity of contact between hard granular powders and corroded metal surfaces might have saved enginemen and shed staff lifetimes of infuriating irritation with sand-pipes and ash-pans.

The screw type reversing gear in the small Atlantics was hard to work because the proximity of the cab-side had restricted the span of the double-handle to 14 in. In No 251 the wide firebox restricted space for screw reversing gear even more and this may have influenced Ivatt in adopting lever-reverse. There was not much room for this either and the driver's physical efforts started a devious way to the weigh-shaft by diving under the ash-pan. The short distance between the cab-front and the tender-front restricted the "throw" of the lever and this limited the leverage to a figure much less than the minimum that might have permitted a driver to reverse the engine in reasonable comfort. Pin-joints in the linkage between lever and weigh-shaft were not easily accessible for lubrication; to the friction of the valves was added the effect of dry friction at the joints.

To move the lever from forward to backward gear you held it with both hands, placed your right foot on a step provided for the purpose and with luck and knack you could move the lever a few inches at a time by violent heaves of the body. To move the lever the other way was harder as you had to push with the sole of one foot against the vertical front of the tender just behind you.

But it was not so bad as this on all the large Atlantics! Some, mostly piston valve engines, might be reversed quite easily; others, mostly flat valve engines, were tough. A driver had to remember which particular engine he was on. (This was one of the advantages of having his "own".) He could do himself harm by heaving on a reversing lever that was hard to move; he could do himself more harm of a different kind by heaving on a lever that was easy.

Reversing a large Atlantic, or changing the cut-off, could be a Herculean operation and naturally gave rise to the practice of setting the lever to give a suitable cut-off in the first few hundred yards of each journey and leaving it there for the rest of the way even if it were for 150 miles. Some enthusiasts believed that the practicability of this procedure was yet another facet of the mystical quality of the large Atlantics. In actual fact any locomotive could be worked in this way, because even with fixed cut-off the regulator could be adjusted to make the engine produce the effort required at any time. Some Atlantic drivers would not always bother to do this and so the down grades on the GN main line might produce speeds that could infect enthusiastic observers with delirious delight.

Drivers could not be criticised for failing to work an Atlantic in strict compliance with copy-book rules; they had enough to do in holding on. There was a swing-link bogie at the front, a rigid wheelbase of only 82 in, and no side-control at the rear beyond what was afforded by the tender and friction between the tops of the trailing axle boxes and the spring-pads. You would think that these conditions would leave the cab-end of the engine free to swing from side to side and you would be right. The Atlantics were unique in rough riding. A sharpish curve might hold them fairly steady but on the straight the front end wandered while the back end wiggled and this went on all the time. You didn't know whether you were on the road or not and after a mile or two you didn't care. At places like Doncaster where Atlantics might run fast over points and crossings their wild antics could terrify observers on the station platform let alone on the footplate, but the enginemen accepted it. Occasionally a very bad lurch would cause a man's head to swing outside the cab so that the wind snatched his cap away and this was just bad luck, but you got so used to the rollicking gait of the big Atlantics that you almost got to like it. The fireman indeed had some reason to do so because in one way it made his job easier. He did not have to take any care in shovelling to spread coal over the whole 31 sq ft of the fire. The tail-wag did that for him. Once the coal was safely through the fire-hole, the fireman could forget about it. Gravity and wiggle spread it over the fire just as well as he could and with far less fuss. Moreover, the tender had perforce to share in the dance and so the coal rolled down to the footplate as fast as the fire could take it. There was no need to stand with semi-scorched bottom in front of the fire hole to reach into the tender; the coal came down to your feet so that you could stand with your back to the cab-side, push the shovel across the width of the engine to pick up the coal and simply lift and put it into the firebox. No need for mighty arm-swings to throw coal in 8 ft flights. The engine almost fed herself, and with careful mounting of a few pieces of steel plate between the tender and the fire-hole might well have done so.

Even after he had developed "Atlantic-legs" a fireman could still expect bumps and bruises now and then, but apart from that his job was easier than usual on engines of Atlantic size and so the driver could thrash a big Atlantic as hard as he liked without causing the fireman to grumble much.

In actual fact drivers did not thrash Atlantics in their early days. They were too cautious for that. Even in the 1895 Race to Scotland the GN enginemen managed to hurry in a sedate way and even the obvious power and speed of the big Atlantics did not beguile them into exuberance. With no special stimulus they were careful not to suggest by any unusual effort that the big Atlantics were any better pullers than the little ones.

On the GN, as on most other lines, no locomotive showed its full power until bigger engines were at work on the same routes. It was not until the Gresley Pacifics had shown what they could do that the Atlantics brought forth their best efforts.

In the early days of the large Atlantics it was common to attribute their apparent lack of hill-climbing power to the small size of their cylinders. This is best expressed by remarking that although the grate area of the Atlantic was 55 per cent more than that of the last Stirling 8 ft singles, the nomimal tractive effort was only about 7 per cent higher. There was some justification for the smallness of this difference in that where very slippery rails made sand essential for any useful pull, an Atlantic was no better than an 8-footer as the weight on the sanded driving wheels was about the same for both. This applied when getting away from rest and when pulling hard against a steep gradient. For equal efforts at speed the Atlantic had the advantage that its much lower combustion rate would make for economy in fuel. But if this possible advantage were disregarded the Atlantic might demonstrate the full power of its 55 per cent advantage in grate area. In time it did so, but even before then Great Northern publicity made great play with the outstanding size of the big boiler of the large Atlantics. Much use was made of an artist's drawing that was a three-quarter front view of a GN train at speed behind a large Atlantic with an imaginatively enlarged smokebox. A comment from an impressed observer was that: "Mr Ivatt's new beauty, bold-bosomed and broad-bottomed, beckons us with promise of power and speed." In mechanical detail the Ivatt Atlantic had nothing exceptional. Steam reached each cylinder past the outer edges of a balanced flat valve and afterwards passed through the middle of the valve on a direct route to the blast-pipe and the chimney. Such valves with "Richardson strips" were in wide use at the beginning of the 20th century. They were a kind of rectangular equivalent of piston valves and they were indeed superior to a good many piston valves at that time.

No 251 marked a big step in development of GN steam by being a notably large and handsome engine, the first of a numerous class that covered all GN main line passenger train requirements for 20 years, and even 15 years later still they were running fast and reliably with the Kings Cross—Leeds Pullman trains. Moreover they deputised in emergency for Gresley Pacifics and in ruthless hands they produced twice as much power as was required of them in Ivatt's time.

For years GN express trains hauled by Stirling singles were among the fastest in the world, despite their six-wheeled coaches on short-railed track. The reputa-tion thus established for the GNR was maintained in the 20th century by the large Atlantics. No locomotive class is more worthy of permanent preservation and it is indeed gratifying that both No 251 and Stirling 8-footer No 1, restored to its original condition so far as that can be established, are preserved in the Railway Museum at York.

No 251 however exhibits one wickedly dangerous feature that she did not originally have, but that was certainly carried by some Ivatt Atlantics in their later years. This is a brass "blow-down" cock projecting from the side of the firebox right at the bottom. It has a screwed end for coupling to a hose and its position is very convenient for the shed-staff when it was used for getting the water out of the boiler. It could, however, be very easily broken off by an acci-dental contact with another vehicle and the subsequent jet of boiling water would convert an otherwise trifling incident into something quite murderous. Danger of this kind was well recognised and designers accepted the consequent necessity of avoiding the use of pressurised projections from the sides of locomotive boilers. That this one was allowed to persist on the LNER shows that quite serious matters can be overlooked even by quite serious people.

The big Atlantics, when working hard, rolled along with a hard rattling chatter from the chimney but if you imagined that they started away from rest like a contemporary GW 4-6-0 you would be greatly mistaken. A GN Atlantic starting "cold" was no impressive spectacle. The regulator was opened cautiously and the engine wuffled gently, with many a hesitant slip, as the train slowly picked up speed. The Gresley Pacifics, being bigger, were better, but no three-cylinder engine had a snappy beat. So when *Pendennis Castle* took her first train out of Kings Cross in April 1925, her gunshot blast and very marked accel-eration over the first 100 yd must have raised immediate doubts of a LNER victory in the ensuing "exchange trials". The last axle under a locomotive should preferably do more than just carry weight when the need is for a strong pull.

But once a large Atlantic had "got them rolling" at about 25 mph the driver could open up pretty rapidly. The exhaust would strengthen and as speed rose it would sharpen till, as some one said many years ago, she was "peppering along!" This she could do all the way, uphill and down, as the centre of a moving circle of sound about four miles in diameter. Yes! A large Atlantic was a slippery bird to get going, a reeling rocking-horse on the road, but so long as you kept pushing the coal into her, Britain's finest foolproof flyer.

In their later years on the LNER the Ivatt Atlantics occasionally produced efforts that would have been incredible before World War I. They were, of course, better adapted to such performances by modifications, made on the basis of experience, to dimensions of valves and superheater, but the real reason for special feats well outside the recognised ability of the engines was largely psychological. By the mid-1930s the capabilities of the Gresley Pacifics had gradually become apparent and a 550-ton express passenger train was not so unusual as to call for special comment from enginemen. They were not frightened by anything in the 550 to 650-ton range.

So on a day in 1936 when a Pacific working a 585-ton train to Newcastle had to abandon it at Grantham because of overheating of the big end of the inside connecting rod and was replaced by an Atlantic, No 4404, the driver, although hardly pleased, did not think that he had the world on top of him. He did not "throw his hand in" and let people know that he was bound to lose time with the much smaller engine, but accepted fate and did what he could. Most fortunately Cecil J. Allen was on the train and took a full record of times and speeds. (See Table 2.) He reported that there was a bit of bother in getting the Atlantic to move at all but once away she ran to some purpose, averaging $63\frac{1}{2}$ mph from Barkston to Selby (64·7 miles) and gaining on the time allowed to York. "Grand engines, these," said the driver (a Gateshead man) on arrival at York, where a helper engine was coupled in front of the Atlantic. Nothing is on record about what the driver had said at Grantham but there is no difficulty in imagining its general gist.

It is most unlikely that either of the enginemen had ever previously worked an Ivatt Atlantic but whether they had or not, they could not have been cheered by their transfer from a Pacific to the cramped comfortless confinement of the footplate of the engine that was given to them. By the time the driver had wrenched that wretched reversing lever several times over its whole stroke in coping with refusals of the engine to go, he can have been in no sweet temper. He would quite reasonably decide that once the train got away he was not going to try to shift that lever for anybody. He would let the engine bash along and wouldn't care much what happened to her. It was most improbable that she would come into his charge again and so it would not matter to him how much hell she knocked out of herself. It is only when a driver has an attitude of this kind that the maximum effort can be expected from any locomotive. Even then that effort will not be realised unless the fireman shovels in the coal as fast as is necessary to maintain it.

On this occasion the fireman did his stuff manfully. It was less difficult to cope with the situation on an Ivatt Atlantic than on most other locomotives because the physical work required per pound of coal fed was small. No need to throw it. Just keep on pushing it through the hole and the wild sway of the engine would spread it better than anything you could do with the shovel.

Engines that could respond in this way to an emergency were obviously very valuable things to have in the motive power department of any railway and to this extent at least railway enthusiasts' admiration for the Ivatt Atlantics is justifiable.

But it may be useful to emphasise that this particular performance (and other comparable ones by Ivatt Atlantics) must not be assumed to have been made possible only by design-features such as low boiler-pressure, short coupled wheelbase, short stroke, wide firebox, Stephenson valve gear or any indefinable subtlety in design. Most important was that the enginemen found themselves on a foolproof type of locomotive with a nice sharp blast and easy to fire at a time when they were going home and were late.

On how many occasions Great Northern men got similar work out of Atlantics will never be known (four or five are on record) but the point about this one is that it was not the result of any intimate acquaintance of the enginemen with the class of engine. They were "fed-up" with the situation and so the driver opened everything wide and the fireman shovelled. This was the standard recipe for making a steam locomotive break records.

And was it any magic in design that made a locomotive "fool-proof" in this way? No! Unless design were bad or the boiler were internally dirty, a sufficiently restricted blast-nozzle would make any engine "steam" better the harder she was thrashed. This would be at the cost of extra coal at normal rates of working and the designer (or at least whoever could change the blast-nozzle) had to decide which he wanted—minimum coal on the one hand or a ready capacity for big overload on the other. Ivatt chose the latter and that's why the big Atlantics responded well to the real thrashing they occasionally got from homewardbound enginemen.

They were not light on coal but, burning about $4\frac{1}{2}$ lb per drawbar horsepower hour, they were no worse in this respect than many of their British contemporaries.

The large Atlantic, one may surmise, was admired by all locomotive enthusiasts. No other British Atlantic gave an equal visual impression of power from a big well-proportioned boiler carefully set on closely packed wheels. The engine knew she was good and protruded her chest in pride. See whether you can discern this in the middle photo on p. 59! Some people can find joy in just looking at a picture like this; others, less fortunate, can see nothing in it but straight lines and circular arcs.

When the same class of engine was fitted with a superheater, the chimney had to be moved a few inches forward and for me the aesthetic magic fled. Some readers will understand this remark; others will be mystified by it. The comparison of the middle and bottom photos on p. 59 may elucidate it for readers who are not distracted by the difference between the photographic qualities of the illustrations, and who can discern beauty of line in a locomotive regardless of colour or dirt. But whether any locomotive is beautiful or not is purely a matter of opinion and no-one should allow his own opinion to be altered by recognition that not everybody shares it.

But, regardless of looks, superheating was worth-while, and the last ten large Atlantics Nos 1452-61 were built with superheaters, with piston valves and 20 in cylinders. All their predecessors were eventually rebuilt in the same way. The earlier superheaters had about 430 sq ft of heating surface; later ones had 570.

Superheating saved coal and water; piston valves (generally) made for speed. The combination was generally so much superior to that of wet steam and flat valves that one may subconsciously form the impression that the latter was not much good. In the GN Atlantics, the balanced flat valves were as good as many piston valves in providing free exhaust. The practice of running with late cut-off assisted in this direction while the throttling of a partly-open regulator dried the steam a bit. So one need not be surprised to learn that the wet-steam Atlantics could be spritely, but of course those with superheaters could be better if the driver were really trying.

CHAPTER SEVEN

Moguls (n65 to n68)

BALDWIN ENGINES (n65)

THE FIRST 2-6-0s and the first eight-wheel tenders on the GN came from America in 1899. Two other British railways, the Midland and the Great Central, also bought American 2-6-0s at about the same time. The reason for this unusual action was that no British locomotive builder could offer to supply urgently needed goods engines in reasonable time. More than one American locomotive builder could do so provided that one of his standard designs was accepted and that is how the GN first used 2-6-0s for jobs that would otherwise have been done by ordinary o-6-0s.

In the country that cradled the steam locomotive, nobody really favoured the idea of importing railway engines and few were inclined to treat such imports with anything like compassion. The engines were stopgaps, everyone knew that Americans never built anything to last and nobody thought it worth while to try to make the American 2-6-0s last as long as British locomotives did.

On every one of the imported 2-6-0s, the feature that distinguished them most violently from the natives was the large cab with backwardly extended roof and two windows on each side besides generous forward look-outs. If the enginemen showed appreciation of how well these cabs sheltered them from bad weather it was not conveyed in a way that induced Ivatt to provide similar cabs on GN engines nor was his successor, Gresley, quickly persuaded in that direction. Gresley did, however, eventually go in for 2-6-0s and the American engines may have done something to guide his mind into that direction.

The distinctly American feature of the engines was the bar frame; the width of the bars forced the firebox to be narrower than in normal British practice.

The quick delivery of 20 locomotives so well satisfied GN needs that they could allow the builders (Baldwin Locomotive Works) to send the last one to the Paris Exposition of 1900 as part of the Baldwin exhibit.

The 2-6-0s were rather less powerful than the average GN o-6-0 of the period and they were said to be more costly in maintenance. They were scrapped after an average life of about ten years.

GRESLEY 2/2-6-0s (n66 n67 n68)

Gresley's first new engines for the GN were required for "mixed traffic". This meant that they were goods engines that could nevertheless undertake many passenger train jobs without knocking themselves to pieces by higher than goods train speeds. For this he built biggish 0-6-0s with biggish wheels.

But a big 0-6-0 at speed wears the sides of the rails and the flanges of its leading wheels and when a bit run down was apt to sway in an unhappy-looking manner. A leading pony-truck could help here and moreover would enable the cylinders to be placed outside the frame-plates in a position impracticable in a 0-6-0 because of excessive overhang.

So Gresley put a fairly large 0-6-0 boiler on a 2/2-6-0 chassis to produce No 1630 (n66), the first of Class K1. This was in 1912, by which time he was sure that a superheater ought to go in, that piston valves were required, that the right place for them was over the cylinders, and that the right valve gear was Walschaerts. A batch of ten such engines were built in 1912-13 and their work matched all reasonable expectations. But somebody thought that a fatter boiler might be better even though the firebox were not enlarged, and this was fortunate as the resulting engine, No 1640 (n67) the first of Class K2, turned out to be the best-looking 2/2-6-0 to be seen anywhere. This at least is the writer's view and he hopes that the middle photo on p. 116 may justify that view in the reader's eyes. Even slight variations in the angle of application of the camera may make or mar the beauty of its picture of an engine. This one could not be bettered.

Rather surprising details of these engines were the use of the Stirling type of pull-out regulator handle and of lever reversing gear; just grip the latch-lever on the handle and she might drop like a stone into full forward gear.

In accordance with a passing fashion in Britain, the 1630s and the early 1640s had piston tail-rods but these were soon removed.

A total of 65 of the 1640s (Class K2) were built before 1922. After the first 20, the design was modified to bring steam to the cylinders by outside pipes in straight casings. The pipe-lines themselves were not straight.

The special purpose of these "mixed traffic" 2-6-0s was the haulage of "fitted freight" trains of vans and wagons fitted with vacuum brakes. This removed the speed limit imposed on ordinary British goods trains by the impossibility of stopping quickly with no brakes beyond those on the engine, the tender and the guard's brake-van. What limited the safe speed of a "fitted freight" was the tendency of 4-wheel vans to wiggle wildly when running fast. For this reason such trains were not supposed to exceed some arbitrary speed figure in the region of 50 mph.

The 2-6-0s might handle any class of train but were not normally to be seen on the best main line express passenger trains. A GN exception, however, was provided by the line from Doncaster through Wakefield to Leeds. The Kings

Cross—Leeds trains nearly all stopped at Doncaster, Wakefield and Holbeck. Because the northbound start from Wakefield and the southbound starts from Leeds and Holbeck were on steep gradients, Atlantics were not the best possible engines for this route; for many years Pacifics were prohibited by the dubious load capacity of the bridge over the River Calder between Sandal and Wakefield. So when the K2 2-6-0s became established they were just about the best possible GN engines for this route; they did not displace the Atlantics entirely, but they surpassed them handsomely in starting and as they could come down past Hampole with a big train at 75 or so they need not lose much time on the way. Although many enthusiasts used to like the sight of wildly scurrying wheels and motion, it does tend to be expensive in demanding a high standard of maintenance in the machinery. In the bad conditions that developed during World War II and after it, one of the connecting rod big ends of a K2 came to bits somewhere near Hampole and the back end of the connecting rod then trailed on the sleeper-ends, but nobody noticed until the rod caught on a rail crossing at Carcroft and then derailed the engine and the train. Before World War II such things were not to be expected and K2s and K3s regularly made spritely speeds between Wakefield and Doncaster.

One can only conjecture about the fastest running made by the K2s but I did note No 1685 to take nine vehicles (about 280 tons loaded) over the 19·8 miles from Doncaster to Wakefield in 20 min 20 sec. I recorded few details because this was a rare occasion in that, after noting the starting time, I went to the restaurant car for some tea. It was an exceptionally rare occasion in that I shared a table with someone more interesting than the scenery or the rail joints. I noted no times but was subconsciously aware from the sound of the exhaust that the engine was working hard and fast. When I observed that that was still the case as we went *down* from Hare Park, I took time off to do a bit of timing and noted a full 80 as we dived under the Midland on the approach to Sandal. It was a roughish run into Wakefield but we stopped at the right place.

I had a word with the enginemen at Leeds. It appeared that at Doncaster, where the train was behind time, a passenger most anxious to reach Wakefield as soon as it could be done had given the fireman ten bob and had promised another to the driver if he got to Wakefield in 20 min. This (according to my watch) was not quite achieved but the passenger paid and everyone was delighted. Twenty minutes would have been an unusually good time in the opposite and easier direction.

The average train-timing enthusiast frowned on this type of thing. His objection was that it could encourage a driver into reckless running and that it could mean unfair treatment of the engine. The real objection, however, was probably that if successful bribery of this nature became known and practised, the best "collections" of runs would inevitably belong to the affluent rather than to the honest.

Reverting now to normal running, it need hardly be added that there were enginemen who were not impressed by the 2-6-0s as engines for goods trains, or even for "fitted freights". They were used to the good old 0-6-0s, they were used to getting underneath them to fill oil-boxes on big ends, they were used to struggling to get at other parts of the inside mechanism, and when they were given an engine that didn't need such awkward attentions they were suspicious. They couldn't see *how* they were being "got at" but they were sure that it must be so. They responded by insisting that the 0-6-0s were better engines and although their disapproval relaxed with time, the 2-6-0s were never fully accepted by all GN enginemen.

GRESLEY 3/2-6-0s (n68)

Even if Gresley had been convinced that the mechanism he had used on No 461 (n77) for deriving the motion of the inside valve from the outside ones was all that it need have been, he was likely to have been shaken by comments made about it in letters published in the technical press. He was probably most impressed by the testimony of H. Holcroft who had studied such mechanisms very thoroughly (and was even granted a patent on one in 1909) and in special consultation was able to suggest a very much more practical mechanism for the same purpose than that on No 461. This Gresley was naturally anxious to try as soon as possible, and he incorporated it in Britain's biggest 2-6-0, No 1000, the first of the three-cylinder Class K3 which in GN days consisted of ten engines, Nos 1000-1009, built with customary GN deliberation in 1920-21 and which was eventually enlarged by the LNER to a total of 193.

At 72 tons she was the heaviest British eight-wheel steam locomotive. In 1920 the closest British competitor was a very different kind of engine, the L &Y superheater 2-4-2T, weighing 5 tons less although nearly 5 ft longer.

The coupled wheels of the K3 carried a full 60 tons. Only the GWR Pacific, *The Great Bear* and the Great Central 2-6-4 Ts had previously attained quite this figure in Britain.

No 1000 was the first engine in Britain to have a boiler 6 ft in diameter at the front end; only one British locomotive (Gresley's Garratt banker for Worsborough) ever surpassed it in this respect.

The boiler barrel was bent from a single sheet of steel. This feature did not persist in LNER-built engines of the K3 class. The plate-rolling fraternity may well have decided that plates twice as wide as usual justified a special price per ton so that it became more expensive to use one plate than to use two.

Alloy steel coupling rods and connecting rods machined down to thin I-form were about 35 per cent lighter than the corresponding members of the Class K2 2-6-0s. Even with the inside connecting rod, the total weight (1880 lb) of these was slightly less in the K3 than in the K2, but the out-of-balance forces at any particular speed were very much less in the three-cylinder engine.

The cab fittings showed some modernisation compared with those of the K2s. The Stirling "pull-out" regulator handle was replaced by twin handles hanging from the ends of a cross shaft. Gresley had seen something like this on the L &Y Atlantics as first built at Horwich near the turn of the century.

The three-bar crosshead design introduced with No 461 was used on No 1000. What was not obvious from outside was that the inside cylinder was much higher than the outside cylinder so that the inside connecting rod and the crosshead could clear the leading coupled axle. The three-bar design of crosshead was distinctly advantageous here, because it permitted the centre-line of the cylinder to be much closer to the axle than is possible where there is a slide-bar below the piston-rod.

Self-aligning ball bearings were used at the big ends of the return-crank rods; they had previously been tried on at least one of the K2 2-6-os. Later on it was found advantageous to use a roller bearing on the main pivot pin of the conjugating mechanism.

The conjugated valve gear introduced some new problems in valve setting and, judging from the uneven beats of Gresley three-cylinder engines, those problems took many years to solve. My first hearing of a K3 suggested that they had adjusted things to get three consecutive beats at equal intervals and left the other three where they had happened to come; their spacing was markedly uneven.

The rounded cab-roof, the short chimney and the low dome suggested that things were being pushed to the limit of the loading gauge, and this may well have been a reason for fitting the bright brass "pop" safety-valves to No 1000.

Outside steam-pipes were to be expected after their adoption in the later K2s. Large holes in the frame-plates were evidence of a desire to minimise weight in relation to main dimensions.

The new features in No 1000 gave food for thought. Her fat boiler suggested power. Her six-beat turning moment applied to six wheels each carrying 10 tons suggested a strong pull. The way she lifted 300 tons out of Holbeck and the way she whizzed through limestone cutting and leafy glade at Hampole at the head of ten of varnished teak showed that she could pull and run. One could hardly see her beating an Atlantic down Essendine if the Atlantic were really trying but the 2-6-0 was evidently fast enough to keep time with any GN express train.

Yes! the 1000s were great engines suggesting what features might be expected in the Gresley Pacific when it should appear, but raising doubts as to whether there was any need for it.

During early trials No 1000 worked some of the heaviest passenger trains on the GN main line and also some of the heaviest coal trains weighing up to 1600 tons behind the tender.

As it happened, the Coal Strike in 1921 came just at the right time for recently run-in 1000s to handle 600 ton passenger trains on brisk schedules on the GN main line, and this they did well.

They took a share in working the Leeds express trains between Doncaster and

Leeds and enthusiastic amateurs could not fail to admire the best of what they did. Enginemen were a little qualified in their praise because, except when newly out of the shops after general repairs, the K3s usually rode roughly at speed. One is said to have touched 90 mph at Sandal on a run specially made to assess the dynamic effect of a three-cylinder engine on the Calder Bridge between Sandal and Wakefield; in ordinary service, however, the K3s rarely exceeded 80 mph.

The early running of K3s revealed an unsuspected defect in the valve gear conjugating mechanism. In accordance with what was then widely accepted practice, the valves were set in full forward gear, giving them maximum travel, when steam was shut off. When this was done at speed on a K3 not in the prime of condition, nasty noises might come from the front end and when the valves and valve gear were next examined it was found that there had been impact between components that no-one thought could possibly touch each other. This led to the realisation that the combination of mass of moving parts, elasticity of metal, and slackness in joints could produce marked "over-travel" of the inside valve. The maximum practicable modification would not completely cure the defect; to make up the difference, drivers were instructed not to advance the cut-off beyond a stated amount when running at speed.

This happened early enough to be taken into account when designing the Gresley Pacific. Most lamentably, the action taken hamstrung that unfortunate locomotive during its period of gestation. Even with a good example set by the Great Western nearly 20 years earlier, the significance of valve/cylinder proportions had not been generally appreciated in Britain before 1922. Those of the 1000 class were just about right but, it would seem, by accident rather than design.

If I were to venture an opinion on appearance, I would say that the K1 was an adolescent, that the K2 was a shapely adult and that the K3 was an adult awkwardly aspiring to be a giantess; she could look well if you chose your viewpoint carefully. When, after 1922, the 2-6-0s were cut down to the general LNER loading gauge, the K2s lost their elegance and the K3s became unmistakeable giantesses, only just able to get under the bridges, and distinctive in their unashamed portliness.

CHAPTER EIGHT

Pacifics (n69)

THE LARGE ATLANTICS were good engines in many ways, but getting away from rest in adverse conditions was not one of them. Four-coupled wheels in the middle of an engine don't grip the rails like four-coupled wheels at one end and so the Atlantics were not such good starters as were the biggest British 4-4-0s in 1914. By that time six-coupled main line passenger train engines were well established on several British railways and it was clear that the GN must eventually move in that direction.

World War I imposed such demands on railway workshops that it was hardly to be expected that any new design would materialise until after the war ended, and on the GN that was indeed the case. Gresley drafted a design for a Pacific in 1915, there were rumours about a 2-6-2 and in 1920 the striking 2-6-0 No 1000 was built at Doncaster, but still no six-coupled locomotive specifically for fast trains.

The London & North Western Railway and the Lancashire & Yorkshire Railway amalgamated at the beginning of 1922 and this was recognised as probably presaging more widespread merging of the railway companies of Great Britain. Many were going to lose their identities and those that hoped for preferential treatment had need to show a progressive spirit. Perhaps recognition of this helped Gresley to secure directors' approval of development of a big new engine and almost certainly influenced the decision to name it *Great Northern* as engine-naming was not a Great Northern practice.

The writer's first knowledge of the first Gresley Pacific was obtained from a broadside view in *The Engineer* for April 14, 1922 and no other picture of any engine of the class made a more powerful impression on him. The most striking feature was the "combustion chamber" reaching forward from the wide firebox over the rear coupled wheels into the British record-breaking diameter of 6 ft 5 in at the large end of the tapered second ring of the boiler-barrel. *Great Northern* was outstandingly "new" in this respect.

In designing the boiler of the Pacific the main point was to get adequate firebox volume. The very nature of a wide firebox gives a lower ratio of volume to grate area than naturally occurs in a box that is narrower at the grate than at the centre height of the barrel. For a wide box to be made comparable in this respect to a narrow box it must be extended into the barrel. (A marked extension of this character tends to be called a "combustion chamber" but what else is the firebox?) So the firebox in the Gresley Pacific was given a forward slope in its front plate and a forward bulge at the barrel. The fire tubes were limited in length to 100 times the diameter and that fixed the position of the front tube-plate. This made a boiler in a rather better style than that of the big Atlantic and about 30 per cent bigger.

As the Pacific had one axle more than an Atlantic, length might be a problem as it was with the GW Pacific. There the problem had won to the extent that the engine was normally restricted to the London-Bristol line, which was only a fraction of GW express-route mileage. It is interesting to note that a corresponding restriction of the GN Pacifics to the 156 miles between Kings Cross and Doncaster might not have been much of a hardship as it was on that length that nearly all the hard work on GN passenger trains was done. Nearly all the rest was done between Doncaster and Leeds where, however, the bridge over the Calder at Wakefield was deemed not to be strong enough to take a Pacific anyway.

The GN Atlantics had enough lateral "slop" to get round any curve that they were likely to reach, but no one really wanted to think of a Pacific slummocking along at speed like an Atlantic.

So the weight on the back end was taken by laminated springs through slides inclined to the horizontal plane, to the tops of axleboxes permitted to move obliquely across the engine in straight lines that simulated rotation about a vertical axis about 8 ft ahead. The inclined slides opposed lateral movement of the axleboxes relative to the main frame, but once their opposition was overcome they did not increase it. There was sufficient friction at the slides, although lubricated, to kill lateral oscillation pretty quickly.

This scheme is associated with the name Cartazzi which gave to the Gresley Pacific a specifically exotic touch.

The three-cylinder scheme with conjugating mechanism for working the inside valve was not surprising as it was a natural repetition of the main novelty in Gresley's three-cylinder 2-6-0s and the side-window cab was only a very late recognition of the virtue of a practice long-established on the North Eastern Railway.

The eight-wheel tender was large although no more than proportional to the size of the engine, but all eight hornblocks were attached to the main frame whereas all preceding eight-wheel tenders in Britain had been of the double-bogie type.

Here was a massive yet not ungraceful engine that looked as if it could get heavy trains over the road with speed and certainty; it was something like the 130 per cent large Atlantic that might keep the operating officials quiet for some time to come.

It was inevitable that *Great Northern* would be compared with the only preceding standard-gauge British Pacific, *The Great Bear* on the Great Western.

(The qualification "standard gauge" is necessary as Pacifics were running on small narrow-gauge railways in Britain.)

No one knows for certain just why *The Great Bear* was ever built and as difficulties with her length on curves caused her to be restricted to the London-Bristol routes, it was never possible to try her out on the really "hot" Great Western jobs on the Plymouth and Birmingham routes. Whether she could have "proved" herself in such services will never be known. Nor is it known that in passenger train service she ever equalled the best efforts of GW 4-6-0s. She was not brilliant but that is not to say that she had nothing worth copying.

It might have been suspected that the boiler of *The Great Bear* was not so good as it could have been. Although the grate area was 50 per cent bigger than that of the GW Star the firebox heating surface (158 sq ft) was actually slightly less. Firebox heating surface was less important than the firebox volume; the former figure was usually included in published dimensions of locomotives and might be taken as a rough indication of the other which was not normally quoted. So it seemed likely that the Gresley Pacific would gain by the increased firebox volume suggested by the comparison between the firebox heating surface of 215 sq ft with the 158 sq ft of *The Great Bear*. Its tube length of 19 ft might well be more appropriate than the immoderate 23 ft of *The Great Bear*. (In fact the significant ratio, that of length to diameter of fire tubes, of 101 against 108, only slightly favoured the GN engine.)

A scarcely-noticed innovation in the Pacifics was the "drop-gate". This means that the firebars in the front 15 in of the grate were carried on a frame that could be swung downwards, dropping the fire on it into the ashpan, and leaving a space to push the rest of the fire through. This eliminated the hot, laborious and tricky job of lifting the remains of a fire out of the box through the fire-hole.

The drop-grate was no new idea, but it was adopted in Britain only slowly and reluctantly and after a very long delay.

It is probably true to say that either no rational consideration was given to determination of dimensions of the valves of *Great Northern* or its conclusions had been over-ruled. Cylinders 20 by 26 had been used in the 1640 class 2-6-0s and 8 in diameter valves in the 1000 class 2-6-0s; they were put together in the Pacific and it was said in attempted extenuation, some years later, that an 8 in valve was the biggest that could be accommodated alongside a central 20 in cylinder. Even if this had been true (and it may at least be doubted) the importance of valve dimensions could have justified a non-central placing of the inside cylinder, although this might have been regarded as an outrageous suggestion at the time. Churchward's staff at Swindon had got valve design rationally sorted out but there is little evidence that that was the case on any other British railway.

It is said that Gresley had been inspired in boiler design by study of the Pennsylvania K4 Pacific and test-results from its boiler. He could have had equally valuable guidance in valve design from Swindon practice, but did he seek the essential information, which had been published? To accept guidance from a foreign country exhibits a progressive broadmindedness but reliance on a near neighbour is very ordinary. How many locomotive engineers at that time recognised the importance of valve dimensions in establishing the GW's lead in Britain? How many recognised that Swindon had a marked lead in locomotive design?

On matter of this kind, the publication in the *Railway Magazine* of a perpetual series of articles on British Locomotive Practice and Performance had established a rather strange situation. Amateurs could be better informed than professionals on the subject of comparative running of locomotives on British railways. These articles, started by Charles Rous-Marten and developed much more extensively by Cecil J. Allen, had built up an ever-growing collection of facts about the daily running of trains on British main lines. Anyone who intelligently studied these facts was led inevitably to the conclusion that GW 4-6-0s could beat the main line locomotives of any other British railway in the haulage of express passenger trains. The writer is unaware of any other source of information on this point and so he is inclined to believe that many professional locomotive engineers who did not read the *Railway Magazine* articles had no reason to think that study of GW design might be specially worthwhile. Had Gresley accepted the valve/cylinder proportions of the GW Saint and Star designs and based on the average of them he would have in 1922 attained in this respect what he did not achieve until he produced the A4 design in 1935. With boiler pressure of 180 lb/sq in he would have needed cylinders 21 × 28 to give a nominal tractive effort of 35000 lb (corresponding to best cylinder performance for 2000 indicated horsepower between 45 and 60 mph) and 11 in valves with 1¾ in lap to get best valve performance between 40 and 80 mph. Such valve dimensions might well have given him pause and in fact they were never matched on British railways until after nationalisation in 1948. But rational design on the basis of Churchward achievements would have suggested those figures in 1922.

What was actually done was to remember that 8 in valves worked all right in the three-cylinder 2-6-0s except that in full gear at high speed the over-run permitted by slackness at joints in the valve gear had caused some bother. So in the Pacific the same valves were used but with lap reduced from 1½ to 1¼ in which reduced the travel (*and the port opening*) at any particular cut-off, and with full gear cut-off limited to 65 per cent instead of the usual 75 to 80 per cent. The product of valve diameter and lap was 10 sq in whereas it should preferably have been about 18.

It is hard to believe that trouble with valve over-run in the three-cylinder 2-6-0s could frighten anyone into restricting the valve-travel in an entirely new design of locomotive that was to be a big "modern" engine, the latest pride of the GNR. But that's how it seems to have been. Certainly the early Gresley Pacifics had valves that half-strangled them whereas, in starting on a clean sheet, they could have been given Great Western proportions.

This did not mean that No 1470 wouldn't go, but that she was not a "flyer" in the GW sense and could not achieve the GW standard of overall thermal efficiency. The early Pacifics were good strong reliable engines that established a new standard of haulage power on the GN and as one admirer said rather ambiguously, they left scope for further development.

In the Pacific, the general arrangement of cylinders, motion and valve gear was, so far as possible, identical with that of the three-cylinder 2-6-0s, but the difference in wheel arrangement and in diameter of coupled wheels enforced a difference in cylinder layout. The outside cylinders were necessarily much further from the driving axle and so an inside cylinder centre-line projected from the driving axle at the minimum slope that would clear the leading coupled axle, would have caused an inside cylinder over the centre of the bogie to be in the smokebox. So the inside cylinder was set to the rear of the outside cylinders and in fact slightly behind the rear bogie-axle. In consequence the front inside valve spindle gland was a bit entombed. To get at it, a good little 'un was better than a good big 'un but as only exhaust steam could leak past the gland and, under the smokebox, would not be noticeable anyhow, there was no need to be pernickety about adjustment of the gland-packing. Apart from that, accessibility of mechanism was excellent.

As in the 1000s, alloy steel was used in the Pacifics for connecting rods so that weight could be saved by using thin flanges and thin webs. "Weight could be saved" means that the rods could be made lighter than would seem to be safe in less strong steels but in one sense the sentence is misleading. The piece of steel required to make the lighter rod may be just as heavy as that for the heavier rod. The lighter rod is lighter because more metal has been cut from the original piece of steel to produce the thinner shape. The light rod is very much more expensive than the heavy one because: (a) the price of alloy steel per hundredweight is higher than that of "plain" steel; (b) the cost of machining the alloy rod is higher, firstly because it is harder to cut and secondly because more metal has to be cut from it: and (c) the cost of heat treatment is higher for alloy steel than for plain steel.

It may be added that, cubic inch for cubic inch, alloy steel is just as heavy as plain steel.

On p. 146 it is explained that these light rods might easily be buckled by compressive loads that could be applied to them. They were expensive and weak. Post-Gresley practice did not include them.

A special feature in the early Gresley Pacifics was that each piston was made in one piece with the piston rod, which was bored out to save weight. This meant a very expensive forging in a very expensive material, and rather expensive machining. The product was much lighter than the corresponding conventional assembly of piston and rod fitted together and locked with a nut, but was it worth the extra cost?

Gresley is thought to have obtained the idea of adopting this scheme from the similar one adopted in the Pennsylvania Pacific which had been developed with special care and had been described and delineated in extraordinary profusion of detail in a 7-part article in *Engineering* in 1916. But that was a two-cylinder Pacific and lightening of reciprocating parts was valuable in that it permitted reduction of the balance weights fitted to offset horizontal forces set up by the reciprocating parts and therefore of reduction of their hammerblow on the track.

In a three-cylinder engine the horizontal forces largely balance themselves and it is not necessary to use any balance weights in connection with them. So hammerblow need not have been any greater with mechanism of conventional design than with the specially lightened mechanism.

The "running gear" of a Gresley Pacific was mechanically elegant, beautifully light and damnably dear. The three-bar type of crosshead was like that of the Pennsylvania K4s, but Gresley did not copy the hair-pin proportions of its valve gear.

Lightness is usually a virtue, but not always. It is vital in any aeroplane that is to operate for profit. A locomotive, on the other hand, relies on weight to get a grip on the rails and so lightness of the complete machine may not be entirely advantageous.

My first sight of the Gresley Pacific was at Doncaster station when she came from the shed ("Carr Loco") tender-first on the down main line and stopped between the platforms. Perhaps because she came in behind the big tender, very highly built up with coal, she did not look so large as I expected (and anyway a bigger engine had been running on the Great Western for 14 years). Her short chimney was the best indirect indicator of size, but we had been made used to this by the three-cylinder 2-6-0s; it was the tapering-out of the boiler from smoke box diameter to something distinctly larger at the hefty firebox that suggested plenty of power.

Then she started ahead and limped across the up main to an up loop, there to await the train she was to take to Kings Cross. Uneven beat and connecting rod clank were accepted as endearing trifles rather than as imperfections, and even after they had persisted for years in dozens of Gresley Pacifics I found no reason to regard them as significant defects.

As the GNR was merged in the LNER group only about eight months after No 1470 was built, there was no real chance for enginemen to become sufficiently well-acquainted with her or her sister No 1471 to show what they could really do before they ceased to be Great Northern engines. Gresley had stated that the Pacifics had been designed for 600 ton trains and No 1471 demonstrated this on a special test-run by taking 20 vehicles (610 tons) from Kings Cross to a stop at Grantham in 122 min (see Table 1, p. 197). This, however, was not markedly better than what the three-cylinder 2-6-0s had shown they could do.

Like No 990 a quarter-century earlier the Pacifics were too long for the Kings Cross turntables and had to go to Hornsey to turn, till a 70 ft turntable (vacuum-operated) was installed by the LNER at Kings Cross near the end of 1923.

When working hard the big Atlantics were said to be "peppering along".

The GN Pacifics peppered 50 per cent faster and 30 per cent harder. Their approach at speed was heralded by a roar. In 1922 I awaited one from a vantage-point east of the main line on the Gainsborough road out of Bawtry. A north west wind was blowing and this gave earlier notice of the approach of a train from Doncaster than might otherwise have been the case.

I first noticed a distant roar when the train must have been nearly four miles away. The noise gradually grew stronger for an uncannily long time until a steam cloud appeared on the far side of Bawtry station, when the exhaust roar was suddenly slightly diminished as the driver notched up for the down-grade. Nevertheless the Pacific had still a harsh voice as she swept along the brick viaduct, accelerating down the grade to Scrooby troughs. I took in what I could of the form and details of this new engine and was rather surprised at the amount of "daylight" that came through the large holes in the frame-plates. It was indeed a moving picture of a very notable giantess profitably employed in getting a Leeds and Bradford train to London and seeming to find it harder than one would have expected of one so large. It was a picture that I saw many times later and that I should like to see again. But the most surprising circumstance was the harsh noise from the chimney. It suggested that something would have to be improved before one could say that the GN Pacifics were a match for anything else in Great Britain. All the same, with a boiler like that, the Pacifics had a clear power potential. As the Pennsylvania boys might have said to Gresley— "You got somep'n there, Bert. She'll go places once you gotten the bugs outa her." And so she did, but not within the lifetime of the GNR. It had less than half a year to run.

I found the side elevation of the Gresley Pacifics very eyeable, and the cutting down of chimney dome and cab in later years to enable Pacifics to run on any LNER main line, made them look more powerful. The smokebox might have been extended with advantage to appearance and perhaps to operation in providing more room for smokebox "char". I always felt that the wheelbase was there to be filled and I have ventured in Fig. (c) p. 125 to depict a 180 lb Pacific as it might have been in 1922, cut down for general service on British main lines and provided with cylinders and valves for Swindon level of performance. To leave room for the inside valve, the inside cylinder might have had to be set an inch or two off centre and this would have superheated the purest purists without any detriment to the engine.

But the actual Gresley Pacifics were sufficiently novel to delight the average enthusiast. During 1922 they did all that was asked of them without much trouble and so no-one could grumble. Some might remark that a good deal of what work they were doing was within the scope of an Atlantic, or a three-cylinder 2-6-0. The Pacifics might be doing it on less coal than the smaller engines would require but no-one was at all sure about it. No-one could say that the Pacifics were light on coal and no results have ever been published of any quantitative tests that may have been made in those very early days.

The fact that neither of the Pacifics was ever reported to have attained any notably high speed was readily explained by saying that they ran so well uphill that it was unnecessary to go fast downhill. They were in this respect comparable with contemporaneous big Atlantics; they occasionally reached 80 mph but did not exceed 85. They naturally beat the Atlantics up the gradients from Kings Cross to Finsbury Park and no-one could have suspected at that time that they themselves were to be decisively beaten on this stretch by a six-coupled "foreigner" in 1925. One could only guess how they would compare with the North Eastern Pacific that began running late in 1922.

CHAPTER NINE

Eight-coupled Engines (n70 to n77)

2/0-8-0T (Avonside 1866) (n70)

THERE IS NO DOUBT that for start-and-stop service a locomotive should have all its weight carried by coupled wheels and plenty of them. So Sturrock's trial of two 0-8-0 tank engines for running GN goods trains through the Metropolitan Railway tunnels between Kings Cross and Blackfriars was very sensible.

These engines, built by Avonside in 1866, were formidable for their day and had strength and power well above anything used on the underground service at the time and indeed for a long time afterwards. They represented a big step forward, but it is sad to say that big steps are not always successful. After the spate of courageous and often outrageous quick steps in the early days of railways, the general pattern of development subsided to the form of small steps with intermediate pauses for reflection.

The Avonside tanks ran for 14 years but no more were built and this combination of circumstances makes it hard to judge whether they were "successful" or not. Over 20 years elapsed before any other GN eight-coupled engine was sent "down the drain" and it was certainly not successful in that region.

The Avonside tank engines were of Avonside design and the outside cylinders were the most distinctive departure from GN practice. Both the leading and trailing axles had spring-controlled side-play but only to the extent of less than an inch each way and this was probably as much as crosshead clearance allowed in the leading axle. The rear axle was not similarly constrained and more play could have been allowed, perhaps with hinged rear coupling rods, modified brake hangers and a narrowed frame.

The general appearance of these engines was very workmanlike. Long side tanks gave high capacity for water for boiler-feed and for condensing exhaust steam. There was, however, no space specifically allotted for coal and one wonders indeed whether each engine normally ran with a tender.

0-8-0 (n71)

Where a need arose for something bigger than a 0-6-0 for goods traffic, the obvious move was to provide a longer firebox and a fatter boiler barrel. If the weight could be carried on three axles without exceeding the maximum axleload permissible on any of the routes where more power was required, then the engine could be a 0-6-0; if not, the 0-8-0 was the obvious development. In this way was designed GN No 401 which appeared in 1901 and by the end of 1906 44 similar engines had been built.

There was inadequate room for valves between 20 in cylinders and so link motion with rocking shafts and levers drove balanced flat valves above the cylinders.

The boiler was generally similar to that used on the small Atlantics but the ashpan had to be modified to clear the rear axle.

There was no special distinction about this design. It was the result of placing the biggest existing standard boiler on the smallest number of small wheels that would take it and using as many other standard parts as possible. The 401s did the heavier work that was expected of them but there is no suggestion that they ever showed any special distinction.

The 401s beat the biggest existing GN 0-6-0s by 38 per cent in grate area, by 34 per cent in adhesion weight and by 50 per cent in nominal tractive effort. They were therefore about 35 per cent stronger and more powerful and might be expected to do a bit more work per pound of coal.

They were fitted with superheaters and piston valves in their later days and in 1918 one of them (No 420, n73) was given a fatter boiler of the type used on the larger 2/2-6-0s (n67)

0-8-2Ts (n74, n75, n75A)

After a couple of years' experience with the earlier 0-8-0s, Ivatt used it in making another stab at the problem of working GN trains over the Metropolitan underground line. In 1903 he produced a "super" tank engine (n74) with what looked like a bigger boiler than that of the 401s. This was an optical illusion produced by a 9 in cutting down of chimney and dome.

The new engine, No 116, was in fact a 401 class 0-8-0 extended to take a bunker and fitted with long, high side tanks. As a full complement of water and coal alone added 13 tons to the total weight, the tank engine could be expected to be about 20 tons heavier than the tender engine. According to the official figures it was in fact 24 tons heavier and once the engine was running, the civil engineers were able to say that it was too heavy to be tolerated on the Metropolitan line.

Before any alteration was made, however, someone noticed that the huge outer vertical wall of each side tank could be a good billboard and No 116 was photographed with large current GN posters pasted to one of its side tanks. The number of the engine was erased from the bunker and its place taken by the legend "This space to let". Here was a sign perhaps of Britain's laboured struggle out of the slough of solemnity ordained by the wishes of Her lately-deceased Majesty.

To get down the weight of No 116, Ivatt replaced the boiler by a slimmer one with firebox no bigger than that of the 0-6-0s, and shortened the side tanks enough to sacrifice 500 gal of water capacity. The nominal coal capacity was reduced from 4 tons to 3, but as no difference was made to the bunker, that was just a pious hope. Unless carefully watched, enginemen would load tenders and bunkers with enough coal for the bridges to trim the heap to size.

All succeeding 0-8-2Ts were built to this modified design. Ten of them worked goods and passenger trains in the Metropolitan tunnels but most of the others were used for short distance goods and mineral trains in the vicinity of Nottingham and in the West Riding of Yorkshire. Later on the first ten engines were transferred from London to Colwick (Nottingham).

It was said that a reason for withdrawing the 0-8-2s from London suburban passenger trains was that they were not fast enough. This presumably means that to make acceptable speed downhill they had to be worked harder than the other GN engines. No suburban train schedule demands anything very spritely up-hill and the 0-8-2Ts had sufficient pull to do all that was required in that direction. They could beat the 4-4-2Ts uphill, but with smaller and more numerous coupled wheels they were naturally less free-running downhill at equal cut-offs. But it is hard to believe that the big engines would not have run fast enough if given cut-off late enough to avoid undue restriction of exhaust. This sounds like a complaint invented by enginemen to reinforce others that they had.

And they had plenty to complain about in the cab. From the top of the door (and of the tank) to the under-side of the archway was only 18 in. From the top of the wooden pedestal was only 5 ft 5 in.

From the back of the boiler to the front of the bunker was only 4 ft 4 in, leaving the fireman only a hamstrung swing for a 7 ft 6 in grate.

There were lookout windows in the rear wall of the cab, but nothing could be seen through them when the bunker was full of coal, and very little when it was empty.

The greatest width of the whole engine was at the top of the bunker but the driver had to push his head out further still to get any view of where he was going with bunker leading and had to put up with the coal-dust.

Whatever the merits of what are normally regarded as the major technical features of its design, no engine with defects of this kind has any chance of being successful in service. The enginemen will see to that.

The arrangement of blastpipe and petticoat was noticeably non-Goss* and change here might have permitted such enlargement of the blast nozzle as would have made the engine faster downhill. But nothing of this kind would make as much difference as a couple of turns on the reversing screw.

*Professor Goss (Purdue University) whose research before 1904 on front-end design was very valuable to any locomotive engineer who bothered to examine its results. Churchward, on the Great Western, had done so by 1906, and most of the others by 1950.

In their later days and other places these tank engines were given boilers of the original diameter but this tended to be concealed by the fact that the chimneys used were taller than the original ones and the cab roofs were raised. Superheaters were provided and the position of the snifting valve showed that the tube-plate was set well behind the back edge of the smokebox wrapper plate. The engines retained over-cylinder flat valves exhausting vertically through the "back" (that is to say the "top") directly into the blastpipe.

A noticeable effect of superheating on these engines was that the economy of water enabled them to take coal trains from Colwick to New England (Peterborough) without any need to stop to refill the tanks. This was one of the rare cases in which saving in water was specifically advantageous. Superheating also cut coal-consumption by some 15 per cent.

Later on some of these engines were relegated to empty-coach working into and out of Kings Cross.

The bottom photo on p. 122 shows the bunker rails arranged to give a backward view from inside the cab.

2/2-8-0s (n76)

Being satisfied that a 2/2-6-0 with outside mechanism was superior to a 0-6-0, Gresley was obviously likely to prefer a 2/2-8-0 to a 0-8-0. So there was little surprise when in 1913 the first GN 2/2-8-0 No 456 appeared. The outside Walschaerts valve gear was to be expected after Gresley's use of it on the early 2-6-0s but a new GN feature was the feeding of each steam-chest by a pipe that came out of the smokebox about halfway up. The shape of the heavily lagged casing of the pipe suggested that it might be straight and very widespread use of this feature in later years led some commentators to imagine that by cutting out a bend or two, a straight pipe could give an engine quite a bit of "zip". Actually the advantage of "outside steam pipes" was simply that of reducing the pipe joints and general clutter in the bottom of the smokebox. The pipes might not, in fact, be straight.

In sharp contrast to this "modern" feature, the feed of boiler-water through a clack box on about the middle of each side of the barrel was a reversion in No 456 to 19th century practice. It did not persist on the GN.

In No 456 the GN had a close counterpart to the 2800 class 2/2-8-0 on the Great Western but with the advantage of more readily accessible valve-gear.

These GN 2/2-8-0s were about 10 per cent bigger than the 0-8-0s but they were less numerous as only 20 were built. This was because by the time the batch was completed, Gresley had fallen for the three-cylinder principle and he applied it to his subsequent eight-coupled locomotives.

3/2-8-0s (n77)

No doubt noticing the development and multiplication of classes of three-cylinder locomotives on the adjoining North Eastern Railway, and seeing the probable future necessity to use more than two cylinders, Gresley built a three-cylinder equivalent to his 2/2-8-0 in 1918. It differed in that all three cylinders drove onto the second coupled wheel-and-axle assembly instead of onto the third. A special feature was a conjugating mechanism that enabled the valve for the inside cylinder to derive its motion from those of the outside valves each driven by Walschaerts valve gear in the usual way. This mechanism was kinematically passable but it did not evoke warm approval from every locomotive engineer. Its many rubbing surfaces and short links suggested that normal wear

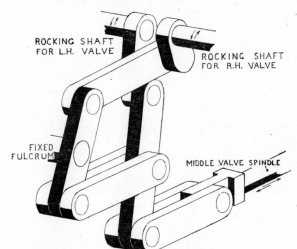

ROCKING SHAFT
FOR L.H. VALVE

ROCKING SHAFT
FOR R.H. VALVE

FIXED
FULCRUM

MIDDLE VALVE SPINDLE

Fig. 2. Diagrammatic view of conjugating mechanism used in 3/2–8–0 No 461.

might produce perceptible inaccuracy in the motion of the inside valve. Whether such inaccuracy would have significant results was not seriously considered at the time.

No 461 had about seven per cent higher nominal tractive effort than No 456 and, in some circumstances at least, this would give her an advantage, quite apart from any that might come from three cylinders, and so would help Gresley to convince himself that the three-cylinder principle was worth adopting. He did adopt it and used it widely in many of the locomotives he afterwards designed.

A feature that No 461 introduced to the GN was the use of the "three-bar crosshead" (Fig. 3). This is a convenient name for a crosshead made to work under a broad slide-bar and over two narrow slide-bars one on each side of a web that connects the sliding element to the gudgeon pin in the small end of the connecting rod.

The particular form of conjugated valve gear used in No 461 was not repeated.

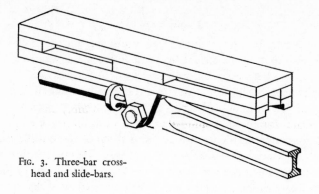

FIG. 3. Three-bar cross-
head and slide-bars.

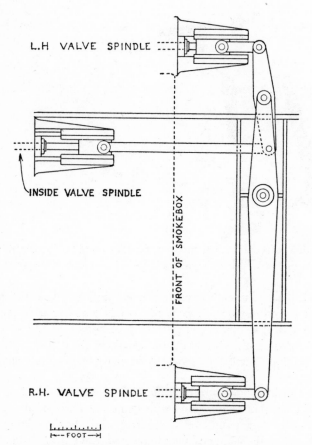

FIG. 4. Plan view of Holcroft-Gresley conjugating mechanism that
derives the motion for the inside valve from those of the outside valves.

A much less objectionable alternative was used in the 3/2-6-os introduced in 1920 and it was also applied to the 3/2-8-os built by the GN in 1920-21 and by the LNE after grouping.

The regulator was worked by a double-handle horizontal lever in the old Stirling style. The reversing handle was attached to the upper end of an elongated nut rotatable about a nearly vertical axis. From the nut, the screw extended downwards to its connection with a bell-crank lever, of which the vertical arm was connected by the usual long rod to a similar arm on the reversing shaft.

The axial loads imposed on the nut by forces from the reversing shaft were taken by ball bearings.

The handle was locked against undesired rotation by engagement of any notch on its boss with a latch movable by the driver. When the handle was thus locked, the reversing shaft could be locked by a vacuum-operated hand brake provided that there was vacuum in the train pipe. Unlatching the reversing handle also released the reversing shaft by destroying the locking vacuum.

CHAPTER TEN

Tenders and rail-coaches

TENDERS

GREAT NORTHERN PRACTICE complied with general British convention in that tenders were outside-frame six-wheelers. Also conventional was early limitation of height and loading with coal to permit a man to stand on top within the height of the loading gauge. This could never have been a necessity and with increase in power of engines and consumption of coal, tenders were gradually built bigger till they overtopped the boiler.

Sturrock tenders had outside sandwich frames. The frames of the early Stirling tenders were made mostly of timber. They were outside the wheels and outside the axleboxes; the springs were over the axleboxes between the frame plates and the upper parts of the wheels, and were invisible with the tender in any running condition. Only the inside of the boiler would have been a more effective hiding-place for the springs. Features at this level of intelligence (and they are dotted here and there over a wide range in British locomotive practice) inevitably make one wonder whether the perpetrator had any personal acquaintance with the realities of keeping locomotives going.

In 15 years or so Stirling was persuaded out of the buried-spring atrocity on tenders and after 1882 new GN tenders fell into line with what became general British practice in having laminated springs over axleboxes outside steel frames, themselves outside the wheels.

Over the years, modifications to this design of GN tender raised the water capacity to as much as 3850 gal with a loaded weight of 43 tons. Such tenders were attached to the last 8-footers built in 1894. Ivatt tenders were generally similar to these, though none had quite so large a water capacity. The laying-down of water-troughs on the GN main line permitted Ivatt to adopt a 3500 gal tender as standard but it was inadequate for Atlantics handling the heavier passenger trains that were run during World War I. The difficulty was reduced by laying additional troughs at Langley, and it was only with the Gresley Pacifics that larger tenders appeared on the GN.

Great Northern tenders were higher than their contemporaries on other railways and whilst this would hinder the driver's view when running tender-first, it could also be a welcome protection from the weather. A lamentably small number of British tenders had a weatherboard with look-out glasses to alleviate the enginemen's discomfort when the tender led the engine. The GN never made any concession in this respect, but the tenders attached to Gresley Pacifics were high enough to do all that was possible without being specially designed to that end, and earlier GN tenders were nearly as good.

In the ordinary way there was not much working of passenger trains by engines running tender-first, but it was common enough with goods trains and mineral trains; perhaps the lower speeds of such trains were held to excuse the absence of weatherboards from British tenders.

STURROCK'S STEAM TENDERS

The second-favourite type of British locomotive was the 0-6-0 tank engine. All its weight was on coupled wheels and so it all helped the engine to get a grip on the rails. For many purposes the "all-adhesion" locomotive was ideal.

The top favourite British locomotive was the 0-6-0 tender engine. Again the whole weight of the engine was on wheels that would help to pull the train. But the tender, which accompanied the engine wherever it went, gave no such help. It was heavy enough to give a lot of help if something would drive its wheels. And why not? Put some cylinders under the tender to work a cranked middle axle, connect all the axles by coupling rods and feed the cylinders with steam from the boiler through a flexible pipe. At least it was worth trying and Sturrock tried it.

If you liked the look of a fly-cranked 0-6-0 making a purposeful way along the line at the head of a coal train, you would have liked to see a Sturrock 0-6-0 and steam tender similarly engaged. Even better would have been a train "double headed" by two such double-engines.

Whether or not Sturrock like the look of engines with steam tenders he allowed himself to be impressed by the results of his early trials. The enginemen did *not* like them. They had reason for objection before the engine left the shed because they had twice as much mechanism to look after as they had in a normal 0-6-0. Moreover the "works" under the tender could be got at only from underneath; those under a boiler could be reached from above. On the road the steam tender could be a great help in getting away from rest up a steep gradient and especially on greasy rails. But could the steam tender help in running at steady speed?

The answer depends on what that speed is. If the engine alone has to be run at late cut-off to maintain the speed, then the steam tender can be advantageous because by passing some of the steam through its cylinders, the required pull on the train can be maintained with an earlier cut-off in the four cylinders than is necessary in only two cylinders. This may enable a perceptibly higher cylinder-efficiency to be attained, so that coal is saved.

In general a steam tender is advantageous only where the engine itself would have to "slog". This means either in accelerating from rest or in pulling hard up a steep gradient.

This could well be useful as many goods engines did a lot of starting from rest and, in some districts, did a lot of slogging up steep gradients. So, although a steam tender might not help much on level lines such as Peterborough—Spalding—Lincoln—Doncaster—York, there was a lot of hard pulling to be done in the West Riding. In that district a steam tender would enable an engine to be trusted with a bigger load than it could reliably take without such aid. This is true at least in connection with climbing the gradients, but what about coming down? On a hilly route the maximum load of an unbraked goods train may well be limited to what the braking of the engine, tender and brake-van can hold back; total weight on braked wheels is what matters. In this respect a steam tender is no better than an ordinary tender. So on a hilly line the steam tender might not enable the maximum permissible of the engine to be increased. Its advantage would be limited to that of faster and more reliable starting in adverse conditions.

Perhaps this had not become clear during the experimental running, from 1863, of a few steam tenders before a need for more goods engines arose. Sturrock must have been reasonably well satisfied at that time that steam tenders were worth having, but even so it was surely excessively optimistic to specify a steam tender for each of *seventy* new 0-6-0s ordered from various builders, to be delivered in 1865 and 1866.

These engines (n47) had fireboxes very distinctly larger than any others ever used in any other GN 0-6-0s and this was necessary if the tenders were to be usefully employed in continuous pulling. The figure of 23·6 sq ft for grate area is quoted in Table 5, p. 203 with some reservation as it is compatible with published length of outside firebox only if the water spaces were very narrow at the grate. A suggestion that some of these engines had 26½ sq ft of grate area is rather difficult to believe.

Stirling reported that the boilers specially made with long fireboxes to provide extra steam for steam tenders frequently had red-hot smokeboxes. It seems from this that the increase in the size of the firebox was not accompanied by appropriate increase in the heating surface of the tubes. So the gases reached the smokebox without having given the usual fraction of their heat to the water. The extra residual heat made the smokebox red-hot but served no useful purpose The engine may well have lost more heat in this way than could be balanced by (possibly) higher cylinder efficiency of four cylinders.

The pistons in the two cylinders under the tender were of 12 in diameter and 17 in stroke. Steam reached the cylinders from the boiler through a pipe of such length (23 ft) and curvature as to be able to yield without excessive stress to relative motion of engine and tender. Exhaust steam from the auxiliary cylinders was condensed in tubes submerged in the water in the tender, at least until that water became too hot, when uncondensed steam passed into the open air.

Comparative tests run in 1866 showed GN 0-6-0s with steam tenders pulling 35 wagons to burn about 12 per cent more coal per unit of work done than did similar locomotives with ordinary tenders pulling 30 wagons. The former locomotive used about 60 per cent more oil than the latter.

Whilst delivery of the engines was still proceeding, experience with the steam tenders convinced some of the early doubters that they were justified in uttering a warning word into some director's ear. The result was a modifying order to the builders to the effect that no more steam tenders were to be supplied; any undelivered steam tenders were to be deprived of the mechanism before delivery in company with locomotives.

At the end of 1866, Sturrock retired and lived happily ever afterwards, if 42 years be regarded for this purpose as being equivalent to "ever".

Steam tenders might have been more readily accepted on the GN if they had had inside frames and outside cylinders because the "works" would then have been more readily accessible. If Sturrock had gone further and fitted outside valve gear even less objection would have been raised. But, . . . and imaginative pessimism is never wasted . . . the men might have become so delighted with the unwonted accessibility of such mechanism as to grumble because it was not a feature of all GN locomotives besides steam tenders.

But—still another but!—outside valve gear was almost unknown in Britain in 1863 and the difficulties in designing, making and "proving" a reliable mechanism might well have deterred Sturrock from such innovation.

EARLY FLIRT WITH PETROL

Although inconsistently with the title of this book, mention may be made here of two four-wheel petrol-engine-driven railcars tried on the GN Hatfield-Hertford branch in 1905. Design and operation had the personal supervision of the General Manager, Oliver Bury; the running was the personal responsibility of a Doncaster apprentice, Oliver Bulleid.

The body of each car was externally similar to that of a typical four-wheel tramcar of the period, but the chassis was higher and the wheelbase longer than in tramcar proportion to the body.

Each car had two 36 hp Daimler engines designed for 30 mph on the level and it could do 50. The engines are said to have run well, once a good strong arm had started them, but there were interminable troubles with the transmission and the cars ran in service for only a few months.

The *Railway Magazine* early took a very derogatory view of the experiment. In particular it predicted that the vibration would be found objectionable. Vehement agreement will be felt by those whose travel in BR dmu vehicles has had a multiple castanet accompaniment from the "modern" luggage racks in which loose metal bars have replaced the old-fashioned silent knotted string.

The GN, however, was not deterred but worked the Hertford branch for some five years with petrol-driven coaches (Nos 3 and 4) built by Kerr, Stuart & Co.

STEAM RAIL MOTOR COACHES NOS I AND 2

After the unsuccessful trials of the petrol-engined coaches on the Hertford branch, and following a current fashion, the GN built, late in 1905, two steam-engined coaches for trial on that branch and similar ones.

The general design was that of the coaches afterwards extensively used for many years by the Lancashire and Yorkshire Railway. A very short 2/0-4-0 locomotive of conventional design had provision over its rear axle to support one end of the frame of what would otherwise have been a 50 ft eight-wheel bogie-coach. The locomotive in fact was virtually a "power-bogie" most of which was ahead of the coach.

The boiler had $9\frac{1}{2}$ sq ft of grate area and Walschaerts gear worked flat valves over cylinders 10 in $\times$ 16 in driving 44 in wheels.

Fifty-three passengers could be seated and this would cover normal requirements on a good many GN branches. On the other hand, the same three men with a standard tank engine and six standard six-wheel coaches could take more than five times as many passengers at little greater running cost.

If men's wages formed an appreciable part of the running cost, a railcar showed no very great economy over the ordinary branch train. Worse, it had the great disadvantage of inability to cope with an occasional doubling of the passenger load. The engine complained bitterly about an extra coach and in fact might be unable to keep moving with such an overload on any considerable gradient.

This, at least, was the common complaint of train-operating departments about them. Nevertheless the GN ordered from Kerr, Stuart & Co two steam rail motor coaches (Nos 5 and 6) and from the Avonside Engine Co two others (Nos 7 and 8). These were generally similar to Nos 1 and 2, built at Doncaster. They weighed about 41 tons and were designed to be able to pull a trailer car up gradients as steep as 1 in 40 although not, it would seem, at any high speed.

These coaches were used on the branch lines to Edgware, Hertford and St Albans. To the stations between Louth and Grimsby were added six "halts" and the coaches were tried on that 14-mile line. There they encountered nothing steeper than 1 in 300, and so running conditions were easier than on some of the GN branches. Nevertheless the GN stock of steam rail motor coaches never exceeded six in number and the vehicles had all been withdrawn from service by 1926.

CHAPTER ELEVEN

More than two cylinders

FOUR-CYLINDER ENGINES

Most steam locomotives had two cylinders because it was not practicable to get by with only one; in that acme of simplicity an engine that happened to stop with the crank in line with the connecting rod could not get moving again without help. It was sound practice to use the smallest number of cylinders that would suffice, and that number was two. Why then did Ivatt build a locomotive (n36) with four cylinders? So as not to appear to have been left a long way behind!

Manson had produced a four-cylinder 4-4-0 for the Glasgow & South Western Railway. Webb had done likewise to have a single-expansion locomotive that his four-cylinder compound engines could be shown to be able to beat. Pursuit of prestige rather than power was behind this multi-cylindering.

Later on locomotives might have to be so powerful as to need more than two of the biggest cylinders that could be got in, but this had not happened in the Victorian regime. The only advantages of a four-cylinder engine over the equivalent two-cylinder engine were the smoother fast running resulting from the better balance of reciprocating parts and the reduced horizontal loads on driving axle boxes. In 1900 some engineers thought that these advantages might justify the complication; 50 years later British Railways were sure they did not.

In 1902 Ivatt produced No 271, which was virtually a small Atlantic with four cylinders. It was not quite that, as the distance from the bogie centre to the leading coupled axle had been increased by about a foot in order to provide reasonable room for connecting rods to drive crank pins at 10 in radius on the leading coupled wheels and in the crank-axle. Someone thought that while extension was being accepted in one part of the engine, it might usefully be applied to the next part to increase the less-than-sixpence clearance between the flanges of the coupled wheels by some two inches. This made a gap that would shame nobody and therefore need not be hidden. So the footsteps could be moved from their position in the 990s to a more useful one just ahead of the leading coupled wheels.

One may find the heating surface of the boiler of No 271 quoted to the last half of a square foot, but with no comment on the arrangement of the valves.

There were only two troublesome piston valves, each serving two cylinders, one very badly through "crossed ports". This scheme is bad in principle and worse in practice. Within a year Doncaster had had more than enough of it and by 1904, No 271 was running with new cylinders each topped with a flat valve. The inside valves were worked by Stephenson-gear through rocking shafts. The outside valves were worked by some of the earliest Walschaerts valve gear to be made and used in Britain in the 20th century. After seven years of this, a clean sweep was made and No 271 appeared in the Horwich Atlantic style with piston valves above inside cylinders, and no outside cylinder at all. In this form (n40), with a superheater, No 271 survived till 1936.

It was rather odd that in originally developing No 271 from No 990, and in altering the wheel spacing, no one noticed that the springing should have been altered. In accordance with common practice, No 990 had laminated springs except at the driving axle where the livelier coil springs were used. It was commonly thought valuable to minimise the opportunities for wheel-slip to start from loss of contact of driving wheels with the rails at "low spots", whilst retaining the vibration-damping characteristic of the friction in laminated springs at all other axleboxes.

In No 271, the leading coupled axle was the driving axle and that was where the coil-springs (if any) should have been. They were, however, placed as in No 990 under the rear coupled axle and there they remained for the life of the locomotive. It is hard to believe that any designer took No 271 seriously at any point in her devious history.

Although practically no joy had been derived from No 271 in her four-cylinder forms, Gresley thought that something of this kind might have to be made to work eventually and that some further trial was warranted. Driving directly onto the leading coupled axle of an Atlantic meant lengthening the engine. Could the drive from four cylinders be taken into the second coupled axle? In a rebuilding of big Atlantic No 279 (n41) in 1915, he showed that it could.

In this engine, two inside cylinders were placed over the second axle of the bogie at such height and inclination as enabled the connecting rods associated with them to clear the leading coupled axle and to drive cranks formed on the second coupled axle. The piston valves for the inside cylinders were placed horizontally below them and parallel to piston valves above the outside cylinders. Walschaerts gear drove the outside valves whence tail rods, links and rocking shafts ahead of the cylinders worked the inside valves. Getting at the inside valve spindle glands was no picnic.

No published information showed No 279 to have any advantage over the standard big Atlantic. The higher nominal tractive effort offered the possibility of economy in coal, but none was ever announced. The reciprocating parts in the rebuild were obviously far better balanced than those of the standard engine, but only the enginemen and the track could benefit from this and in a way not susceptible of quantitative assessment.

No other locomotive was made like No 279, she was not normally used on top jobs, and even after rebuilding in 1936 with two cylinders as used in Class K2 2-6-0s her performance remained undistinguished.

In 1915 Gresley sketched out a Pacific with four cylinders arranged as in the rebuilt No 279. Fig. (a) p. 125 is based on a diagram published in the book by F. A. S. Brown on the subject of Sir Nigel Gresley. This design is simply No 279 extended to form a Pacific. The modest increase in grate area from 31 sq ft only to 36 is surprising. To match a 50 per cent increase in adhesion weight the grate area would be 46 sq ft, but 30 years had to elapse before Doncaster designed a Pacific with so big a grate as that. But 36 sq ft for the grate and only 150 sq ft of firebox heating surface would have made a poor Pacific.

The tube-length of 23 ft equalled that of *The Great Bear* and there would have been nothing wrong in this if the diameter of the tubes had been at least $2\frac{3}{4}$ in.

GN COMPOUND ENGINES

The idea of getting steam to do work on the piston in a cylinder, then passing on to another bigger cylinder to do work there, and passing on to yet another cylinder to do still more work there, and so on, was tried early in the history of the steam engine. At least as far back as 1827 Jacob Perkins used triple expansion of steam in cylinders with central exhaust on what became known many years later as the "Uniflow" principle. This was far too elaborate for 1827 and many years elapsed before compounding became an accepted feature of practice in stationary engines and marine engines.

Although there is not really enough room in a steam locomotive to strew extra cylinders about, compounding was tried now and again in various places; some engineers kept on with it, most did not. H. A. Ivatt had tried it in Ireland but found no advantage in it. When Churchward's 1902 purchase of a French four-cylinder compound 4-4-2 for the Great Western had started a flurry of British interest in compounding, the GN dare not be left behind and Ivatt was persuaded, beguiled or ordered to have another go. Being already convinced that compounding would never be worth while, the first compound engine he produced for the GN was designed in such a way that it could not possibly be so effective as his standard large Atlantic. The volume of the low-pressure cylinders was even *less* than of those of the standard engine which themselves were already small in relation to the boiler. The first GN compound, No 292 (n37) had twice as much mechanism as the standard Atlantics and burned about as much coal as the competing standard engine No 294 in doing the easy work prescribed for the test runs.

No 292 had flat valves exhausting through the back, with Richardson strips. Walschaerts valve gear worked the valves over the outside (high-pressure) cylinders through rods sliding in two guides mounted on each upper slide-bar. Stephenson gear worked the valves between the low-pressure cylinders.

Ivatt may have reflected that the restriction of the low pressure cylinders in No 292 to 16 in diameter was perhaps too obviously an anti-compound artifice and perhaps someone pointedly commented on it. An increase even only to 18 in left inadequate room for balanced valves between the cylinders and so in No 1421 (n39) a modified form of No 292, two extra sets of Walschaerts valve gear worked valves above the inside cylinders. Perhaps to improve access to the front ends of those cylinders, the smokebox extension was shortened. This gave No 1421 a very woebegone appearance. She looked a rather depressed member of the large Atlantic family.

No published information suggests that No 1421 achieved any laudable distinction except perhaps in confirming Ivatt's belief that nothing good could come out of compounding. Like No 292, she remained at work for some years but not on top rank main line trains and it cannot be assumed that these engines equalled the standard Atlantics in availability. Repairs must have been more costly. No 292 was scrapped in 1927, but No 1421 was rebuilt to the standard Atlantic form in 1920.

VULCAN COMPOUND NO 1300 (n38)

Every thoughtful student of the steam locomotive must have wondered why commentators—even the most voluble—seem to have agreed not to comment on this engine. All existing literature confirms that it was not designed by the GN, that it was a sort of de Glehn compound, that in tests in comparison with GN compounds it was not the best, that nevertheless it was kept in some kind of service for nearly ten years before being rebuilt as a two cylinder simple. But no one made any comment on the fact that its firebox was in the wrong place. It is as though all biographies of some celebrity omitted to mention that he had three arms. The usual dimensions were quoted, but nothing was said about the extraordinary layout.

The normal attitude in discussing locomotives tends naturally to be that of uncritical objectivity engendered by copying lists of figures and, generally speaking, this is right. Why should anyone but a professional locomotive engineer publish anything about locomotives? I don't suppose it's allowed in Russia. But in less disciplined countries, imagination occasionally shows itself and it may be time it did so in connection with No 1300.

The rear axle assembly of that engine looks as if it were added as an afterthought and confirmation of that surmise is to be found in The Engineer for February 2, 1906. In a letter to the Editor, H. A. Ivatt stated emphatically that he was not responsible in any way for the design of No 1300. He went on to say that no part of the engine was built at Doncaster except the rear wheels, axle, axleboxes and springs. What was the background to this? No official statement about it seems ever to have been published and why should it? There is no difficulty however in imagining what kind of thing went on.

One may visualise an advanced stage in some directorial Bacchanale when someone said—"We can build you a bloody compound twice as good as any you can make. Gimme a bit o' paper an' Ah'll show you. . . . Ah'm no good at drawing but Ah can draw this one. . . . There y'are, we can do it for four grand."

After the GN had naughtily taken up this offer, some unlucky designer at Vulcan had to work out a de Glehn 4-4-0 as depicted by a bleary hand on the back of an envelope. If it were to beat the GN compounds it would need to have at least as big a grate area and so, as its firebox could not be wide, it had to be long. The result might well have been something like what is shown in Fig. 5(a) p. 106, a long 4-4-0 looking rather majestic on well-spread axles, but so big as inevitably to load the coupled axles well above the current allowable limit of 20 tons.

The civil engineer could not accept 23 ton axle loads and so someone had to supply an extra axle. Vulcan's price didn't cover five axles and so the compromise was that Doncaster would send to Newton le Willows some spare parts for big Atlantics. It was agreed that these should be worked into a revised design and No 1300 came out as a dishevelled Atlantic.

This is speculation, soundly based on knowledge of what goes on in industry, and it fits the facts. It may seem a little fantastic but so also was the engine.

The redesign packed the coupled axles more closely together and the outside cylinders were pushed into a position where they had only a dubious hold on the frame-plates.

The cylinder-arrangement was that extensively used in France and associated with the name of de Glehn. Each cylinder had its own set of Walschaerts valve gear. A single reversing screw could be used at the driver's will to fix the cut-off in either the high-pressure cylinders or the low-pressure cylinders after the other set of gear had been clamped in its cut-off setting. When running slowly in clear weather a driver could have much fun in trying a variety of combinations of regulator opening and cut-offs in the two pairs of cylinders; when running fast in fog he would have other things to think about.

The large size of the low-pressure cylinders provided plenty of room for steam to expand and so to give compounding a good chance of showing to advantage, but in fact No 1300 did not beat the other GN compounds which were much less well endowed in this respect.

Whatever one may think about the looks and origin of No 1300, she did not disgrace herself in the coal consumption tests on easy work in comparison with Nos 292 and 294.

Relative to compound No 292, the standard engine burned about eight per cent more coal per unit of work done in pulling the train while No 1300 burned 10 per cent more. Running costs of Nos 292 and 294 were equal; No 1300 cost about 8 per cent more.

Charles Rous-Marten noted No 1300 to take 300 tons from Kings Cross over Potters Bar at a minimum of 47 mph to reach 80 at Hitchin and 82 at Biggles-

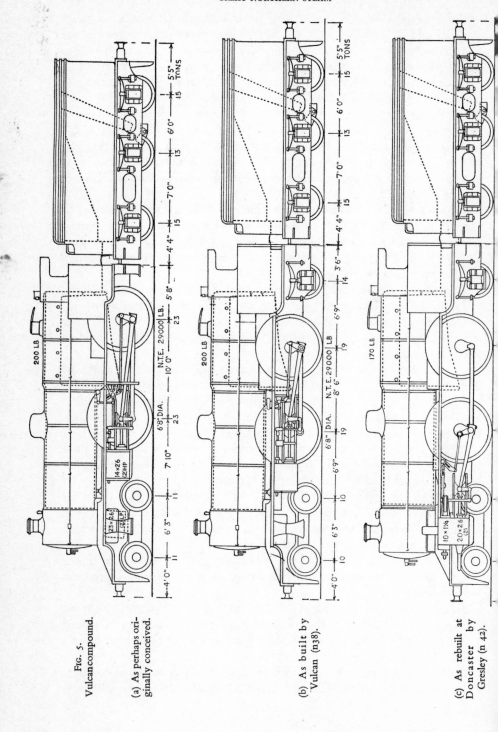

FIG. 5.
Vulcancompound.

(a) As perhaps originally conceived.

(b) As built by Vulcan (n38).

(c) As rebuilt at Doncaster by Gresley (n 42).

wade but to stop at Sandy because of a hot big-end of an inside connecting rod. This seems to be the only published record of any run by No 1300 in ordinary service. She showed no advantage over the Doncaster compounds and it is unlikely that this either surprised Ivatt or distressed him.

In 1917, with cylinders needing replacement, but the boiler still with some life left, No 1300 was rebuilt by Gresley as a two-cylinder simple with drive onto the leading coupled axle by cylinders similar to those of the Class K2 2-6-0s. She ran like this until her non-standard boiler had got past economical repair and she was scrapped in 1924.

General Comments

Looking over these compound engines one sees No 292 as a large Atlantic with very small cylinders and some untidy looking mechanism, No 1421 as No 292 with bigger cylinders and shortened smokebox, and No 1300 as an unfortunate incident. Ivatt must have obtained as much quiet satisfaction from the compounding jamboree on the GN as Churchward had from the failure of the French compounds on the Great Western to beat the competing Swindon-built engines.

THREE-CYLINDER LOCOMOTIVES

A steam locomotive of the conventional type could not get by on fewer than two cylinders, because it could never be sure of starting with only one. Two cylinders sufficed for the vast majority of all the steam locomotives that were ever built; why complicate matters by using more than two? Was it ever necessary to use more than two?

When a designer had decided on a particular nominal tractive effort and a minimum diameter of driving wheels, these quantities decided what must be the product of boiler pressure and total cylinder volume. When he had decided what was the highest boiler pressure he would use, that decided the cylinder volume. Then he had to see how he could provide cylinders of that volume in the available space. Perhaps he could do it with two inside cylinders, or with two outside cylinders. If not, then he simply *had* to have more than two cylinders, and three cylinders had fewer moving parts than four except for one thing. Four valves could be worked by two valve gears and two rocking levers or rocking shafts. Three cylinders, however, were initially assumed to require three valve gears and many three-cylinder engines were so provided. But this was not essential as a three-cylinder engine could work with two valve gears and a "conjugating mechanism" to drive the third valve. On this basis, a three-cylinder engine might—just—have the edge over a four-cylinder engine.

But was there any advantage in using three cylinders where two would suffice? Well, yes! A big two-cylinder engine did pound its axleboxes and its balance weights did bash the track at speed. A three-cylinder engine of equal power had lighter piston thrusts and lighter balance weights and so it was easier on the axleboxes and the track. (Only late in the history of the three-cylinder engine came the realisation that it did not *need* any "reciprocating balance weights" at all.)

The three-cylinder engine had lighter piston loads and for the same reason, lighter exhaust beats. At high speed this was neither here nor there, because beats in quick succession tended to merge together, but at very low speed, each beat ended before the next one started, and the lighter beats of the three-cylinder engine pulled less loose coal out of the fire.

The three-cylinder engine had an advantage in that there was less fluctuation of its propulsive effort during a revolution of the driving wheels than that of a two-cylinder engine. This meant that if the engine was strong enough to make its wheels slip, a very skilful driver, adjusting the regulator opening to go right up to the slipping limit, might get 6 per cent greater mean pull with the three-cylinder engine.

So the three-cylinder engine had three potential advantages, one that is hard to assess, one that was probably very small and one that was hard to realise in practice.

Against these was its higher cost in construction and maintenance. So the overall advantage was too small to be discernible, but nevertheless Gresley was "sold" on it and carried out some tests in which a three-cylinder engine burned about 8 per cent less coal than a competing two-cylinder engine.

It is very tempting indeed to believe that this distinct advantage was obtained by using three cylinders instead of two, but this is unjustifiable unless it can be shown that: (a) the engines differed in no other way that could explain a difference in coal consumption and (b) some feature peculiarly associated with the three-cylinder engine could explain the advantage.

Under (a) it may be noted that the nominal tractive effort of the three-cylinder engine at the common boiler pressure of about 162 lb/sq in quoted in the results was about 7 per cent the higher. This would give the three-cylinder engine an advantage of over 5 per cent if the cut-off was anything like the 47 per cent quoted in the results.

Under (b), the gentler blast of the three-cylinder engine would give it a small advantage in reduced loss of coal from the fire, but as the combustion rate itself was low (round 60 lb/sq ft of grate per hour) any advantage must have been very small.

But it is important to note that the mean coal-rate of both engines was about 5 lb per drawbar horsepower hour, whereas good superheated engines in good condition would have returned a figure of 3 instead of 5. Differences of this sort were common enough in the 1920s and later investigation showed that leakage of steam past valves and pistons could explain them. Engines identical except for condition of piston-rings and valve-rings could very easily show far more

than 8 per cent difference in coal consumption. In other words, a test intended
to reveal what was recognised could be only a small difference in performance
between two locomotives of different design might well be just a comparison
of their leakages.

So what the coal consumption-test proved was that both engines were bad
and that the two-cylinder was perhaps the worse. The 8 per cent difference was
little more than the inevitable uncertainties in the measurement and the test
was unfair in that the three-cylinder engine had a distinctly higher nominal
tractive effort.

Subsequent general experience showed that 3 lb of coal per drawbar horsepower hour was a good standard attained by a wide variety of steam locomotives
irrespective of number of cylinders.

Any difference in this respect between two cylinders and three was less than
the "scatter" of test-results in this vicinity. The three-cylinder engine *could*
justify itself, but not by saving coal.

CHAPTER TWELVE

Some Details

CHIMNEYS

No PART OF A LOCOMOTIVE more strongly affects the general character of its appearance than does the chimney. (Not all observers agree with this, but those who do are fervent about it.)

Sturrock brought from the Great Western the markedly bell-mouthed chimney and retained it on the GN after Swindon had abandoned it in favour of a more elegant style.

Stirling brought his "built-up" (or pseudo built-up) style of chimney from Scotland, but from 1876 began very gradually to use a much more elegant one-piece type of cast iron chimney which Ivatt continued for a time before going back to the built-up type.

A Stirling practice was to load the front of the engine with a fifth lamp-bracket attached to the chimney, and very unhandsome an engine looked with a lamp in this position. It reminded one of a dog carrying some treasure in its mouth.

Gresley continued the built-up appearance even in the short chimney of the three-cylinder 2-6-0s which was actually in one piece, but he later reverted to a smooth external style.

DOME? AND SAFETY VALVES

If one imagines that the surface of the water in a locomotive boiler was always flat, one deceives oneself and the truth will escape one. When an engine was working hard, bubbles of steam, large, fast and numerous, were violently disturbing the water surface and, even in the most favourable conditions, were causing a lot of splash. Chemicals in some waters made matters very much worse and much of what was intended to be steam space could be filled with froth. In such circumstances a great deal of water went with the steam into the cylinders and the boiler was said to be "priming".

As conditions in the cylinders are adversely affected by moisture in the steam, it is very desirable to collect steam from the boiler in such a way that the minimum quantity of water comes with it. Quite clearly the first step in this direction is to collect the steam at a point as far as possible above the surface of the water. That is why most locomotive boilers had domes. Inside the dome, near the top, was a pipe leading steam out through the front tube-plate and down to the steam-chests for distribution to the cylinders. In most cases the valve (the "regulator") that controlled admission of steam to the steam chests was placed at the end of the pipe in the dome; in other cases it was in the run of the steam pipe, where it entered the smokebox.

But a dome was not essential as steam could be collected through a lot of small holes on the upper side of a steam pipe running close to the top of the boiler barrel. Many GW broad gauge engines had this feature. The Churchward taper boilers had a collecting point of each of the two front corners of the outer shell of the Belpaire firebox. On the other hand, many Dean boilers on the GW had huge domes.

It may be concluded that in the ordinary way it did not matter which method of steam collection was used. In bad conditions, however, the highest steam collection point, and therefore a dome, made the best of them. A domeless boiler compelled the engine-men to be far more fussy about boiler-water level than would suffice with a dome.

As the temperature of gas inside the fire-tubes is lowest at the smokebox end of them, disturbance of boiler-water is least there and so there is an argument for placing the dome close to the smokebox. In rare cases this was done. On the Great Eastern any boiler barrel made in two rings had the dome on the front ring.

Another point to be mentioned is that hard braking, strong acceleration or a steep gradient may pile the water in the boiler at one end of it. For that reason the dome should be kept away from the ends of the boiler, that is, it should be placed in the middle.

For that reason also, the safety-valves are preferably placed halfway along the boiler. A sudden uprise of water under a safety-valve that is blowing off steam can cause a Niagara of dirty hot water to fall on any bystander if the engine is stationary or nearly so.

In spite of this, safety valves were normally mounted on the firebox, near the cab, and an early justification for this was that it placed within easy reach of the enginemen an "easing lever" projecting from the safety-valve. Up-and-down blows on the lever could "unstick" safety valves that seemed reluctant to move from their seats. As against this it may be recorded that some enginemen preferred safety-valves to stick a bit as they liked to have the boiler-pressure as high as they could get it regardless of that the designer intended should be the maximum. Furthermore some enginemen knew that if they took care not to cause the safety-valves to blow off for a week or two, they could stick more than somewhat and quite a lot more than official steam pressure could then be developed in the boiler and this could be useful at times.

But there was no argument for retaining the firebox position for a safety-valve that did not have an easing lever. Nevertheless there the safety-valve was placed on most locomotives.

The general conclusion is that a locomotive should preferably have a dome. This, and the safety-valves that it must have, are preferably placed near the middle of the whole length of the boiler, but even so, well clear of each other to avoid unnecessary concentration of outflow of steam.

Patrick Stirling affected to find an argument in favour of not using a dome, in a complaint that Great Eastern engines were apt to "prime" when they had taken water at Doncaster. He pointed out that Great Eastern engines had domes whereas his (GN) locomotives did not, and yet Doncaster water did not cause them to prime. What he did not mention is that a mixture of Doncaster water and other water might cause any engine to prime even though neither water separately might do so.

Stirling's early practice was to use the "Salter" type of safety-valve held down by a vertical spring acting through a long horizontal lever. The valve was near the cab and the lever extended through the cab-front to reach the spring which was attached to the back of the boiler. A tall, approximately conical brass casing guided steam from the valve to reach the atmosphere above cab-roof level.

After about 1877 Stirling used Ramsbotton-type safety valves of the conventional two-column type, inside an elegant brass casing similar to that applied to his Salter-type valves. Such enclosure of Ramsbottom valves was unusual. It made "blowing-off" less noisy for everybody and it made it very difficult for unauthorised persons to tamper with the adjustment of the safety-valves.

Ivatt used Ramsbottom-type safety-valves in cast-iron casings and those fitted to his earlier engines had distinctly shorter columns than the average in British practice.

Gresley continued with Ramsbottom-type safety-valves before switching to "pop" valves on the K3 2-6-0s in 1920. This was while the "pop" valve craze was sweeping Britain. Even the usually immutable North Western succumbed to it; only the Great Western, having tried it and rejected it 20 years earlier, remained resolutely unseduced.

When the steam pressure under a safety-valve of the normal type approached the blowing-off point, steam began to escape from the valve in gently "sizzling" fashion and this might go on for a long time. A "pop" valve, however, would suddenly lift well away from its seat when boiler pressure rose high enough, and steam would then roar noisily from the valve until the pressure in the boiler had dropped by two or three pounds per square inch. Then the valve would suddenly close and everybody got a bit of peace.

The "pop" safety-valve was one of the most outrageous nuisances inflicted by railways on their passengers. This was clearly admitted by the application of the word "muffled" to some "pop" valves by their manufacturers.

The excuse for this type of valve was that it was claimed to save steam by cutting out sizzling. But misbehaviour of "pop" valves to the extent of dropping

No 139 (n57) Stirling 0-6-0ST (1890).

No 167 (n63) Gresley 0-6-0T (1913) "Ardsley tank".
[British Railways.

No 1578 (n61) Ivatt 0-6-2T (1911) with condenser.

No 1606 (n62) Gresley's superheated version (1920) of (n61).

No 1200 (n65) Baldwin 2/2-6-0 (1900). Note bar frame, smokebox on saddle, and tender on two four-wheel bogies.

[G. B. Herbert.

No 1636 (n66) Gresley 2/2-6-0 (1912).   [W. J. Reynolds.

No 1655 (n67) Gresley 2/2-6-0 (1914).

No 1000 (n68) Gresley 3/2-6-0 (1920).   [W. J. Reynolds.

No 879 (n8A) Stirling 2-2-2 (1894) with train near Potters Bar.   [C. Laundy.

No 872 (n8A) Stirling 2-2-2 (1892) with Ivatt domed boiler passing Stirling 0-4-4 WT at Potters Bar.

[C. Laundy

No 112 (n24) Stirling 0-4-2 (1883) with train near Hadley Wood
[C. Laundy.

No 1515 (n33) Ivatt 4-4-2T (1899) at Nottingham (Victoria) with
train for Basford via Gedling. [T. G. Hepburn.

No 424 (n71) Ivatt 0-8-0 (1903) rebuilt with superheater, Gresley-type snifting valve and mechanical lubricator.

No 420 (n73) Gresley reboilered form (1918) of (n72).

No 472 (n76) Gresley 2/2-8-0 (1913) with superheater, snifting valve and piston tail-rods.   [W. J. Reynolds.

No 461 (n77) the first Gresley 3/2-8-0 (1918). Note inside cylinder-cover, markedly inclined outside cylinders and highly loaded tender. [F. W. Goslin.

No 477 (n77). Generally similar to No 461 but with superior conjugated valve gear, and outside cylinders nearly parallel to the rails.

No 473 (n70) Sturrock 2/0-8-0T (1866) with condenser for use when working underground on the Metropolitan Railway.   [BR.

No 116 (n74) Ivatt 0-8-2T (1903), the only one of its class, before finish-painting. This locomotive was too heavy for Metropolitan Railway. Note large ventilator on cab-roof and the very restricted space for side look-out. Lever on smokebox controls direction of exhaust to atmosphere or to condenser.   [BR.

No 133 (n75A) Ivatt 0-8-2T as rebuilt for main line goods traffic. Note raised cab-roof and lengthened chimney and dome.   [T. G. Hepburn.

No 753 (n18) Stirling 2-4-0 (1884) with Ivatt domed boiler on train near Hadley Wood.   [C. Laundy.

No 668 (n9) Stirling 2/4-2-2 with train near New Barnet.
                                                          [C. Laundy.

No 1008 (n11) with northbound train passing signal-gantry with elaborate background hoarding on approach to Hitchin.

No 990 (n34) passing imperfect signals, incorrectly worked at Hadley Wood.   [C. Laundy.

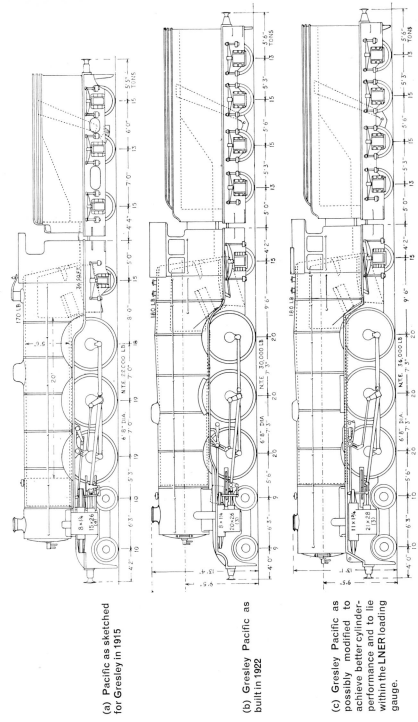

(a) Pacific as sketched for Gresley in 1915

(b) Gresley Pacific as built in 1922

(c) Gresley Pacific as possibly modified to achieve better cylinder-performance and to lie within the LNER loading gauge.

125

One of the first large Atlantics to be rebuilt with superheater. Note double safety valves, well above cab-roof, the double "thimble type" snifting valves behind chimney, and cable leading from superheater to temperature-indicating pyrometer in cab. Note also the blow-down cock with screwed outlet pipe at bottom of firebox, mechanical lubricator on running board ahead of leading splasher, footplate on cylinder, lubricator for gland in front cylinder-cover, and piston tail-rod not sheathed. Ahead of bogie-wheels are guard-irons attached to main frame and others attached to bogie-frame. The locomotive is fitted with steam sanding gear and helical springs under leading coupled axle.   [BR.

Interior of cab of early Gresley Pacific.

1. Cut-off indicator
2. Regulator-handles
3. Vacuum brake-handle
4. Reversing handle
5. Hand-wheel for steam sanding
6. Handle for vacuum locking of reversing shaft

[BR.

Newly built No 1471 (n69) at Doncaster in 1922.

[T. G. Hepburn.

the boiler pressure by 30 lb/sq in at one "go" could outweigh a great deal of sizzling.

It must be added that some "pop" valves, eg the German Knorr type, worked inoffensively. Britain's record in the other direction was probably the case in which the uproar produced by a Southern Railway Pacific blowing-off at Waterloo Station could be heard in the Strand.

Fig. 6.

(a) Salter-type safety-valve in conical casing.

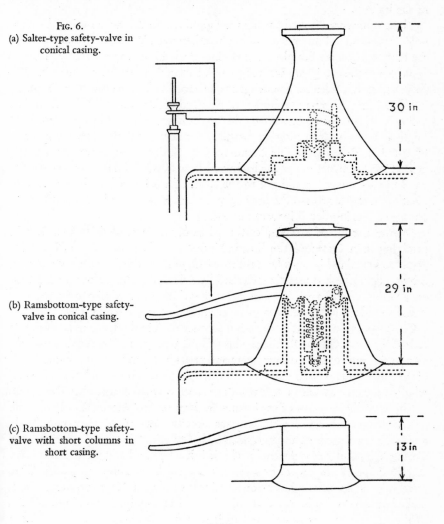

30 in

(b) Ramsbottom-type safety-valve in conical casing.

29 in

(c) Ramsbottom-type safety-valve with short columns in short casing.

13 in

CABS

There is little to be recorded under this heading in respect of Sturrock. He didn't believe in cabs and his enginemen had to manage without them unless they were working 0-4-2 well-tank engines on the underground line. On each of these the footplate was roofed by a sheet bent also to form weatherboards fore and aft. Sturrock believed in clean rain but not in dirty droppings from tunnel-roofs.

Stirling's concept of a cab was a pair of side sheets extended upwards and bent inwards to meet each other and so to form a roof. In some early examples each side had a circular hole at about shoulder height above the footplate. This looks rather odd in pictures and would look odder still with a man's head sticking out of the hole.

These cabs were disliked for the very good reason that when using the porthole all you had to lean on was your chin or jawbone. Well into the 20th century the Hull & Barnsley bought 0-8-0 engines made in such a way that you had to come out of the cab if you wanted to look back along the side of the train. One may well doubt whether the designer concerned had ever been on an engine.

The Stirling cab was too short from front to back to act as a shelter from rain falling vertically or blown across the track. It was also far less effective than might at first appear in running forward. Air does not flow smoothly past any obstruction. When an engine is running fast, vortices of air form immediately behind local obstructions to the backward flow of wind. So even if you were to stand as close as you could get to the front of a Stirling cab there would be plenty of lively air round the back of your neck at speed and you could not be certain of keeping dry if it were raining.

On the last lot of 8 ft singles the cab-roof was extended backwards by a grudging 10 in. Ivatt took the hint; in his first 4-4-0 he made the roof-extension about 20 in and in his 2-4-0 he went to about 30 in. In this way the style of Ivatt cab was developed. It was characterised by a flat roof, well below the loading-gauge limit, after the Stirling pattern, so that chimney and dome towered above it and so indeed did the safety-valve even on the large Atlantics.

Gresley continued Ivatt's cab design practice until in the 3/2-6-0s he distinctly arched the roof. On the Pacifics he broke new GN ground by arching the cab-roof to the limit of the loading gauge and providing windows in the side-sheets of the cab. It had taken 62 years for W. Bouch's good example in building a side-window cab on a Stockton & Darlington locomotive to bear fruit in Doncaster.

Although the reaction of enginemen (at least before World War I) to a cab newly designed for more shelter was usually opposition, they commonly devised, or accepted, extra protection in heavy rain. That condition inhibited photography and this is probably why it is hard to find any picture of a locomotive draped with canvas or sacking between the cab and the tender. This, however, was common practice on all railways and the GN was no exception. It looked scruffy—even before that adjective had been coined—and high officials of the railways naturally objected to it on that account as well as because it obviously suggested that the management didn't care a damn whether enginemen got wet or not. In fact on many railways it was only the enginemen's own grumbles about tentative moves towards better shelter that left them condemned to an open-air-and-water life.

CAB FITTINGS

Regulator. Sturrock brought to the GN the Great Western practice of admitting steam to the cylinders through a "regulator-valve" in the smokebox and of working that valve by a "pull-out" handle on a lever extending horizontally across the back of the boiler. A driver standing in line with his front look-out found the regulator handle close below it. Because of its considerable leverage over the valve, the handle was not hard to move and not too difficult to set in any position the driver desired. This type of regulator-handle was used throughout Stirling's time on the GN and indeed on many GN locomotives built afterwards. In later versions the handle extended in both horizontal directions from its pivot so that the regulator could be opened from either side of the footplate and so that both enginemen might combine to move a very tight valve. Ivatt provided a double handle on a longitudinal shaft to work the regulator-valve in the dome.

With the 3/2-6-0s, Gresley introduced a different design in which a vertical lever hung from each end of a horizontal shaft extending across the width of the boiler. From a box near the middle of the boiler it had a lever-and-rod connection with the regulator valve in the dome. Here again the fireman could conveniently help the driver to work a stiff valve and moreover it was sometimes necessary.

Reversing Gear. Ivatt's general rule was to use screw-type reversing gear but the vast majority of GN locomotives had lever-type reversing gear. For those engines built before 1900 it was adequate but for the larger locomotives that came later it left a lot to be desired. In the large Atlantics the wide firebox was an obstruction that led the designer to include extra levers in the connection between the reversing-lever and the reversing-shaft and this contributed to the great resistance that the mechanism opposed to any attempt to move the reversing lever. Once having got his train on the move a driver would set the reversing lever where it might stay for the rest of the journey. That was the way to cope

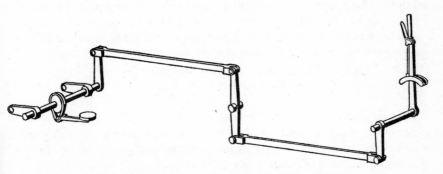

Fig. 7. Main elements of reversing gear in large Atlantics.

with a reversing lever on a GN Atlantic and its success was probably the reason why nothing was ever done to improve the gear.

Not all GN reversing gear was in this class. Indeed on some engines the mechanism would set itself in full forward gear with but slight encouragement.

Screw reversing gear was applied by Stirling to his 0-4-4 tank engines and to the last half-dozen 8ft singles. Ivatt used it on the small Atlantics but he reverted to the lever in the large Atlantics, perhaps because the wide firebox complicated matters, perhaps because it was a feature of American practice, by which he was being impressed at about that time.

In designing the layout of cab-fittings in many steam locomotives there was difficulty in finding room for them in places where they could be conveniently controlled by the enginemen and inevitably some awkward circumstances were sometimes unavoidable.

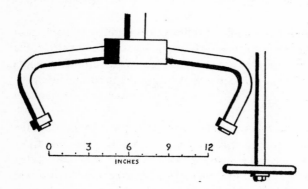

FIG. 8.
Plan view of reversing-handle and blower hand-wheel in small Atlantics.

Fig. 8 is a plan-view of the handle on the reversing screw of a small Atlantic. The hand-wheel and spindle for the blower are also shown, but as the spindle was higher than the reversing screw, the two were not so close together as this plan-view may at first suggest.

One may marvel at the ugly bends in the bar that formed the double handle on the reversing screw and perhaps even more at the two rings shrunk onto the bar at its ends. These rings may have restrained the driver's hands from slipping from the handles whilst he struggled to rotate the screw, but their primary purpose was to try to remind him that the screw worked the "wrong way". This was emphasised by an inscription on the central boss; the driver was instructed to turn the screw anticlockwise to set the valve mechanism in "fore gear".

This suggests a difference in this respect between this class of locomotive and other GN classes with screw-reverse. It would seem better to have chosen the hands of the screw threads in the various screw reversing gears so that they had a common direction of rotation to reach fore gear.

An Ivatt mechanism for holding the reversing shaft against the tendency of the valve gear to give it vibratory rotation was in the form of a brake applied by a piston loaded by atmospheric pressure on one side when the other side was connected to the vacuum chamber.

In his larger engines eg (n68 and n77) Gresley applied the vertical screw reversing gear that he had seen on L &Y Atlantics in his younger days. He used this principle also in the Pacifics and in some of his LNE designs.

Firedoor. Stirling used a firedoor that swung about a vertical hinge-pin to the right of the fire-hole and had a large rectangular slot that could be opened, or partly opened, by using the shovel to tilt a plate about a horizontal axis. A ratchet-notched circular-arc piece in a longitudinal vertical plane could hold the plate at any one of a number of inclinations to the horizontal. The original purpose of this was to provide adjustable admission of air above the fire, but it was found possible to feed the fire with coal through the slot in spite of the plate. Modified to facilitate this procedure, this type of door continued as a GN standard and indeed a subsequent LNE standard. It was not nearly so bad as it looked, especially when made with the part of the fire-hole above the pivot line of the plate well blanked off to keep the air out.

FRAMES AND CRANK AXLES

In most British locomotives the frame was built of two long iron (or steel) plates connected by the cylinder-block at the front and by cross members fore and aft of the firebox. The main plates were about an inch to an inch and a half in thickness and they looked very weak in relation to the general bulk of the engine. The frame lay between the wheels and was called an "inside frame" in distinction from the earlier "outside frame". This was identical in general form with the inside frame but was wide enough for its plates to lie outside the wheels and consequently to hide a lot of each wheel. An outside frame tended to make the engine look strong and massive in its lower parts.

The "double frame" was a combination of an inside frame and an outside frame and the wheels were contained in the narrow spaces between the long plates.

A "sandwich frame" might be an inside frame or an outside frame. Its distinction lay in the fact that each "plate" was a wooden plank between two iron or steel plates, much thinner than the normal single plates. So the "sandwich" might have more lateral flexibility than had the corresponding single iron (or steel) plate.

Each axle was loaded by at least two "axleboxes" guided by "hornblocks" each attached to a frame-plate. The axleboxes in an outside frame engine lay outside the wheels and the axles themselves had to be extended outside the wheels for this reason. Coupled axles had to be extended further still to take "fly-cranks" and of course the crank-pins projected further again.

The construction was expensive but it was magnificent for the watching enthusiast. The frame itself looked as strong as a battleship, with bolt heads or rivet heads in shining array and the fly cranks flopped round and round in a very purposeful-looking manner.

Axleboxes in outside frames on a non-coupled axle were very much more easily accessible than those in inside frames and this feature might well justify the use of outside frames for "single-driver" locomotives.

In most double-frame engines the crank-axle had *four* axleboxes, one at each frame-plate. This was because in the early days crank-axles were liable to fail in running and the consequences were likely to be disastrous if, as usual, the axle had only two axleboxes. But with an axlebox close to each side of it, a wheel could be retained in its proper position even if the axle broke in its weaker part between the inner axleboxes. There was therefore early justification for the double frame, but with improvements in material and manufacturing technique, crank-axles ceased to be specially hazardous and double frames became super-fluous. Some British railways, eg the North Western, early settled for the cheap and simple inside frame.

From the Great Western, Sturrock brought to the GN the outside sandwich frame and retained it in all his engines. They had additional iron frames between cylinder and firebox to accommodate inside axleboxes for the crank-axle.

Sturrock's successor, Patrick Stirling, went in for inside frames in general, but used double frames for 2-4-0s and 2-2-2s. But (another variation!) he limited driving axles (even though uncoupled) to axleboxes in the inner frames and other axles to axleboxes in the outer frames. He built no absolutely new engines with fly-cranks but that feature was used in a number of Stirling "rebuilds" that can have included very little of the original engines. Among these were Nos 67 and 70 (n25), very impressive-looking outside frame 0-4-2 engines which were nominally rebuilds of 2-2-2 engines known as "Small Hawthorns" dating back to 1850.

Rather against his natural inclination, Stirling was persuaded to use outside cylinders in his most famous locomotive design and this had no crank-axle. The same remark may be made about the practice of Stirling's successor, Ivatt. Even though a crank-axle had ceased to be a dubiously safe component of a locomo-tive it was always an expensive one and in time (quite a long time) this fact began to impress designers. As standards of living gradually rose during the twentieth century, some things that used to be taken for granted became too expensive to make. Double frames were "phased out" in the first ten years or so. When nationalisation of British railways came in 1948, crank-axles had become pro-hibitively expensive luxuries and new standard designs were exclusively of the two-outside-cylinder type to which American practice had been limited since the start of railways. (There were of course exceptions to these general rules.)

Gresley had an early habit of saving weight by cutting big openings in the frame-plates, but in such frames too many cracks appeared too soon and so later hole-cutting was more restrained.

SPRINGS

No ride on a steam locomotive ever suggested to a novice that it was carried by springs, but it was.

Most locomotive springs were "laminated" ie in the form of a pack of plates (see Fig. 9a) of lengths adjusted to match the variation of bending moment across the span of the spring.

Alternatives were of the coiled (or helical) spring (Fig. 9b) and the volute spring (Fig. 9c).

Friction between the plates of a laminated spring caused it to "kill" quickly oscillation produced by running over a bump and this was good. But friction also caused the spring to be just a trifle slow in following a wheel down into a

FIG. 9. Springs.

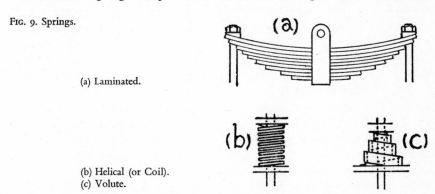

(a) Laminated.

(b) Helical (or Coil).
(c) Volute.

quick local dip in the rail. This was not good, firstly because loss of contact of wheel and rail might let the flange climb the rail, and secondly because, if the wheel was a driving wheel and the engine was pulling hard, it could start a "slip".

Helical springs and volute springs had much less friction and so locomotives were quite commonly provided with such springs under the driving axles, but with laminated springs at the other axles.

In some Stirling 0-6-0s, 0-4-2s and 2-2-2s, six short volute springs pressed down on a trough-shaped beam that spanned the two rear axleboxes.

LOAD-SHARING BEAMS

If you place a four-wheel vehicle, without springs, on two rails, at least three of the wheels will touch the rails; the fourth wheel may also touch a rail. Which of the three wheels touch is determined by the position of the centre of gravity of the vehicle. If it is close (in plan view) to one of the two diagonals connecting the centres of the wheels, then the vehicle may find it hard to decide which wheel it shall not place in contact with a rail. If the vehicle and the track are geometrically perfect, then each of the four wheels will touch a rail. But three wheels will touch rails, however uneven the track may be.

Now if the vehicle has springs that are sufficiently flexible, then all wheels will touch rails, provided that track errors are smaller than spring deflection under a quarter of the total weight. The main purposes of springs in any rail vehicle are: (a) to enable all the wheels to touch reasonably well laid rails and (b) to diminish the shock of running over gaps at rail-joints and at the crossings of rail-tracks.

This suffices for four-wheel vehicles but not necessarily for vehicles having more than four wheels to be run on not specially good tracks. Because of this, many six-wheel locomotives in the early days of railways had "equalising beams" or "compensating beams". For example (see Fig. 10) the adjacent ends of the springs for adjacent coupled wheels might be linked to the ends of a beam pivoted on a pin fixed to the frame. In any static condition, equality of the lengths of the two arms of the beam meant equality of the loads on the adjacent ends of the springs, and therefore equality of the loads applied by the springs to the axleboxes. If the locomotive came to a low place in the track, the freedom of the beam to rock on its pin allowed each coupled wheel to go down to the low spot whilst still carrying a load equal to that on the adjacent coupled wheel. So the beam was an "equalising beam" even on uneven track. A "high-spot" on the track was similarly countered at least at low speed. At high speed the equalising beam also helped because it allowed the shock to be shared by two springs instead of being concentrated on one.

In some circumstances it might be useful to load one axle more heavily than its neighbour. This could be accomplished by using a compensating beam with appropriately unequal arms. It was then literally an "unequalising beam" ensuring a preselected ratio of one axle-load to the other. Many of the early GN engines had this "unequalising" feature and it is seen in Fig. 10. Because a beam could be designed either to equalise the loads on two springs or to make them unequal in a predetermined ratio, the adjective "load-sharing" is preferable to "equalising".

Many GN locomotives built before Stirling's arrival had load-sharing beams. Fig. 10 refers particularly to a Hawthorn 2-4-0 design (n14).

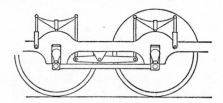

FIG. 10. Springs connected by a load-sharing beam. If the arms of the beam had been equal, it might properly be called an equalising beam.

By the beginning of the 20th century British practice was moving away from "equalising" mechanism of any kind. In general track was so well maintained that the errors were not big enough for equalisation to justify its cost in construction and maintenance.

BRAKES

As on many other British railways until well into the second half of the 19th century, the subject of braking was regarded rather casually on the GN in its early days. Many locomotives were built without brakes at all. All the engine-men could do to slow down was to apply a handbrake on the tender and to try to set the engine into reverse, which is not easy with the lever-type reversing gear used on most GN engines at the time.

After having used the Smith non-automatic type of vacuum brake in passenger trains from 1876, the GN decided round about 1887 to standardise the automatic vacunm brake and by 1889 all GN passenger vehicles and all GN engines intended to haul such vehicles had been converted accordingly.

BOILER PRESSURE

There is a persistent legend that after Sturrock had left the Great Western he told Gooch (or was it Brunel?) that he intended to adopt a boiler pressure of 150 lb/sq in in a big engine he was building for the GN. The other man commended this as a progressive move from the 100 lb/sq in which was common at the time, but added a recommendation not to tell anyone. It is natural to conclude from this that all Sturrock's GN engines worked at 150 lb/sq in, but Mr F. A. S. Brown reported that his attempts to find any confirmation of this were unsuccessful. The evidence is that Sturrock adopted boiler-pressures gradually rising from 120 lb/sq in in 1850 to 150 lb/sq in in 1860.

Afterwards Stirling went gradually up to 170. Ivatt advanced to 175 except when playing with compounds when he used 200. Gresley adopted 180.

These last steps were slow, cautious and sensible. There was in fact no technical value in voluntarily going higher than 180, but fashion can overrule technology as a compound-craze showed and as other crazes showed after the grouping of 1923.

The non-technical reader of the account of Sturrock's adoption of higher boiler pressures than were used in contemporary British locomotives inevitably tends to admire this man as a progressive go-getter in this respect at least. Sturrock didn't worry too much about the troubles that high pressure might bring. He just made the boiler, pipes and cylinders a bit stronger (and, of course, heavier), screwed down the safety-valve more tightly than usual and watched how the engine behaved in service. To the amateur it may seem obvious that "high pressure" is what every engine ought to have; after all it was pressure that pushed the pistons and so the higher the pressure the better. Alternatively one could get more piston thrust by enlarging the cylinders and retaining the original pressure, provided of course that room could be found on the engine for such enlarged cylinders. If not, higher boiler pressure might be the only means of getting the desired increase in piston thrust.

But if (say) 120 lb sq in gave all the thrust that was useful in a particular case, was there any point in adopting a higher boiler pressure, with correspondingly reduced cylinder size? The answer to this question depended on consideration of economical use of steam. To get work out of steam it had to be allowed to expand whilst pushing a piston. The more it expanded the more work it did and accordingly the cooler it got. On its way out of the cylinder it cooled the metal of the valve, the ports and the adjacent cylinder-end. It took away from them heat that the next incoming charge of steam had to replace. Because of this, increase in the expansion ratio of steam beyond a certain point would lose more than it gained. In the normal working conditions of steam locomotives the highest useful expansion ratio was about 4. Corresponding to this the highest useful steam-chest pressure was about 6 times the blastpipe pressure, which never needed to be more than about 10 lb/sq in above atmospheric pressure, or say 25 lb/sq in absolute. So a steam-chest pressure of:

$$6 \times 25 - 15 = 135 \text{ lb/sq in}$$

was high enough to allow steam to be expanded to the greatest useful extent.

Opposing the motion of the piston for about three quarters of each stroke was the "back pressure" associated with the pressure of steam at the blastpipe. (For the remaining quarter of the stroke, the steam in the cylinder was trapped by the closure of the valve to exhaust, and it retained the work that was done in compressing it.) This is where high pressure had an advantage over lower pressure. The ratio of back pressure to steam-chest pressure was lower and so the proportional loss of energy was less. But the higher the steam-chest pressure, the less there is to be gained in this way by raising it further by any particular amount. Moreover, steam leakage (conveniently ignored in elementary examin-ation of the physics of the subject, but actually of perceptible magnitude when cylinders and steam-chest liners had worn past their best) was worse with higher pressure.

As far back as 1904, Professor Goss (Purdue University) concluded after a great deal of careful testing that if a boiler pressure of 180 lb/sq in could give you all the tractive effort you wanted, there was nothing to be gained by going higher. On the contrary, the necessity for a stronger boiler increased the weight (or, alternatively, the boiler had to be smaller to come within any prescribed weight-limit) and there was an operational loss by more rapid deterioration of the boiler. The higher the pressure, the hotter the water and the faster the corro-sion.

So GN practice in respect of boiler-pressure was entirely rational.

TOP FEED

In 1911 Churchward on the GW adopted as standard the practice of feeding the boiler with water through valves at the top. Other British locomotive engineers naturally tried this and Gresley did so on some GN 0-6-0s in 1917. In his scheme a pipe was led from each of the injectors on the back-plate of the boiler through pipes under the lagging sheets to clack valves on a dome immediately ahead of the steam dome. Within the secondary dome the water encountered plates that compelled its descent to be in tortuous sheet form so that it would be well heated by the steam before it reached the water already in the boiler. The two domes were under a common casing which neatly hid the clack valves, but which rather prohibited the smart hammer-blow that was the simplest means of dealing with a clack valve that had not shut down when it ought.

Gresley apparently found no advantage in top feed as he applied it to only a few GN engines.

SUPERHEATER

The striking coal-economy achieved by superheating and demonstrated by the comparative tests made by D. Earle Marsh on the Brighton line in 1908 caused every railway in Britain to make an early trial of superheating on the basic Schmidt system. All sorts of variations in detail were tried with varying advantages in construction and maintenance; one common belief was that when the regulator was closed immediately after a spell of running under steam, air had to be allowed to flow through the superheater elements in order that they should not be burned by the hot fire. So a "snifting valve" was fitted between the regulator and the superheater and on GN engines it was just behind the chimney. External evidence was provided by two thimbles (eg on No 1428, p. 126) slotted to admit air but not any sizeable solid body. Later on Gresley superseded this design by one with a cover of mushroom-head form.

Ivatt had fitted superheaters to various locomotives by 1909 with such success that in a year or two a superheater was regarded as a normal component of new engines of most GN classes.

The full advantage of superheating was obtained if it were high enough to prevent the steam from condensing in spite of the cooling effect of its expansion in the cylinders. This could be achieved with everything in good order by a superheating surface about 10 times the grate area. But as things did not long remain in good order in ordinary service, a bigger superheater was needed to make sure that it would do what was required even with fire-tubes partly blocked with cinders. So ratios of 13 to 18 instead of 10 represented average practice and variations within that range were not significant.

To use higher superheat than was necessary to prevent steam from condensing in the cylinders was entirely disadvantageous; it meant greater loss of heat in the flue-gases and it weakened the oil-films in the cylinders. When, in post-GN days, Ivatt Atlantics with large superheaters were thrashed into stirring performances, it was the thrashing, and not the superheater, that produced the performance.

The harder an engine was thrashed, the less the steam was cooled by expansion in the cylinders and so the lower was the minimum superheat that would suffice to prohibit condensation in the cylinders. Anything higher than that minimum was dead loss.

This is one of several facts resented by some uncritical students of locomotive practice. They are convinced that if a little of anything is good, a lot of it must be better.

Application of superheater

Early trials of superheating were naturally made by taking a locomotive of well-established type and rebuilding the boiler to take a superheater and (usually) replacing cylinders with flat valves by cylinders with piston valves.

Because it was recognised that steam expands when superheated without change in pressure, replacement cylinders were usually larger than the original ones. To retain the original nominal tractive effort of the engine, the boiler pressure was lowered and this would reduce rate of deterioration of the boiler and therefore its maintenance cost. In many cases, however, the original boiler-pressure was restored and the consequent increase in the nominal tractive effort was usually advantageous to the locomotive. In some cases, however, the heavier piston loads noticeably increased the maintenance cost of axleboxes and connecting rod bearings not designed to take them.

So the relationship between cylinder-diameter and its published value was not rigorous and there would be no point in trying to split hairs in deciding what figure should be recorded in such places as Table 5. Technically, cylinder-diameter is not at all critical and variation of an inch by reborings during the life of the cylinders was nothing unusual.

CYLINDER COCKS

At the bottom of each end of each cylinder in every locomotive was a valve or "cock" that could be opened by the engine driver to allow the steam to blow out any water that had formed by condensation in the cylinder. This was necessary because a large enough "slug" of water struck by the piston would burst the end cover of the cylinder.

The connection between the cock and the handle in the cab was usually a system of rods and links and levers. It was always a bit difficult for the designer to find room on the engine for this essential ironmongery and especially if the engine had a wide firebox.

On the first Gresley Pacifics the cylinder cock levers were linked to a cross shaft connected with the operating spindle in the cab by wires in Bowden cables such as are widely used in brake systems on bicycles. Bowden wires work quite well even when laid in sinuous paths but they are apt to snap when overloaded.

FIG. 11. Balanced flat valve with Richardson strips.

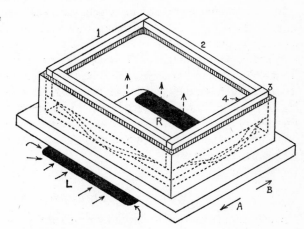

BALANCED VALVES

Till Ivatt took charge at Doncaster, the valves in GN engines were of the conventional D type working against a flat face.

Ivatt favoured the "balanced" flat valve which takes up too much space to be placed between the inside cylinders unless they are small in diameter. When used with outside cylinders or when placed above inside cylinders, this type of valve can be arranged to discharge the exhaust steam through the back, affording a shorter and straighter path to the base of the blastpipe than is possible with the D valve.

The valve (see Fig. 11) is a rectangular frame that rests on a flat "port-face". When the engine is running, the valve is moved to and fro in the direction of the arrows A and B.

In the position shown it has uncovered at L part of a "port" leading to the left hand end of the cylinder and at R a port leading from the right hand end.

"Richardson strips" 1, 2, 3 and 4 are shown protruding from the valve's top face, which is in the form of four narrow rectangles of which the visible parts are shaded with vertical lines in Fig. 11.

The strips are pressed down against the resistance of a leaf spring under each of them, by the flat underside of a cover-plate attached to the top of the steam chest. The top surfaces of the strips are then nearly flush with the top surface of the valve and their contact with the cover-plate makes a reasonably steam-tight joint with some automatic compensation for wear of the sliding surfaces.

When the regulator is open, the valve is surrounded by steam which, with the valve in the position shown, passes down the port L into the left hand end of the cylinder. At the same time steam in the right hand end comes up through port R and escapes to the blastpipe through a large hole in the cover-plate.

By greatly reducing the area on which steam-chest pressure acted to clamp the valve to the port face, the "balancing" of a valve in this way reduced the load imposed on the valve gear by friction at the valve-face.

Whether the advantages of "balanced" valve outweighed its greater leakage from steam-chest to exhaust may well be doubted. Piston valves could be expected to be better, but they took longer than might have been expected in developing into really practical form; while that was going on, Ivatt used flat valves with Richardson strips. When superheating came in, piston valves became almost imperative; certainly very few railways got acceptable results from flat valves with superheated steam.

PISTON VALVES AND SNIFTING VALVES

The steam pressure on the back of the old flat valve held it firmly in its working face and the valve gear had to transmit a pretty big force to overcome the friction between the sliding surfaces. Everybody knew that this was undesirable and, certainly as far back as 1835, Robert Stephenson had tried a valve in the form of two pistons sliding in two cylinders under the control of a common spindle worked by the valve gear.

The piston valve offered the convenient possibility of a wider port than a flat valve would normally give and (one could reasonably expect) less friction.

But the difficulties in making piston valves that would not quickly begin to leak badly were greater than could readily be imagined. Many people tried them before 1900 but came back to the flat valve.

But superheating brought great trouble to the lubrication of slide valves and it virtually compelled engineers to get right down to it and develop some reasonably good piston valves.

Then came another difficulty. When an engine was running with the regulator closed, the movements of its piston caused them to suck from the steam pipes any small amount of steam that leaked into them and in doing so exerted a braking effect on the engine. Ordinary flat valves avoided this by lifting from their seats as soon as the pressure in the steam pipes fell the least bit below atmospheric pressure, so that gas in the blastpipe got back into the steam pipe. The engine drifted on, with valves clattering on their seats unless the driver gave the valves something like their maximum travel when they ceased to clatter.

The obvious way of preventing a piston valve engine from creating a vacuum in its steam pipes was to fit a valve that opened inwards as soon as the internal pressure fell below atmospheric pressure. The old "atmospheric" engine had a valve that let air into the cylinder at the lower end of each stroke. It was called the "snifting valve" no doubt because of the hiss of the ingoing air and the same name was given to the automatically opening valve on the steam pipes (or the superheater-header) of a locomotive with piston valves. If you wanted to refer in writing to such a valve you might call it an "anti-vacuum" valve and this is an appropriately descriptive name, though lacking a little in punch and snift.

Where to put the snifting valve (or valves) on a superheater-fitted engine was a matter of opinion. On the "wet" superheater header it allowed cold air to sweep through the superheater, keeping it from over-heating, but getting hot itself so that it kept the valves and cylinders warm (which was good) but tended to carbonise their oil and this was bad.

On the downstream side of the superheater the snifting valve allowed the incoming air to cool the valves and cylinders (which was not the best thing to do) but not to harm the oil, while leaving the superheater full of stagnant steam or air which did nothing to cool it, although with the regulator closed the fire did not remain fierce for very long.

Some railways did one thing, some did the other. Ivatt and Gresley on the GN adopted the first alternative. On the Great Western, Churchward used the second method but still found that oil could be carbonised by hot gas sucked down the blastpipe when the engine was drifting.

The proper procedure was to fit a small snifting valve anywhere between the regulator and the valves, and never to close the regulator completely so long as the engine was moving. Many enginemen on the GW complied with the second condition but it was rarely observed anywhere else in Great Britain.

The snifting valve used by Ivatt looked rather like that on the Vulcan compound No 1300 (n38). Gresley continued to use the Ivatt pattern for some time before introducing his own design.

VALVE GEAR

Stephenson-type valve gear was normal on GN locomotives until 1911 when Walschaerts valve gear was adopted and became standard for valves over outside cylinders.

The general remark applies to the locomotives bought from outside in the early part of Sturrock's time, but some at least of the locomotives of his design may have had the approximately equivalent Gooch valve gear.

Some thought was given by David Joy to the application of Joy valve gear to a GN 8 ft single. Its use there would have brought all the "running gear" into readily accessible positions outside the wheels, but Stirling would havenone of it. He said it would spoil the looks of the engine.

The Walschaerts valve gear applied by Ivatt to the outside cylinders of No 271 looked very compressed and this is difficult to avoid when the connecting rod is short. On compound Atlantics Nos 292 and 1421, the Walschaerts valve gear had more elbow-room and better use might have been made of it.

In Walschaerts gear as applied by Gresley the radius-rod was extended behind the curved expansion-link and in that region was slotted and supported by a die-block on a pin connecting the two halves of a double reversing-arm.

Joy valve gear was applied to No 265, one of the Ivatt singles (n12A) but not to any other GN locomotive.

THREE-BAR CROSSHEAD

This is a convenient name for a crosshead (Fig. 3, p. 94) made to work under one broad slide-bar and over two narrow slide-bars, one on each side of a web that projects downwards to support the gudgeon-pin below the lower bars.

Such a crosshead can be made much lighter than the corresponding conventional one that lies between two slide-bars. The three-bar type has less bearing area for force associated with piston-load when the engine is working cab-first than for pulling in the forward running condition, but this is not detrimental in a main line engine as it does little work in backward gear.

As there is very little of a three-bar crosshead below the centre-line of the cylinder, it permits the designer to set the centre line of an inside cylinder closer to the axle that precedes the crank-axle than is possible with a slide-bar below the crosshead.

Two-bar crossheads on a locomotive with outside cylinders and a leading truck obstruct access to the leading crank-pins in many angular positions of the coupled wheels. The three-bar crosshead has a distinct advantage here.

The inertia of any crosshead that is not symmetrical about the cylinder centre-line imposes an alternating bending moment on the piston rod when the driving wheels are rotating fast, and Churchward on the GW is said to have rejected such designs on this account. The effect is, however, quite small and easily calculable.

The proximity of the three bars enables their rear ends to be conveniently supported by a single bracket attached to the frame.

The sliding surfaces of the top and bottom bars face each other over a narrow gap and this minimises the opportunities for dirt and grit to settle on them.

SOLID-END CONNECTING RODS

The early K3s (n68) had what were basically marine-type big ends to their connecting rods, but the heads of the bolts were hidden within the outline of the cap and the nuts were at the front ends of the bolts. This general form was used for all connecting rods for inside cylinders in Gresley designs.

A big-end to work on an inside crank had to be made in at least two parts, but this was not necessary for a big end on an outside crank-pin. This had been well recognised in America in the 19th century and the advantage of something that can't fall to pieces is so great that it was bound to be accepted eventually in Britain. It had been adopted as a standard by Churchward on the GW in 1904 and he had not turned back from it and so it was probably all right. So, although he may have shared the common British reluctance to copy anything from Swindon, Gresley went in for "solid" big ends for all outside connecting rods and the early K3s also eventually got them.

ALLOY STEEL RODS

A feature of Gresley's Class K3 3/2-6-0s and of his Pacifics was the use of "alloy steel" in making connecting rods and coupling rods. As alloy steels are in general stronger than ordinary steels one can readily believe that a rod for any particular job can safely be made thinner in alloy steel than it could safely be made in ordinary steel. If that were done, then the alloy steel rod would be lighter than the other, not because alloy steel itself is lighter than ordinary steel, but simply because there was less material in it.

   All this would be perfectly sound, if the most destructive load imposed on the rod was one that tried to pull it in two, that is, a pure tension.

FIG. 12.
A. Cross-section of connecting rod for 2/2-6-0 Class K2 (n67).
B. Cross-section of connecting rod for 2/2-6-0 Class K3 (n68).

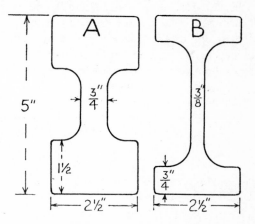

   For example, Fig. 12 shows the cross-section of the connecting rods of the Class K2 2/2-6-0 while Fig. B similarly applies to Class K3. The area of section A is about twice that of section B and so if two such rods were made of similar material A could take twice as big a tensile load as B. But alloy steel is about 50 per cent stronger than plain steel and so rod B could take a tensile load equal to about 75 per cent of the maximum safe load on A. The area of the K3 pistons was about 86 per cent of that of the K2 pistons and so the thin rod was about right for its smaller tensile load.

   But tensile loads were not the worst thing that happened to connecting rods.

They received as many applications of compressive loads of the same magnitude as the tensile loads. A compressive load can cause a long thin rod to fail not by being pulled in two, but by bending and buckling.

Now it is the *stiffness* and not the *strength* of the material of a rod that decides whether it will buckle or not and the sad thing is that *all* steels, plain or alloy, weak or strong, soft or hard have the same stiffness.* For that reason, a rod of section B, no matter what steel you make it of, is only half as strong as A in resisting failure by buckling laterally, which is its weakest direction. The designer was evidently satisfied with the weak section B and a plain steel rod would have been just as strong in this respect as an equal one of alloy steel.

It is the impact of the piston on water trapped in the front end of the cylinder that puts the most destructive load on a connecting rod. As an intended safeguard against excessive cylinder-pressure, relief valves were normally provided, but they often failed to cope and the cylinder-cover was burst. This was what usually happened, but if the connecting rod were weaker than the cylinder it could buckle, bend, twist and split in striking fashion.

After one has seen a 68 in wheel engine, such as a K2 or a K3, running at nearly 80 mph with connecting rod whirling round six or seven times a second, one realises that the centrifugal forces on it are tending to bend it and perhaps to break it. One looks at Figs A and B, reflects that the centrifugal force on B is less because it is lighter but also that it is the weaker of the two. It works out that these effects almost cancel each other and that the stresses due to centrifugal force at any particular speed are nearly equal. So far as this is concerned there was no object in using specially strong steel in making the light rod with cross-section B; whatever steel sufficed for cross-section A would be equally good for cross-section B. Moreover, one can work out that such stresses would not be serious in any ordinary steel at any speed below about 120 mph with a K3.

The significant essence of these remarks applies equally to coupling rods as their normal mode of failure was by buckling.

Careful study indicates that the extra expense of the alloy steel used in making the skimpy rods of Gresley engines was waste of money; ordinary steel would have been just as good. The rods looked to be much weaker than rods of conventional thickness and so they were, but they were evidently strong enough as their failures were not alarmingly numerous.

EXHAUST SOUND

Great Northern engines with flat valves had an exhaust beat that sounded like "cheng" or "chang". It had a quality that suggested impact between two biggish pieces of bronze and cast iron as for example a flat valve and its seat. It certainly seemed to be affected by metal-to-metal impact somewhere.

*This is hard to believe, but professional engineers ought at least to know it.

The blast-nozzle seemed to have been adjusted to produce a pretty strong draught, as is necessary for easy steaming, but which did, however, inevitably tend to spark-throwing unless the smokebox were well extended. A passenger near the front of a train being pulled hard through a tunnel by a GN engine could easily notice the noise and the sparks without opening the window.

Better chimney-blastpipe-smokebox design would have enabled adequate draught to be produced by softer exhaust. Smokebox extension (as on the big Atlantics) could have cut down spark-emission with any particular draught.

FIG. 13. Typical indicator-diagram.

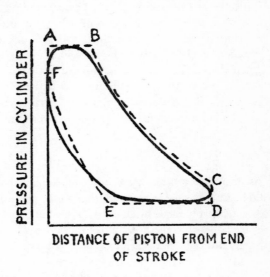

DISTANCE OF PISTON FROM END OF STROKE

INDICATOR DIAGRAMS

As the piston moves in the cylinder of a working steam-engine, the pressure of steam in the cylinder varies. The variations of pressure can be ascertained (with some uncertainty) by an instrument called an "indicator". It displays its findings in the form of a pencil-line on a sheet of paper; the line forms a closed loop of the general form shown in Fig. 13.

What is sometimes called the "ideal diagram" represents the result of calculating the variation of steam pressure on the basis of some simplifying assumptions, two of which are that: (1) the valve opens and closes ports instantaneously and (2) there is no leakage of steam anywhere.

The ideal diagram corresponding to the closed loop in Fig. 13 is the dotted-line loop A, B, C, D, E, and F.

Because assumption (1) cannot be realised in practice, the corners of the ideal diagram at A, B, C, D, and E are inevitably rounded off. Because of normal leakage of steam the full-line loop crosses the dotted-line loop between E and F.

The useful work done by steam on the piston during one stroke is represented by the area of the diagram and this can be conveniently measured in various ways, no matter what its shape.

From the "area of the indicator diagram", i.e. the area enclosed by the loop, the "indicated horsepower" (or ihp) may be calculated. This quantity has often been quoted with high superficial precision but only in very special circumstances can it be obtained from an indicator diagram with any uncertainty less than about 5 per cent in each direction, and the diagram itself can be much further from the truth than this. Hair-splitting calculations based on it are meaningless.

Ideally, an "indicator" should be mounted on a cylinder-cover of the engine under test, so that the passage connecting the inside of the cylinder to that of the indicator-cylinder is very short. Applications of indicators to locomotive-cylinders were usually very far from ideal in this respect. A consequence was that when the engine-piston was moving fast (near the middle of the stroke) the change of pressure in the indicator was lagging behind the change in the engine-cylinder. The indicator diagram was therefore fatter than it ought to have been and the indicated horse power was an overestimate.

FUEL

As steam locomotives were first used to haul coal from collieries, coal was the fuel naturally used in them. Burned in the primitive fireboxes of the early days, coal inevitably made black smoke at least in the period after application of a new charge of coal to the fire. Smoke might be tolerated near collieries—or perhaps hardly noticed—but when locomotives were attached to passenger trains smoke could be a very objectionable nuisance.

So coke came to be the normal fuel for locomotives on passenger trains. It worked very well, though expensively, and as time went on attempts were made to find means whereby coal might be burned without producing too much smoke and a number of different artifices were adopted.

Smoke is largely carbon that ought to have been burned in the firebox, and would have been burned there, had there been enough oxygen mingled with the flames just above the surface of the coal and had there been something very hot to prevent the flames from directly striking the relatively cold roof of the firebox.

The problem was solved best by Markham on the Midland Railway in 1859. First, you compelled the flames to pass under and then over a brick arch that attained yellow heat with sustained running of the engine. Second, you fitted inside the firebox and over the fire-hole a downward-pointing deflector plate that directed towards the underside of the brick arch a stream of air that had passed through the fire-hole. So, in hot surroundings, fresh air was mixed with the ascending flames, providing enough oxygen to burn up all the carbon in them and thus to eliminate smoke.

The general principle of this scheme was soon seen to be simple and effective and eventually was universally adopted. But there is nothing to stop the firemen from closing the fire-hole door immediately after putting a lot of coal on the fire, and in those circumstances it may make smoke despite the brick arch.

Even from a single coalfield, coal may come in great variety, and in 1860 Sturrock said he wanted for his engines hard coal from specific collieries and screened in a specific way. Happy days for enginemen! It was practicable to lay down such specifications for locomotive coal until well into the 20th century, but every such refinement disappeared in the general degradation precipitated by the winning of World War II.

In the ordinary way, GN locomotives naturally used coal from South Yorkshire or Nottinghamshire. There was a wide range of choice in quality but it could all be classed as "bituminous" and would respond to appropriate action by a fireman in response (for example) to a request by a photographer to make a lot of black smoke when passing some defined spot.

Whilst coal could be bought on "calorific value", that property was less important to a fireman than were the sizes of the biggest and smallest pieces, the proportion of ash, and the resistance of the ash to fusion. If much of the coal was too big to go through the fire-hole, it meant extra work for the fireman in breaking it. For handling and burning, 6 in cube was about the ideal, but enginetenders rarely received much coal of that size.

At one time, GN locomotives working in the Metropolitan tunnel were supplied with Welsh coal which was less liable to produce smoke than were the bituminous coals. Even apart from this characteristic, certain Welsh coals were excellent fuels for locomotives, but cost of transport naturally made them more expensive to the GN than were coals mined in its own territory.

WATER

A big steam locomotive used a lot of water (about a ton for every five miles) and provision of supplies was an undertaking. Quantity was the main problem but in some localities quality was equally a difficulty. It took British railways over half a century to become convinced that it could be worthwhile to apply chemical treatment ("water-softening") to supplies of water for locomotives and it was near the very end of steam before it was applied in Britain under such fine control as to produce a marked saving in boiler-maintenance.

"Bad" water might produce scale or sludge at unusually high rates or it might severely corrode the metal of the boiler, or it might offend in all three ways. Nearly all natural supplies of water are detrimental to boilers. Some mixtures of natural waters react chemically on each other in such ways as to produce foam and thus to cause water to be carried away with the steam, increasing the consumption of water and tending to cause bother in the cylinders.

It was natural in the first instance to use the local authority's water for supplying locomotives at running sheds and at stopping places on main lines, but most railway companies eventually found it advantageous to pipe water from their own private sources. In 1904, for example, the GN laid down a pipeline from Bawtry to supply water for locomotives at Doncaster.

The GN began to provide water-troughs in about 1902 and the spacing of them at first seems very odd until it is realised that the selection of sites may have been strongly influenced by the qualities of the local waters and the absence of much British experience at that time with softening of water for locomotives.

From Kings Cross the first trough was 80 miles away, immediately beyond Werrington Junction and so just not available for an engine going to Spalding. Then followed an interval of 43 miles to Muskham, and only 23 miles from there to Scrooby. In the up direction the need was to reach Potters Bar, 68 miles from Werrington, with the boiler at least half full even if the tender then had no water, as a train with no stop from there to Kings Cross could if necessary run down without using much if any steam. With a heavy train even by pre-1914 standards this meant that the tender had to be filled at Werrington. To pick up the maximum possible quantity of water from a trough requires a speed not higher than about 30 mph and this is very trying for the driver of an up train at Werrington as normal speed over the trough would otherwise be over 70 mph. And so many a lively descent from Stoke had to be prematurely "killed" just to go slowly enough over Werrington trough to be sure of filling the tank. Even so, a robustly-bashed Atlantic could boil its tenderful of 3500 gal in covering the 68 miles to Potters Bar.

So here was a reason why the Atlantics never showed their highest sustained power south of Peterborough till additional water-troughs had been laid down between there and London. This was done at Langley in 1919, reducing the crucial 68 miles to $53\frac{1}{2}$ miles. On this point an earlier proposal to lay the additional troughs at Tempsford would have been preferable in reducing the 68 miles to 33 but quality of local water may well have been an overriding factor. As it was, the Langley location reduced the critical mileage by 20 per cent, but the climbing—which is what really used water—by only 13 per cent.

To give to enginemen a positive indication of their approach to a water-trough (and perhaps to remind them that they might be needing water) the GN erected a white-painted board with a black zig-zag. This was possibly conceived as conjoint Ws or as a hint of the waves a fireman might make if he liked to take a dip. The board was lit at night.

It was not common practice among other railways to provide such advance-notice of water-troughs, and it was not normally necessary, but it could be very useful when visibility was bad.

SAND

The maximum sustained pull that a locomotive may exert on its train cannot exceed the backward push that its driving wheels and coupled wheels exert on the rails. This is limited by the product of the total weight on the coupled wheels and the coefficient of friction between the wheels and the rails. If tyre and rail are clean and dry, that coefficient is about 0·25 and may be as high as 0·3. If the surfaces are not clean and dry the coefficient of friction may be less than 0·05. This happens, for example, when a fine film of water, condensed from the air, mixes with fine dust on the rails to produce a lubricant where it is not wanted.

But any such lubricant can be cancelled by sand and it was standard practice to provide every locomotive with "sanding-gear" whereby a trickle of sand can be dropped on each rail immediately ahead of the leading coupled wheels.

If the sanding gear is properly designed and made and if the sand in the sand-box is quite dry a modest flow of sand to each rail brings the coefficient of friction up to its value in the ideal dry condition, however slippery may be the rails ahead.

There have been many occasions on which slippery rails have been blamed for failure of a locomotive to climb a gradient whereas the true culprit was sanding gear that failed to deliver the sand. Perfectly dry sand will flow down a steeply inclined pipe but by its very nature it does not flow like a liquid and it is liable to block the pipe at any sudden change in direction. Damp sand will not flow at all, but different sands varied in their sensitivity to any departure from dryness.

So the provision of reliable sanding was not so easy as it may appear at first sight and in many cases the problem was not given all the attention that its importance warranted. Some engines had no sanding gear for backward running. Many Stirling 0-6-0s had no sand-pipe for the leading wheels or trailing wheels.

Because the tender could add very substantially to the brake-power of a locomotive that was holding back a goods train on a steep down-grade there was a strong case for fitting sand-pipes at the back of the tender so that it might reliably contribute to braking when running ahead of the engine, but few British tenders were so provided.

The subject of sanding is mentioned here because of its special importance to any locomotive that was liable to be loaded to the limit of its adhesion as the GN singles certainly were in their later days.

In "dry sanding" the sand is allowed simply to trickle down pipes and to drop on to the rails. "Steam-sanding" means the use of a steam-jet to blow sand from the bottom of the pipe to the contact-line between wheel and rail. The speed of the projected sand prevents it from being seriously misdirected by strong side-wind. On the other hand, if the wind is strong the rails are unlikely to be slippery and so sanding may not be necessary.

Steam-sanding was rarely more effective or reliable than dry-sanding. Damp from leaking steam could cause the sand to become clogged in the pipe.

Steam-sanding began to be applied to Stirling singles in 1886; it is not certain whether this was an advantageous change from dry sanding.

To anyone who has seen how helpless a locomotive can be on really slippery rails the absence of properly-designed sanding-gear from many British main line locomotives tends to confirm the common suspicion that detail design of locomotives was often left to men unacquainted with the worst realities of practical railway operation. On the other hand, omission of sanding-gear for backward running may have been deliberately based on the attitude that if the operating department think that they are going to use our noble main line engines to pull trains tender-first even for only a quarter of a mile, let them get on with it.

SIGNALS

To the older student of locomotives and railway-working, the word "signals" means "semaphore signals", boards about 5 ft × 1 ft, pivoted at one end on a tall post, and by their inclination to the vertical, giving to engine-men an instruction or a suggestion about what they should do next. For a century, signals of this type controlled the movements of British trains.

The signalman moved the board from the horizontal position (its most restrictive aspect) downwards through an angle of about 45 degrees to the position that gave drivers permission to pass. The signalman did this by pulling a lever that increased the tension in a wire spanning the distance (it might be more than half a mile) from the signal box to the signal. A wire is admirable for transmitting tension but it can do nothing useful with compression. So the reverse motion of the arm from its "clear" position up to its horizontal position was accomplished by a "counterweight" on a lever pivoted on the signal-post.

Highly sophisticated engineers in years to come will tell each other that no device of such appalling crudity could possibly work reliably over any distance more than about 20 ft, but nevertheless it did, with occasional exceptions. A disastrous one occurred on the GN main line at Abbots Ripton in 1876. A heavy fall of freezing snow piled so thickly on signal arms that the weight was too great for the counterweights to overcome. Signalmen restored their levers to the normal position after the passage of a train, the wires slackened but the snow held the signal arms down, wrongly indicating "clear".

The Abbots Ripton accident was widely reported at the time and although it was obvious that the cause of it could be repeated at any time in winter, nobody but the GN (and the Taff Vale) did anything about it. The GN signals were altered (or replaced) so that in the new conditions the arm was pivoted at its mid-point; no weight of snow that was uniformly spread along the arm could prevent the counterweight from restoring it to the "stop" position when the tension in the wire was relaxed.

This was a good move, but it would have been *easier* to make a *better* one and, 50 years later, it began to be made in Britain. That it was not made by the GN at a time of change was just one of the numerous demonstrations of the inertia of the human mind. When the reason for the change was being discussed, did it not occur to anyone that the signal could be arranged so that weight of snow would *help* the counter-weight to pull it back to the horizontal position?

All that had to be done was to give the "clear" indication by pulling the arm from the horizontal position *up* into what in later years came to be called the "upper quadrant".

The centrally pivoted arm was adopted by the GN and its new signals were called "somersault signals"; their "clear" position was vertical although any inclination within 20 deg of the vertical was in practice accepted as being vertical.

Whilst the somersault signal may well be regarded as a "good thing" it is hard to admire certain other features of GN signalling practice. Some of them were very costly, as indeed was signalling on the North Eastern Railway, and as both of these railways bought signals from the Worcester firm of McKenzie & Holland, one begins to wonder. Did these railway companies hand the whole business of signalling over to this firm, who in the interest of turnover specified as much hardware as their salesmen could "flog"? This is an impression that the writer formed at the age of about fourteen and he has seen no reason to dismiss it.

The feature of GN signalling that was quite absurd was the mounting of signals well up in the sky. One example (Bib. ref. 2, p. 101) was associated with the signal box called "20-mile down" (near the mile-post 20 from Kings Cross). It was a structure carrying two "distant" signals, one for each of two parallel running lines, the right hand one being the "main" line and the other the "slow" or "relief" line.

The arm for the main line was pivoted at a height of about 60 ft above the track; the low arm for the slow line was only 55 ft up. The heights of the associated lamps were 27 ft and 23 ft so that they also were invisible to any engine driver in thick mist. It took over 50 years for British signal engineers to become convinced that signals are most easily seen by an engine driver when they are set as close as possible to the paths of his eyes as he stands in his normal position on a moving engine. Moreover, the signals should be set at such positions on the track as to give all necessary information even if atmospheric conditions prevent the driver from seeing a signal until he is just about to pass it.

But at "20-mile down" the signal engineers managed to work in about 150 ft of lattice-work columns to support two signal arms and two signal lamps where they could not be seen in fog. With this example in mind the tonnages of signals erected at wayside stations on the North Eastern Railway can be recognised as only minor feats of salesmanship.

The object of setting a signal very high was to present it to the driver's view with a "sky background". Where that was deemed desirable, but impossible even with 60 ft high signals, an alternative was to build an artificial sky in the form of white-painted boards (see p. 124 upper). This artifice was not, however, limited to high applications; a white board, not much bigger than the signal itself, might be placed behind it where the background (e.g. a brick tunnel-face or bridge-abutment) did not contrast sharply in colour with the face of the semaphore arm. Some British railway companies erected such boards, others did not.

Apart from the somersault semaphore, artificial skies and some lofty signals, GN signalling practice was not markedly unconventional, but of course some odd things happened at times.

In the *Railway Magazine* for September 1915 was a picture of *Henry Oakley*, the first small Atlantic, taking a train past Hadley Wood and a strikingly unusual combination of signal-arm angles. The picture is reproduced in this book (see p. 124 lower).

The most striking feature of the picture is that the "stop" signal is "on" and the distant signal is not "on". The interlocking in the signal box prevents the corresponding signal levers from having positions with that inter-relation. One must conclude that the stop signal lever was restored to "on" very quickly after the distant signal lever was restored and that the counterweight for the distant signal was not big enough to do its job briskly.

Now even if the train were running at only about 30 mph, the signalman must have worked very quickly indeed to make those two movements after the engine-driver passed the signal-post. The only justification the signalman could have had for such a rush was receipt of some late emergency information that required him to stop the train there and then. Apart from that, the rules required him to leave the signals "off" until the whole train had passed them.

If the guard had been doing his duty and had seen the signals go prematurely "on" he would have stopped the train by applying the vacuum brake. It would be interesting to know what did happen, but unfortunately the photographer made no note on this subject.

The probability is that the signalman was simply in a hurry to get back to what he had been doing before the train came along and that the guard was engrossed in his journal or something.

Any railway official who noticed this picture and ascertained the date of the incident from the photographer might have used it as the basis of an enquiry. Very strict discipline was what maintained the high standards of safety and speed on British railways and there had been no relaxation before 1915. So it is quite probable that the signalman was questioned over this affair.

CHAPTER THIRTEEN

In the West Riding

In the Railway Magazine for July 1915, E. L. Ahrons wrote

"The final section of the GN to be considered is that in the West Riding. Here the character of the railway changes entirely with the change in the features of the country. The green fields of the London to Doncaster section give way to the collieries, ironworks and mills of the lines north and north-west of Wakefield. The West Riding branches radiating from Bradford may be described as a series of "White City" switchbacks on a large scale, but with this difference that though there is a vast amount of switchback, there is no whiteness".

The last remark is literally true. There are pockets of greenery even in the Keighley-Leeds-Wakefield-Halifax part of the West Riding served by the GN, but there was in GN days a fair amount of blackness. There is less of it now but still no whiteness. The uplands are bare and the local stone (Millstone grit) is impermanent and attracts black dirt like a small boy. Consequently old buildings tend to be black. The result of cleaning the outside of Sheffield Town Hall some years ago astonished everybody. One local inhabitant remarked that he had always believed the Town Hall to have been built of coal.

GN lines in the West Riding are shown in map on p. 156. The most notable features were perhaps the numerous junctions at and near Laisterdyke (Bradford) and the double-entry into Halifax from Holmfield over lines shared with the L&Y. The GN had running powers over certain L&Y lines such as those from Low Moor to Wakefield (Kirkgate) via Heckmondwike and Thornhill. The latter was in fact over part of the L&Y main line from Thornhill to Wakefield, a section which, by its gentle grading down the Calder valley from Greetland, was in marked contrast to every other railway in the district.

Ideally the map would include contour lines, but at 50 ft intervals, they would be so numerous and convoluted that the railway lines would be swamped. Apart from the use of colours to mark different height-ranges it would be hard to present on a flat sheet of paper any useful picture of the severity of the railway gradients in this area. A relief-map would be impressive, at least to anyone who could believe it.

The topography of the industrial part of the West Riding compelled most

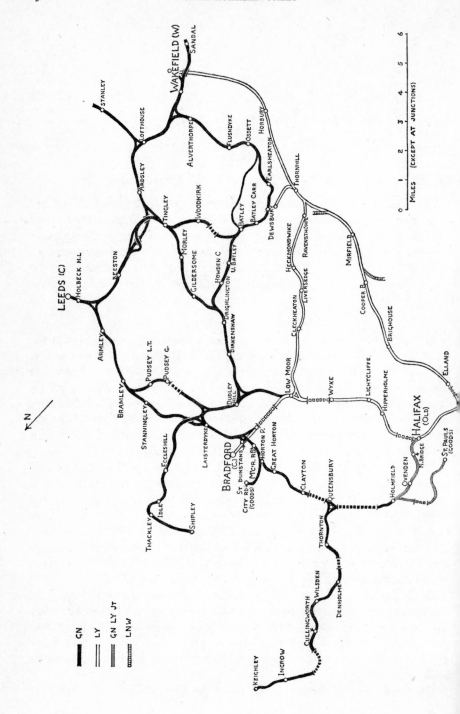

railways to be curved both horizontally and vertically and the GN lines were perhaps the worst of all in this respect. Anything less steep than 1 in 100 on the GN in this district was deemed flat and a half-mile straight was looked on as an undesirable incentive to reckless speeding. A traveller on the very hilly main road from Leeds to Halifax may well be astonished that at its highest point, over 600 ft above sea level, it lies *beneath* the GN line from Bradford via Morley to London.

Out of Bradford, that route makes a steeply climbing detour through Laisterdyke to reach almost the top of the ridge at Dudley Hill and then goes up more gently to cross the 650 ft contour near Birkenshaw. But this is not the steepest GN route in this region.

From Bradford to Queensbury the GN line averages about 1 in 65 for $4\frac{1}{2}$ miles in reaching the 800 ft contour above sea level and there it is in a deep cleft in the hill side. The route to Halifax then enters Queensbury Tunnel, nearly $1\frac{1}{2}$ miles long and nearly the longest on the GN. A mile-and-a-half away, the local eminence of Soil Hill is 1320 ft above the sea and nearby the main road from Queensbury to Keighley crosses the 1200 ft contour line.

Queensbury station was one of those rarities, a triangular junction with a platform adjoining each of the six link-lines. To follow the by-road from the station to the main Bradford road at Queensbury meant half a mile up at an average of 1 in 9.

While people down in Bradford were enjoying the herald of spring brought by a rather balmy evening, tramcars might be held up by snow at Queensbury. A grimmish spot in the Pennines, this Queensbury, not a bit like the similarly-named place on the Stanmore branch of the Bakerloo Line. As an interchange station it must have stood high in the list of candidates for the distinction of being the coldest in Great Britain.

But the GN provided a fair service of trains from Bradford to these less hospitable regions. If, for example, one found it necessary to reach Denholme from Bradford very early on a cold winter's day, one might leave Exchange station by the Halifax train at 4.55 am, get out of the train at Queensbury at 5.14 am, and after an invigorating tramp through the snow, join a train that had arrived at another platform at 5.12 am, after leaving Keighley at 4.48 am. It would be ready to leave at 5.20 am and would drop you at Denholme at 5.27 am, which is early enough for most purposes. During your time at Queensbury you might notice the 4.55 am Halifax-Bradford train which was booked to stand at the Junction from 5.13 to 5.17 am. So if, depressed by the darkness, and stiffened by cold, you felt like calling the whole thing off, you could use this train and be back in Bradford by 5.34 am, the streets by then having become a little aired.

If then mollified by the clement temperature you began to regret your impulsive gesture at Queensbury and to take a calmer view of the situation, you might be glad to find the GN quite prepared for another "go"; you might leave

Exchange at 5.58 am, have a quick three minutes at Queensbury and be at Denholme at 6.26 am, not so early as you would have liked, but better late than never.

If, at the other extreme, your need to reach Denholme had been established very late in the evening you could catch the 11.15 pm "flyer" from Exchange. By missing the usual stops at Manchester Road and Heaton Park, this train made Queensbury in 19 min, leaving you just 2 min in which to sprint round to catch the Keighley train from which you could alight at Denholme at 11.41 pm. If, enervated by your exertions so late in the day, you should fall asleep after leaving Queensbury, you had no need to worry as they would wake you at Keighley and have you out on the platform before midnight, in good time for the 4.48 am train back to Denholme, arr. 5.5 am.

It is romantic, in a chilly kind of way, to think of Queensbury Junction as a pool of light in impenetrable encircling gloom soon after five o'clock on a winter's morning. In quick succession three Stirling 0-4-4 tank engines, safety-valve casings agleam in the gas light, bring in trains and stay for a while. Two of the engines simply stand still, perhaps with steam blowing off if all was well in the firebox, but if not, perhaps not. The engine from Keighley, however, had to run round its train, or indeed to shunt it so as to face Keighley without detaching. It is interesting to consider the various possibilities at a place so liberally tracked as Queensbury Junction but, on the other hand, so infested with trains during the 8 min available for the resorting. For most of the year these meetings, re-shuffling and partings took place in darkness and the depressing chill of Queensbury weather, but in the summer the sun might well be up, and a hillside view of those green engines and varnished teak coaches bathed in morning gold was something to remember and can now be recalled only by memory.

In 1915 the Bradford-Halifax-Keighley service included 24 trains in each direction every weekday, and seven on Sundays, and was rather more lavish than the average of short-distance GN services in the West Riding. It was, however, less intensive than that between Leeds and Bradford where there were about 40 trains a day in each direction over the direct route $10\frac{1}{2}$ miles long. There were in addition over 20 trains a day each way over a $17\frac{3}{4}$-mile route through Morley. Most services in the West Riding suffered from tramway competition even where the journey time by road was much longer than by rail. Between Leeds and Bradford, for example, the fastest trains took only 17 min with one intermediate stop, but even in the *Railway Magazine* for October 1909, H. S. Lawrence could say

". . . whilst some years ago the standard make-up of a Leeds and Bradford train was 10 coaches, today 5 or 6 only are necessary."

A GN train toiling eastwards past Laisterdyke station might bend left to run to Leeds via Stanningley, might turn right to reach Cutler Heights and so reach Leeds via Pudsey, or Dewsbury or Wakefield by Dudley Hill, or might take a middle course and eventually reach a terminus at Shipley. There it would have covered three sides of a rectangle and was alongside a Midland line that also traversed the fourth side.

This GN branch, with plenty of 1 in 60, was no speedway in the ordinary sense, but if a goods train got out of control near Idle some violent impacts at Shipley became likely. On two well-known occasions, Stirling saddle-tanks (No 601 on May 12, 1885 and No 845 on May 18, 1916) were overcome by their trains in this way and there was much damage, but no loss of life, at the GN terminus at Shipley.

It is sad to reflect that a fair fraction of the hard work done by locomotives on lines of this sort was dissipated in nothing more useful than heating and abrading brake-blocks. It was sad, but if it were not done the alternative results could be very much sadder.

There was plenty of gravitational power to recover on the downgrades, time lost on the ups, but achievement in this respect was determined (as is usual on most public highways) by the degree of the driver's contempt for curves. E. L. Ahrons expressed concern about the speed of Stirling 0-4-2s round bends on the descent from Laisterdyke to Bradford. He gave no numerical estimate of speeds but one may safely assume that they rated as "a hell of a lick". Not until over 20 years after the end of the GN, was there published any figure relating to high speed on GN metals in this region. In the Journal of the Stephenson Locomotive Society for October 1946, R. H. N. Hardy estimated that 70 mph was reached by late-running passenger trains on the steep drop from Drighlington to Batley. The only virtue demonstrated by such exploits was the ability to stop correctly at Batley.

GN goods trains on the steep West Riding lines ran slowly uphill and (usually) very slowly down. Only south-east of Wakefield could they be allowed to "go" and there they *had* to go if they were to compete with the fastest Midland goods trains running from Yorkshire to London.

The GN coaches on West Riding services were small six-wheelers weighing about 15 tons each. Hardly any writer has mentioned these vehicles without a comment on their distinctive riding. My own first impression of it was conveyed verbally (without serious thought) by saying that the coaches had hexagonal axles. Ahrons remarked that they seemed to have octagonal wheels. On reflection, I realise that my diagnosis was based on the rather harsh continuous grinding "feel" of the running. It was not that the wheels seemed to be markedly non-circular but that there was friction between surfaces that were rough rather than smooth. It was almost as if the wheel-flanges were "tight to gauge" so that both rails were subjected to flange-pressure all the time. The bumps on rail-joints and crossings were "hard" but at the usually moderate speeds of the local trains there was no undue sway and one could write in the train without much difficulty beyond that arising from lack of inspiration.

Ahrons complained that "the door handles required a pipe-wrench to turn them", but one may be sure that he did not mean this to be taken literally. I do not remember them to be excessively difficult in this respect (I am more disturbed by door handles that turn very easily!) but I was incommoded by the lack of inside handles in conjunction with the average passenger's complete lack of consideration for other people. It seemed to me that only railwaymen ever thought of pulling up a window after having lowered it to reach an outside handle in order to open a door. Until a few years ago, I was convinced that I was the only passenger in Great Britain, apart from railwaymen, who ever thought of closing a window in a railway coach. Recent experience, however, suggests that there are now one or two others.

My riding in GN trains came late in GN days and does not include any trip behind a 0-4-4 tank engine. I was a regular traveller for some years between Wakefield and Dewsbury where the local passenger trains were normally run by 0-6-2Ts (n61) and 4-4-2Ts (n33); in emergencies, 0-6-0 tender engines might be used. Although the booked times were brisk considering the gradients, the usual four-coach train weighed hardly any more than the tank engine and so there was little to move one to the study of "locomotive performance" on these trains. Nevertheless, I was at times inclined to wish that the route could be instantaneously electrified and the train transformed into a powerfully-motored mu that would cover the ground in half the time allowed on the timetable. This happened when the train I was using was running late; the usual reason for this was that its start had been delayed so that it maintained an advertised connection with a main line train. In particular, I was concerned that the punctual running of the 9.30 pm train from Wakefield to Leeds via Dewsbury and Batley depended on the time at which the 5.45 pm from Kings Cross to Leeds reached Wakefield.

The period concerned was a year or two after the grouping of 1923, and so there was no Great Northern Railway, but there had been no departure from GN practice in the West Riding except for the replacement of those letters by LNE.

It is well known that since 1860 or so a train left Kings Cross for Edinburgh at 10 am on every weekday. Similarly a train left for Leeds at some time between 5.30 and 6 pm; in the 20th century it was usually between 5.40 and 5.50 pm; during the period of my particular interest it was 5.45 pm. The main train ran to Leeds and Harrogate; it included a Halifax-coach that was detached at Doncaster. It also included a three-coach Bradford portion, detached at Wakefield where the main train was scheduled to stand from 9.15 to 9.18 pm. Then a tank engine backed down on to the detached Bradford portion and took it away at 9.22 pm. This left a nice margin of 8 min before "my" train left at 9.30 pm.

Now if my journey had ended at any station between Wakefield and Leeds on the route of the 9.30, a few minutes lateness—or even half an hour—would not have bothered me much. But my destination was Huddersfield and my route included a pedestrian crossing of Dewsbury from the GN station to the LNW station, well over a quarter of a mile, half of it uphill at about 1 in 10, in order to catch a Leeds-Huddersfield train due to leave Dewsbury at 9.55 pm. With everything working in accordance with the timetable it would suffice if I covered this distance in 6 min, meaning an average of about 3 mph, nicely within my scope. But if the 9.30 were 3 min late in reaching Dewsbury, then I needed to make 6 mph to be sure of catching the North Western train and this meant that walking would scarcely suffice. Running was necessary over the initial level stretch and also up some of the 1 in 10. If the GN train was more than 3 min late it meant for me running plus a reasonable hope that the North Western train would be late.

Now let me say at once that there was usually no trouble. As I approached the Wakefield (Westgate) station at about 9.23 pm I heard the "cheng-cheng-cheng" of an Ivatt 0-6-2T fussily hastening the Kings Cross-Bradford train on its last lap, and I knew that there was nothing to stop the 9.30 from getting away on time. But sometimes it was not so. Perhaps the main train for Leeds was only just leaving and the question then was "How long will it take to get the Bradford engine down, to couple it up and to get the train away?" The answer was "Not long". Everything was done with as much zest as if everyone was as interested as I was in getting the 9.30 away on time. If the Leeds train was any later than 9.28 in leaving, the Bradford portion could not be off before 9.30 and so the 9.30 train was allowed to slip away whilst the Bradford engine was backing down on to the coaches left by the 5.45. Such a departure from normal sequence of operations to effect a punctual departure during a very short interval in which it would not impede any other train was something outside common railway practice and I was glad of it.

But if in spite of all the 9.30 was more than a couple of minutes late in leaving, with what mental attitude should one make the journey? Should one forget all about time till the train is running into Dewsbury and then concentrate on getting along those stony streets as fast as ever one can? Or should one mentally exhort the driver to pick up a bit of time on the way? Or should one look out at every station in case one may see a chance of expediting departure by leaping out and closing a door before the station-staff could have reached it?

Usually I just sat and listened. The engine had been standing for some time before 9.30 and so was not really "hot". But I never got any impression that she was "cold". We left the platform quite briskly—in fact sometimes too briskly for a comfortable divergence onto the Dewsbury line at Balne Lane and we had worked up to quite a speed on the dip to Alverthorpe before steam was shut off for the stop. Very often the safety-valve was blowing off before we restarted. For the engine, the hard part of the journey was the rise from Alverthorpe to Flushdyke, about 1¾ miles at something like 1 in 60. Was he really pushing as much as he might? I didn't think so! If he knew how hard I was going to have to run up a far steeper gradient in Dewsbury perhaps he would really open her out. She could do better than this. After all a 66-ton engine should be able to pull a 60-ton train without noticing it. We're not doing above 25 mph and for the whole 126 tons up 1 in 60 this speed doesn't mean much power. How much? Well . . . 25 mph is about 37 ft/sec and that multiplied by 126 and divided by 60 is about 75. Multiply it by 2240 to get it to foot-pounds per second, and divide by 550 to get it to horsepower . . . this means multiplying by about 4 and so you get 4 times 75 which means 300 hp. It doesn't seem very much for a biggish tank engine. With about 18 sq ft of grate area she ought to be able to do 50 indicated hp/sq ft for a minute or two. That would be 900 hp! At 300 hp she's only playing!

What about tractive effort? It's about 17000 lb for an N1, getting on for 8 tons. If you divide the total moving weight of 126 tons by 60 you get just over 2 tons, only about a quarter of what the engine can do if she really tries. Try it again . . . two tons at 37 feet/sec means about four times (2 × 37) horsepower, or 296. So 300 hp is about right.

But here we are at Flushdyke. We don't usually stop for more than about 15 sec here. That's right, we're off again. Come on George, give her some stick! He does, but not so much as he might. I wish I was on the job. I'd show 'em what an N1 could do with four six-wheelers. But of course the thing is to save time in stopping at the stations on a milk-round like this. I must say the GN are on top of this kind of job. The driver blows the whistle just before he gets to each platform-end to get the station staff off their bottoms. This knocks a bit out of the station-time and that counts when you're snatching seconds.

Here we are at Ossett. This is a bigger station in the status sense than those on each side of it and I feel that they are not too anxious to let a train go. There's something undignified about a snappy stop and start. They don't have them at places like Wakefield and perhaps Ossett thinks that they ought not to put up with them there. Still, they've done us pretty well tonight and the driver is getting her going with a good burst for a fast swoop down to Earlsheaton. A quick bump-bump at Runtlings Lane Junction and away we go. Let her run and make a quick stop at Earlsheaton. And the driver does! I think he is inclined to pick up time rather than to drop it tonight. Earlsheaton doesn't hold us. How are we doing? Dare I look at my watch? Might as well, but be ready to be shocked. I look and find we're about 2 min late and we can knock a bit out on the mile into Dewsbury. So collect your belongings, find your ticket and keep it in your hand. Don't be too impressed by the need for all speed through the town. Before that you've got to get off the train in one piece and in good working order. Be ready to jump out but remember that there's no sense in doing it while the train is going faster than you can run. Here we are! He's doing a fast run-in. I hope he doesn't run past the subway steps. No! Just right! Ticket to the collector. Careful down the steps. Off we go across town. Pretty quiet, thank goodness, but don't go too hard on the level. You don't want to start the big pull out of breath. Town Hall clock says 9.53 pm so we should be all right. I keep running up the rise, but it gets tough half way and so I drop to a brisk walk. If the other train's not already in, I can hear it run in from here, and might make another effort. But I think we're all right. And so it proves.

This was an easy night, because there was no need for difficult decision. That arose when the GN train reached the GN station at the same time as the North Western train was booked to leave the other station. Did the probability that it was 3 min late justify one in making the big effort required to catch it?

If it were decided (or indeed proved) that it could not be caught, what was to be done? Well, Dewsbury, although only a small town, was well provided with railway stations and at that time of night one might repair to the L&Y station whence a train left at 10.10 pm to take the frustrated traveller for 1½ miles to Thornhill on the L&Y main line. There he could join, at 10.32, the 10 pm train from Normanton to Sowerby Bridge and would alight from it 8 min later at its next stop (at Mirfield). Thence he might travel to Huddersfield, arriving at about 11 pm, by the Kirkburton "motor" or "push and pull" which had popped down to Mirfield in order to take back a through coach dropped there by the Halifax and Huddersfield portion of a train from St Pancras. This train stopped at Thornhill, but to set down only.

If the arrival at Dewsbury were after 10.10 pm the traveller might still catch the 10.32 from Thornhill after covering the intervening distance either on foot or on a single deck tramcar that usually rode like an Ivatt Atlantic without running quite so fast. But if it seemed at Wakefield that the 9.30 was going to be more than 20 min late, the easiest course was to intercept the 10 pm from Normanton before it left the Kirkgate station at 10.15 pm.

These details are mentioned to give an idea of the multiplicity of alternative railway facilities in this part of the West Riding in the late evening. To make full use of them you had to know your way around and to know not to join a train that was booked "Stops to set down only" until it was too late for anyone to stop you.

As Dewsbury has come prominently into these notes, it is perhaps pertinent to mention that it had a fourth station—by far the newest of the lot—owned by the Midland Railway and reached from the Royston-Thornhill line by a spur crossing the L&Y main line by an expensive viaduct. This terminal station was limited to goods traffic.

It is more interesting to recall one's adventures in mitigating the effects of late-running of trains than it was to endure them. One did not really relish the occasional necessity for combining thinking and guessing in trying to establish how to get home with the least distressing combination of lateness and physical effort. The basic reason for being compelled to do it was the dependence of a local train on the running of a main line train. Even a slight imperfection in the action of any member of the railway staff or of any item in the mechanical equipment in the 175 miles between London and Wakefield might make it impossible for the (nominal) 9.30 from Wakefield to reach Dewsbury by 9.49 pm. It might, of course, make a lot of more important things impossible also, and that emphasises the point, which is that punctuality of local trains is very hard to achieve consistently if they are advertised to "connect" with long-distance trains. Nevertheless, that was normal railway practice and failures of the particular "connection" described above were remarkably few.

In the nineteenth century, GN passenger trains in the West Riding were worked by 0-4-2s, 2-4-0s and 0-4-4Ts. Goods trains were taken by 0-4-2s, 0-6-0s and 0-6-0STs.

GN singles were used for some passenger trains between Doncaster and Leeds, but such engines did not normally run on any other route in the West Riding.

Early application of Ivatt 4-4-0s was to the express trains between Doncaster and Leeds, but singles could still be seen on the lighter trains many years later. When Ivatt 4-4-2Ts and 0-6-2Ts became numerous, they displaced the Stirling 0-4-4Ts. This was perhaps the most noticeable difference between GN West Riding practices in the 19th and 20th centuries. With it was the appearance of domes and the disappearance of Stirling's bright brass safety-valve covers.

The main GN shed in the area was at Ardsley, where all but a few of the locomotive "strength" were goods engines. Locomotives for passenger trains between Leeds and Doncaster were shedded at Copley Hill, to the south of Holbeck.

Locomotive "performance" on fast passenger trains in the West Riding was limited to the Doncaster-Wakefield length of about 20 miles. This line climbs the foothills of the Pennine range, and after Wakefield the feet become rather large. No passenger train normally ran northward through Wakefield with stopping. The restart on a 1 in 100 gradient that persists for nearly four miles made the engine cough in a way that suggested to the traveller from London that he had reached a different style of country, in which there would be no fast running except perhaps downhill. Top speeds on GN lines north of Wakefield were determined by the character and current mood of the driver rather than by any feature of the locomotive. A mile a minute was rarely exceeded; when it was, the discerning traveller was moved to hope that it was not due to failure of the brakes.

CHAPTER FOURTEEN

On the Road

SHE RUNS HERSELF

THERE'S NOTHING LIKE a big Atlantic (said the fireman) for any sort of job on the GN. They're the best engines we ever had and if any other railway has anything better they're lucky. They've got their faults of course—who hasn't?—but once they get away you can thrash them as hard as you like and they'll steam as long as you like to keep pushing coal into them. Keep putting plenty on, that's all you have to do. It doesn't matter where you put it—the engine sorts it out to suit herself. You can't go wrong. A big Atlantic can keep time with thirteen or fourteen on and I believe she'd get along with twenty at a pinch. So you can guess what an easy time you can have with some of the short trains.

We used to have a turn from Grantham to Doncaster first stop, a very nice job, only seven or eight on as a rule and the train would nearly run itself. You'd got to pull from Newark on the flat and up past Tuxford, of course, but after that you didn't need to put any more on the fire or touch the injectors or anything.

After a few trips I found that if you put plenty on just after Newark, that would get you through to Doncaster. Later on I tried putting plenty on at Claypole and that worked. So I tried putting plenty on before we got to Barkston and that was just as good. The engine didn't seem to mind and of course it's easier to fire while she's getting up to speed than when she's really going. There was only one thing better still and that was to fill the box before we left Grantham. So I tried that and it was just as good.

You couldn't have done it with a little engine, but the box on an Atlantic is big enough to take all the coal she needs for fifty miles without piling much above the bottom of the fire-hole.

So what I did was to keep sprinkling round the box every five minutes while we were preparing the engine at the shed and finished up with a heavy round of the box as we moved out for the station. The only trouble was that you'd make a lot of smoke if you weren't careful to keep the blower on and the door open. Our boss could be a bit fussy about smoke and about blowing-off too, and so you had to watch your step as long as you were in sight of the shed. I usually fixed things so that I could give her a sharp burst with the blower to bring the boiler up to blowing off just as we hooked-on.

The fire was not properly burned through before we got away and steam generally dropped on the way out to Barkston, but that didn't matter as it's level followed by downhill and we hadn't much to pull anyway. The boiler-water dropped as well, and that meant that I could start an injector at Barkston and with a bit of luck in getting the right setting, it could stay on all the way.

Down the hill to Newark, water and steam would both come up and the fire was really burned through by the time we were past Muskham. Getting up to Tuxford would bring the water down, but not the steam. As like as not she'd be blowing-off on the way down to Retford. On the flat past Sutton, I might have a look at the fire, just for something to do, but it never needed anything doing to it. It would be white-hot and getting a bit thin, but there was enough to get us over Piper's Wood and there you were as good as in Doncaster. All you had to do was to decide when to shut the injector off.

If my mate opened her up a bit more than usual in getting up past Tuxford your boiler water might drop a bit, but if you'd got your injector-setting right, it would be up again by the time you were at Sutton and you could usually get by without touching anything.

Old George used to say I'd nothing to do and he wondered how I had the nerve to draw my pay. I reminded him that I was helping him to see the signals and he said he could do that himself. The only help he needed was in working the reversing gear and I couldn't do much for him there. "Oh well," I said, "You only do that for something to do, there's no need to move the lever once you've got going."

This made him think a bit and he soon found that what I'd said as a joke was right. You could do all the alteration that was necessary with the regulator.

So between us we made this the easiest job on the GNR. I put all the coal we needed in the box before we hooked-on, George got his lever set before we passed Barrowby Road, gave the regulator a couple of thumps at Carlton, a couple the other way at Markham, another couple at Scrooby, shut off at Rossington and braked at Balby. I might run the right hand injector as we went down to Retford.

I remember one day we were on this job, I was not feeling too bright—nothing wrong, just a bit fed-up—and George seemed a bit "edgy" as we got the engine ready. So we didn't say much to each other. We were not across, you couldn't say we were "not speaking", but we weren't saying much. We knew what we had to do, there was nothing out of the ordinary to call for any remark and we just got on with it but without even a word for the cat. It just happened that on that day a stranger came to the engine as soon as we had hooked-on, showed an engine-pass to George and asked could he come with us.

This was just a matter of form, really. George couldn't have refused without risking a row with the boss, but he didn't have to be welcoming and he wasn't. He didn't raise any objection and that was about as much as you could say. Honestly, there's no room for a third man on an Atlantic; there's hardly room for two, especially when there's any firing going on. On this trip there wouldn't be much firing, if any, and so a visitor wouldn't matter very much.

This one didn't say what he had come for and we didn't ask him. It was nothing to do with us and we were neither of us in talking mood anyway. As far as I remember I didn't even say "Right away" to George. He was looking toward me when the time came and I just raised my hand.

He set the regulator at about half open and away we went in full forward gear. We were soon up to thirty or so and he started pulling the lever back, bit by bit (it's all you *can* do, on an Atlantic) until he got it where he wanted it. While he was doing it, I started my injector and set it about right. I was used to it and could be pretty sure of what it would do. And so we got away to what you might call a royal start, nice and slow, picking up speed without hurrying.

As usual, we'd got the doors shut and so our visitor wouldn't get thrown off the engine even if he was thrown off his feet. If he hadn't known how an Atlantic rides he would soon find out. He stood on the tender behind Geoge, and it's no worse there for riding than it is anywhere else. A bit draughty, but it wasn't a cold day and so it was all right for anybody who didn't mind fresh air.

We were not going quite as fast as usual as we passed Barkston and so George didn't ease her at all as we started on the downhill. He didn't ease *on* the downhill either and we were really going past Balderton and Newark.

I must have been lucky with my injector setting as the water hardly moved in the glasses. Steam kept steady at about ten pounds below blowing off and she went like a bird on the flat past Muskham. She had slowed a bit by Crow Park but George didn't touch anything and so the rise past Egmanton to Dukeries slowed her down quite a bit and by Markham we had got down to 30 or so. This wasn't like George but we were not far off time and so there was nothing to bother about.

Of course we picked up speed all the way down to Retford and I've never gone faster over that crossing. On the flat after Retford she kept up speed like a swallow, steam and water still steady. I thought of looking at the fire and then I thought, "What the hell, it'll be all right" and so I didn't bother. She slowed a bit in coming up from Scrooby to Piper's Wood but I was pretty sure from the way we'd been going that we were well on time and so it didn't matter that we got down to about thirty at the top.

But we were moving pretty well again by Black Carr and my mate knocked the blower on and shut off at Carr Loco. He let her roll after that and at St James's Bridge we were running a bit fast for a train that was supposed to stop at the station. Then he put the brake handle well down, and up again, just once, short and sharp and we ran onto the platform loop and stopped in just about the right place. Lovely!

I dropped off and brought a lamp from the front and as I came back I saw our visitor get down and buzz off. He looked thoughtful and perhaps a bit morose. As I got her unhooked from the train it struck me that nobody had done anything from Barrowby Road to Carr Loco and nobody had spoken at all. He must have thought we were a funny pair. Or of course if he'd never been on an engine before, he might think that it was always like that. Still, whatever he thought it didn't matter to us, we'd done nothing wrong. We'd not been very sociable, but that was not what we were there for. No! we'd nothing to worry about except perhaps that if this man's story got round, the high-ups might begin to think of running engines without firemen.

As we pulled away from the train, my mate said to me, "See if you can get a late edition as we go back." As it happened, they put us on the platform line and my mate slowed her to a crawl so that I could slip off, buy a paper from the bookstall, and get on the engine without stopping it. "You take her on," he said to me as I gave him the paper. He turned the pages pretty smart and then shut them up. "I've come up at twelve to one on two quid," he said, and he was as good as gold for the rest of the day.

HOT WORK ON A K3

Do I remember the first lot of K3s? (asked the driver). I'll say I do. I'll never forget the first time I had one on a main line passenger train. We didn't call them K3s at that time; everybody seemed to have his own name for them; some called them "thousands" because their numbers were between a thousand and about a thousand and ten; some called them "jazzers" and some called them "fat rag-times". Top-link men never had them in the ordinary way, as they were really goods engines, although of course they did a bit on passenger trains in some places, such as Doncaster to Leeds. As we had any amount of Atlantics for the main line trains nobody thought of using anything else in the ordinary way. They could do anything we had to do, although they were always a bit slow in getting away with big trains. We didn't usually have more than ten on, but we could keep time with thirteen if we had to. Getting out o' Kings Cross was the worst thing we had to contend with. The empty-stock engine would have made all the difference there but everybody said that somebody else had said that they were not allowed to give a push at the back. Nobody knew who said so and nobody knew why.

Well, there was a coal strike in 1921 and although the company had plenty of coal in stock at the start of the strike it began to look as if it was going to be used up before the miners got to work again. So the timetable was altered a bit and some main line trains were shortened and combined so that instead of two ten-coach trains they would run one with seventeen or eighteen on or even perhaps twenty. The passengers might be a bit crowded but you were using only one engine instead of two. Except o' course out o' the Cross. An Atlantic couldn't be trusted with seventeen even on a good rail. She would have to be piloted to Potters Bar and there you were with two engines after all. And that's how they came to think o' K3s for the big trains. A K3 wasn't bothered by having twenty on. Six-coupled engines could shift far more weight than that, but o' course it didn't mean that they could run with it. So they allowed us more time on some o' the hardest jobs. A K3 could get away with 600 or 700 tons and you just had to hope that she could keep time after she'd really got hold o' the train.

My mate wasn't pleased with the idea of having to run a big passenger train with what he called a "goods engine". I told him it was a "fast goods engine" and he said, "Well, it's a goods engine just the same."

The trouble was, not whether it was a goods engine or not, but whether he would be able to fire a long box after so many years on Atlantics and hardly anything else. An Atlantic has a square box and you feel that you can almost touch any part of the fire with the shovel, although you don't have to. In fact you don't often need to throw coal very far on an Atlantic. Get it through the hole and the engine does the rest.

O' course, the narrow grate on a "thousand" has a bit o' slope on it and so you can expect the fire to make its way down towards the front when the engine's going, but you can't rely on it. You've got to keep your eye on what's going on and you may have to throw quite a lot to the front. On an Atlantic you don't need to bother and you don't need to throw; get onto an engine with a narrow box and you have to do both. On top of that, we were going to have to take seventeen or eighteen coaches. A bigger train than we were used to with an engine we were not used to. I could understand why my mate was inclined to grumble and the weather wasn't going to make him any more cheerful. We'd had the driest and hottest spring and summer I could remember and this day looked like being a real scorcher. You were sweating with standing on the floor in the sun, let alone on the engine, and let alone working. It was going to be a bit grim but after all we were only going to Peterborough. That would be far enough on this day even with good coal. I expect they'd fixed it to change engines at Peterborough in case we got bad coal. The way things were in the pits we were soon going to be lucky to get any coal at all apart from what might come from abroad.

I was a bit inclined to grumble myself when we came to preparing the engine. After years on Atlantics you are not used to pushing your way under the engine to get at a big end. On the "thousands" there was some valve gear under the running board ahead of the smokebox but I must say there was no trouble in getting at it after you'd lifted a big lid. You had to get to one big-end underneath and one crosshead but you'd got no eccentrics to bother with.

When we got to Doncaster station we found we had to piece three trains together and our engine was all right for that. The regulator was a bit stiff and that didn't help, but it worked with a push and pull straight in front of you and that's easier than stretching yourself up to reach the handle on an Atlantic. By the time we were ready to leave I'd got the feel of the regulator and I was going to need it as we'd got nineteen on. Nineteen, mind you! Nobody said whether we were expected to keep time. Nobody knew whether we could or not and nobody asked me what I thought about it. I set her in full fore gear and my mate had got her blowing-off. We were both wanting to get moving to make a bit of breeze. With loose shirt necks and no hats we didn't look like enginemen, but we were so far away from the platform that no passengers or station officials could see us.

When we got the right away I pulled the regulator half open and away she went without a murmur. I pulled out a bit more and she pulled harder, no slip or anything like a slip. She had a pretty poor beat, chuffety chuffety, but the nineteen on didn't seem to bother her a bit. So I let her run till she'd got up to thirty or so and then pulled her up to about 40 per cent on the scale right in front of me. That's one very good thing about the "thousands". You can see how hard you're working the engine without counting notches or turns of the handle. And it's nice to have a soft seat! 'Course it might take a bit of getting used to after years on Atlantics where you either stand up and hold on, or use a hard seat on the tender, but it was a nice change and so as we chirruped past Carr Loco I was feeling a bit brighter.

My mate had his doubts about the long box and had not put too much on till he found out what she liked but when she started to blow-off he began to be a bit hopeful. He said he thought that a round of about eight at the back and sides might be about right and I had said it was worth trying. I was safe in saying that, because you're always right with "little and often". What you find out with experience is what's the most you can put on at once, so that you can have long rests between rounds.

We were picking speed up all the way to Rossington and then I pulled her regulator full open to get up to Piper's Wood. She made a lot of noise at that, but you could see nothing at the chimney except for a puff of smoke as my mate put each shovelful on. But no steam! No steam could show in that heat. The sun was blazing down and the air was warm even at fifty miles an hour. 'Course it was all right for the engine and she went up the bank like a hero, pretty well holding her speed all the way, but it was hot work for my mate. He fired very carefully on the way up, but he put plenty on as we started to go down. I notched her up bit by bit as we went down to Bawtry and by then she was going pretty well, not as fast as an Atlantic with an ordinary train, but I don't think any Atlantic could have touched our time to Bawtry with any more than about thirteen on.

She held her speed on the level with about 25 per cent and even blew off for a bit. So my mate started the second injector to get more water into her while she was in the mood, but he didn't put any more on the fire and we ran on to Retford still with plenty of steam. My mate was sat down all the way from Ranskill and leaned out to get a breeze while he had the chance.

We were about right time at Retford but this was just luck. I was on a strange engine and wasn't used to having nineteen on. I just worked her pretty hard and hoped she could take it. Well she could, and keep time as well.

We had to pull up twice at Retford, but that didn't bother her. I just put her in full fore gear, pulled on the regulator and she moved the train for a few coach-lengths without any more bother than if she'd only eight on. As we did this bit my mate did a quick round o' the box and then sat down to get the rightaway. I'd got more of the feel of the engine by then and gave her more than half regulator to get away.

The difference from an Atlantic was marvellous. She just dug her heels into the rails and pulled. She was off beat and I couldn't help wondering whether that helped her. After a couple of revolutions you could feel that she had got hold of them and set off up the bank with a grip on the rails like the Snowdon rack engines. I pulled her up to 50 per cent and opened her regulator wide and the way she crackled her beat out was a treat to hear. But no steam showed at the chimney-top. It was hard to believe that there could be all that noise out of what looked like nothing. That is until my mate had finished a good round of firing. Then she turned out some pretty thick smoke. In fact there was too much but I didn't say anything. Both my mate and I were only just finding our way how to run this new job and it was no use fussing about details. After all they do say "No smoke, no steam" and she was steaming all right against the injector.

It's quite a slog up to Askham and I can't say we went very fast but we could see that nothing was going to stop her. My mate gave her a couple more light rounds on the way up and then plenty on as we started to go down to Crow Park. I kept her working pretty hard to Dukeries and then pulled her up to 25 per cent. We were moving all right at Crow Park, believe me, and I gave her another 5 per cent or so to take her on to Newark. She slowed down bit by bit on the level but we were still doing sixty or so as we picked up water at Musk-ham and we had about kept our booked time from Retford when we stopped at Newark. We were running late because of the time we lost in drawing up twice at Retford, and we lost more for the same reason at Newark.

It was hot standing in the station and I was glad to get on the move again, but not my mate. He knew he would have to keep firing for most of the way up to Grantham and so he was going to be hot whether we were running or not. But it was too hot even for me; it wasn't a day for anyone to have to work on an engine. But this one didn't cause any trouble with starting. Just give her half regulator for half a dozen revolutions, then pull the handle right back, wind her down to 50 per cent, and then you could lean over the side and leave her to it. Nineteen on? So what? She got them moving up the bank without any faltering. She chattered away from an empty chimney into an empty sky while the sun beat down on us till it was hard to know whether you weren't better off in the shade of the cab-roof even though you were then out of the main draught. Yes, the engine was all right; no Atlantic could have touched her on this bit of the road, but the heat was hell.

I was sweating a bit myself and so you can guess what my mate was like with shirt wringing wet and his hair dripping. In Peascliffe Tunnel it was cold and like a breath of fresh air after working hard up the bank. Then out again into the heat and on the level to Grantham. They were in trouble on the Great North Road at Gonerby with melting tar and sticky chippings. As we ran on into Grantham I thought how lucky that steel rails didn't get soft with the sun.

In the tunnel my mate had done a quick strip to the waist and had a quick wash with tank-water in the bucket. This cheered him up a bit, but the effect doesn't last long.

He never did like warm weather and so he was more than fed-up on this trip. He got to doing everything savage-like, and cursing; whereas he would have done better to take things gently. I was glad we were coming off the train at Peterborough. I can't think what sort of a state he would have got into if we had had to go to London. All the same, I must say that he kept on top of the job. The needle was never far from the red line and she blew off once or twice on the way up from Newark.

So when he complained about the heat as we stopped in Grantham station, I said "Well anyhow the old girl doesn't seem to mind it. She's steaming all right and so that's one thing we don't have to worry about."

"Steaming all right?" he said, "So she ought to on a day like this. If we could get the lagging off the boiler, she'd steam without a fire in this bloody sun."

"Never mind," I told him, "We can't get the lagging off, but we'll soon be at Stoke now."

We had to draw up again before they let us go and then I opened her well out and away she started up the bank with just one slip that stopped itself. Oh! she was the sort of engine to have with nineteen on.

I left her to it and she picked up speed bit by bit over the first couple of miles. My mate fired her nice and steady with plenty down the sides and then plenty at the back till he could get no more in.

"That's it!" he said, "I'm doing no more this trip. If she doesn't like it, she'll *have* to like it."

Then he got the hose going. He swilled down the back of the boiler and all over the floor and soaked all the coal in the front of the tender.

He stripped to the waist and slung his clothes on the injector handles to dry. He brought some soap out of his basket and had a thorough wash. Then he drew a bucket of fresh water and as went we into Stoke Tunnel he took his boots and socks and trousers off. I suppose he had as near to a bath as you could expect to have on an engine, while I kept looking where we were going. My mate hadn't finished drying himself as we came out of the tunnel, and I suddenly thought of what the "bobby" would think if he saw a naked man on the engine. So I stepped across to the left side of the engine, to hide my mate, and gave a wave to the man in Stoke box.

I let her pick up a lot of speed down the bank before easing her. Then I gave her about half regulator and thirty per cent or so. She liked it all right, and we came right down to Tallington at 75 or so, just about ordinary Atlantic speed, and that wasn't bad with nineteen on.

My mate had soon dried out in the draught and put his vest and shirt on. He had hung the rest of his clothes on the boiler-back. I think they had dried a bit before he started getting dressed again at Werrington.

She had run 25 miles without anyone touching the fire or even looking at it and so that wasn't bad, was it? What's more, we'd picked up a couple of minutes from Grantham and so everybody ought to have been satisfied. I said as much to my mate, but all he could say was,

"Huh, do it a few more times and they'll be sticking twenty on regular!"

FIRST GO ON A PACIFIC

Oh yes, (said the fireman) I remember the first time I fired a Pacific. The regular man went off sick at the last minute and they put me on the job, 10.51 out of Doncaster. There were only two Pacifics on the Great Northern, and as the 10.51 was one of the hardest jobs they always tried to have a Pacific for it.

I'd heard some bad tales about the Pacifics (you always hear bad tales about anything new on the railway) but I didn't take much notice of them. 'Course you can't expect a big engine to be easier to fire than an ordinary one, but some of the trains were getting too big for an Atlantic and for years people had been saying that it was time we had some six-coupled engines. Mind you, the Atlantics were all right once you got well away, but getting away could be a worry. When you left Kings Cross on a bad rail you never knew whether you'd get to Holloway or not. The engine that had brought the train into the station could have given a push for the length of the platform anyway and this would have made all the difference, but could you get them to do it? No! Every now and then, somebody would natter about this, but you couldn't make any impression. So we could do with something stronger than an Atlantic if it was only for getting quicker out of Kings Cross.

Some said that a six-coupled engine didn't have to be as big as a Pacific and the Pacifics were too big. They burned more coal than the Atlantics on the same work. With their big tenders they weighed 30 or 40 tons more than Atlantics and that's equal to more than an extra coach on the train, but by all accounts they burned more coal than an extra three or four coaches could account for. Anyway, I thought, I'll find out today.

The regular driver was on the job and I must say he didn't seem as pleased as he might have been at having a different fireman. I think he rather liked to bash along a bit and he'd got his own fireman to like it. So he probably felt that a stranger might cramp his style. He asked me had I been on a Pacific and when I said "No!" he didn't look any more pleased than he'd done before. I could see he was thinking that these things are sent to try us.

So I didn't say much as we set about getting the engine ready. I built the fire up and I must say that the size of the box made me think a bit. It looked as if it was going to need more throwing to the front than on an Atlantic, but that was something I would need to find out for myself, unless the driver would tell me something about it. He didn't; I believe he'd made up his mind that the best way to weigh me up was to see how I shaped on my own.

I didn't expect that I was going to have an easy time but at least the cab was a lot better than an Atlantic cab, if you can call it a cab. You might have to throw coal to the front of the box on a Pacific, but at least you had room to swing your shovel. And there was a decent-looking seat that could be all right if you had time to sit on it. And on a cold day you could pull a window back to keep the draught off you. We'd never had anything like that on the Great Northern before.

So I sat on the seat as we went from Carr Loco to Doncaster station. I thought that it might be the last chance I should have till the first stop at Retford.

We had fifteen on out of Doncaster and it was a treat to feel how she got off the mark. Full fore gear with regulator just open and she got them on the move without a slip or anything. Then my mate opened up, bit by bit, to about three-quarters, pulled her back to about 50 per cent, and then he did nothing till he shut off for Retford.

We started with water near the top of the glass, steam just short of blowing-off, and a good fire. I left her alone just to see what she did. Up she came, blowing-off as we passed the shed. So, on with the feed and on with the coal. I spread it round pretty well in that big box and I must say it was a bit frightening at first. You could put twenty shovelfuls on and hardly see that it had made any difference. It looked like being a hard day for me. I did appreciate the elbow-room and it looked as if I was going to need it.

I kept on top of her over Piper's Wood and then sat back a bit. But my mate didn't notch her up at all and she just roared along the level from Scrooby and I had to get down and put a lot more on. A funny driver, this, I thought to myself but I realised afterwards that he was just sulking. Nobody likes to lose his regular fireman, especially on a hard turn, and I think he was just working a bit of mad off. That's all right but it makes a Pacific burn a lot of coal and I could see that she was going to need a thicker fire. So I got plenty on as we went on to Retford. We'd come over from Doncaster in nineteen minutes which was a bit daft when we were allowed twenty-one.

No bother about steam! She was blowing-off as we stood in the station. The noise may be a nuisance to passengers but it's more like a comfort for a fireman and so we struck off from Retford quite happy. The way she lifted fifteen out of the station had all the difference in the world from what you could do with an Atlantic. He opened her well out and she just walked away with them. He kept her pretty hard at it up to Askham and, remembering how he'd run her down from Piper's Wood, I got plenty on as we went up the bank.

But he eased her back in a sensible sort of way as we came down past Dukeries and so I could sit back for a bit and just ride. And what a ride! Just like being in the train except for a roll here and there. After years on Atlantics it was hard to believe and after I'd enjoyed it for a mile of two I began to hope that they would build some more Pacifics.

We flew past Carlton and I felt sure we were keeping time all right. When I looked at the fire I could see that we were not getting our speed for nothing. So I did a quick round before Muskham and got a tenderful of water without any bother.

From Newark up to Grantham you just have to work, whatever you're on, and I'd not much time to look around on that stretch. This is a big engine, I thought, and a pretty big train and so I just have to keep at it. It's hard to judge on a short stretch whether an engine is heavy on coal, but I didn't think this one was too bad, considering the train and the way the old boy was bashing her. Still, I thought, I'll have a better idea of how things really are when we've got back to Doncaster tonight. Mustn't grumble, not yet.

I thought my mate had worked her a bit hard up to Peascliffe but we only just kept time to Grantham. Oh well! I hadn't expected it was going to be easy and it certainly wouldn't be on the next bit up to Stoke.

They put another coach at the back while we stood at Grantham but you wouldn't have guessed it from the way she got away from Grantham; she must have been two minutes faster than an Atlantic over the first mile alone. 'Course I think the old chap was trying to show me how hard it could be. He kept her at it right to the top so I had to keep at it as well, not just to the top but for another mile in the hope of being able to sit down for a bit. And I did. He eased her down to something reasonable and we went down the bank as fast as any Atlantic but a lot more comfortable. You could sit as still as if you were in a coach. Very little vibration from the motion, no rolling, no wiggling, just a smooth ride. It was worth the extra work and I felt I could get to like Pacifics. I let her go right on to Peterborough without putting any more on the fire and apart from picking up at Werrington I had nothing to do on this stretch. We were right time into Peterborough with plenty of steam and water, and I was feeling on top of the job.

I had no trouble for the rest of the way to London. Just a steady slog round and round the box. I found that it did help a bit to have the fire thick at the back but it didn't jiggle down as it does on an Atlantic. You had to throw a lot to the front. So I was glad to see Knebworth and ride in from there on the cushion. We were a couple of minutes early and my mate said that that didn't often happen with the 10.51. I suppose this was a way of telling me that I had been doing all right.

We were relieved in the station, but the two hours to 4 o'clock soon went and when we got back to our engine I looked to see what sort of a fire they'd put into her. I had said nothing about this to the fireman who had taken over from us. I thought to myself that he probably knows more than I do about what to do with a Pacific in the turn-around time. There was plenty of fire in the box, nicely burned, and there was no need to touch it before we started.

The 4 o'clock was always a big train and we had sixteen on for five hundred tons but it was allowed more time than some other trains such as the 5.40. The weather had turned out wet and windy and my mate said we'd better check up on the sanding gear. Even a Pacific could be in trouble with sixteen up to Holloway if the rails were not dry. So he blew through the front sanders while I rapped on the pipes and the sand was coming through all right. All the same, when we got away, he took it pretty easy, or at least as easy as you can if you're to get up to Holloway at all, and we got through the tunnels in fair time and nothing like a slip. But by Finsbury Park he was slogging her again and I thought, "Here we go again," and set myself for a real packet of work up to Potters Bar. We went roaring up the bank as I plugged them into her and when I was just beginning to think that we must be nearly at the top, he knocked the blower on, shut the regulator, blew the whistle and cursed, all at once. I looked out to find a distant "on" just ahead of us. We lost a lot of speed and took it easy but the "home" was "on" till we got to it and the bobby let us go on to the "starter". But there we stuck. After a time I thought I ought to be going back to the box, but it was raining and blowing and a lot more comfortable in the cab with the window drawn. Anyway, I thought, the man in the box must know we're here while he's got the train right in front of him. Very likely some passenger was leaning out to ask why we were stopped. I couldn't do any good by tramping back through the wind and rain. So we risked it, although I must say I felt a bit guilty, and at last the board came "off". So we had to get going again, up the bank from a dead stand, and we were glad we had a Pacific, with her sanders working. But to be honest, it didn't bother her much and we came over Potters Bar at about the usual speed but about six minutes late. My mate said, "we ought to pick this time up, you know," as if he wasn't sure he could without his regular fireman, so I said, without a minute's thought, "Well, it's up to you." And that's how it was.

He kept her going hard right down through Hatfield, pasted her up past Welwyn and Woolmer Green, while I kept plugging the coal into her and thinking it was a good job we could pick water up at Langley. He didn't ease her at all till we were nearly at Hitchin and we must have been doing eighty as we went through. I thought that bashing her along at this speed was a bit crazy and I thought to myself that as there was plenty of fire in the box I'm not going to touch it before Biggleswade. It's time I had a bit of a rest and if I can't have one going down from Hitchin to Biggleswade, where can I expect to get one? So I sat and enjoyed the ride, so far as anyone can on an engine, but I must say the way she rode was a treat. I could have sat there all the way back to Doncaster.

But at Biggleswade I got down again. The fire was white and patchy and so I had to get some more on quick and I could see that there was no question of taking it easy with this bird on the wing. So I covered the thin places and then went round the box, building up.

She rolled a bit round Offord and we came through Huntingdon so fast that we could almost have run up and over Ripton without steam, but he opened her out a bit more all the same and I had to keep piling more into her or else he would have had the lot out of the chimney.

We came over the top at over sixty, I would think. He eased her a bit, but we must have been over eighty down to Connington and I had to keep plugging them in right on to Yaxley. I got into my seat then, and wondered what it was going to be like up to Stoke. He let her run well past Fletton, and then we got stopped outside Peterborough. No wonder! We'd come from Potters Bar in three minutes under the hour and we were well before time. A bit daft, wasn't it?

But they took five off the train at Peterborough, and we got away on time and there was no need to rush. He took her along pretty brisk all the same and as we get on up the bank past Tallington I thought to myself it would be easier on an Atlantic. After we got past Essendine, the old fellow said, "You watch the road. I'll put a bit on."

You could have knocked me down with a feather. But I got onto his seat and he fired her up to Stoke. I don't know whether he thought I'd done enough for a day, or whether he just wanted a bit of exercise, and I didn't care. But it just shows, doesn't it? He'd worked her pretty heavy all day but when he found I could keep up to him perhaps he thought I'd earned a rest. I was ready enough to take one.

After Grantham, it's mostly downhill to Doncaster and with only eleven on it was easy enough.

So I just put plenty on at the back as we got away and then had a nice long sit. After Newark, the steam had gone down more than I would have expected and so I had a look at the fire. It hadn't shaken down as it would have done on an Atlantic and the bars were showing at one place at the front. So I got some coal down there pretty quick and then went round the sides. Steam soon came up again, and so that was all right, but I could see that Pacifics needed firing round the box. This was the price you had to pay for the smooth ride.

Taking it all round, it had been a pretty hard day, and I was not sure what to think about Pacifics. This one rode like a coach, but the box was big and I could see some hard work for firemen in future as the drivers and the traffic people found out what a Pacific could do with a big train. We should have to watch our step, and not be too ready to work them hard.

CHAPTER FIFTEEN

Some Highlights

FOUR TRACKS

UNLESS TRAFFIC IS SPARSE, the running of fast trains and slow trains on a two-track route soon shows its limitations. The provision of an additional line for each direction of running makes matters much easier because, in principle at least, the passenger trains which are expected to adhere very closely to the time table may use the fast lines, leaving the others for goods trains which do not need to be so closely tied to the rubric.

The cost of the extra lines is heavy and in some places prohibitive. The GN suffered badly in this way. At the end of the 19th century, other railways had considerable mileages of four-track main line out of London, eg GW 53, LNW 83, Midland 75, whereas the GN had only about 10 miles. This was from Kings Cross to Greenwood (not to be confused with Wood Green 5½ miles) beyond New Barnet. From there to Potters Bar there were only two tracks and only for 2¼ miles but they included three tunnels and the cost of doubling them was something that only nationalisation could face.

A scheme for "doubling" was instituted in 1881 and completed in 1890 but it was only patchy. For example, the two-mile stretch including Welwyn Viaduct and the two Welwyn tunnels remains undoubled to this day.

There was early recognition of the value of two extra lines over the 11 miles between Essendine and Stoke Summit because there the passenger trains could come down very fast while the gradient could make climbing goods trains very slow. There were also four lines from Peterborough to Werrington Junction but only two from there to Essendine.

There were some odd features here and there. For example, the apparently continuous four-track length from Huntingdon southwards beyond Hitchin was in fact broken at Arlesey and at Three Counties, to avoid any need to alter the stations to admit extra lines.

Before 1900 it was decided that a preferable alternative to doubling the awkward Welwyn bit would be to extend the Wood Green—Enfield branch through Cuffley and Hertford to join the main line near Stevenage. Operationally this would be equivalent to straight doubling only if most of the goods trains used the Enfield loop, instead of the main line, between Stevenage and Wood

Green. The loop might be expected in time to develop a commuter strip that might make heavy passenger traffic for two periods per day, but for the rest of the time there would be plenty of paths for goods trains.

In March 1910 the track had been extended to Cuffley but it was not till 1918 that the loop was completed and even then by only a single line north of Cuffley. It made a burrowing junction with the down main lines at Langley (26 miles from Kings Cross) and a flat junction with the up lines. For a long initial period it was used only by goods trains run on an "Absolute-Permissive" system, which raised some frownful doubts, but no one seemed to get killed after all. It did not become fully operational with passenger trains to Hertford till 1924.

The earthworks involved in laying the line were very considerable and they included the Ponsbourne Tunnel slightly exceeding the $1\frac{1}{2}$ miles length of the Queensbury Tunnel away up in Yorkshire and thus becoming the longest on the GN. The steepest adverse gradient is 1 in 198 and there are about 8 miles of it altogether, but nothing formidable faced a train running from Langley to Wood Green. There was nothing formidable for a northbound train either, compared with the initial climb at 1 in 55 to cross the main lines at Wood Green. This made traffic controllers think before diverting a heavy down main line train on to the Cuffley loop.

THROUGH WORKING

Many of those whose acquaintance with steam locomotives is limited to their later years may wonder why, in the early 19th century, long distance passenger trains in Britain "changed engines" at several stopping places. One answer, applying to the earliest days of railways, was that the engines could not be relied upon to run very far before "breaking down" by loosening of nuts and other fastenings, or by failure of lubrication. Before starting its day's work, every early locomotive had to be carefully examined, adjusted, tightened-up, oiled and otherwise cossetted, with the knowledge (or suspicion) that some of this would have to be done again after a hundred miles' running. With details improved in the light of experience, weaknesses were overcome, but traditional engine-changing continued in many cases long after there was any technical need for it.

Mr F. A. S. Brown records (Bib. ref. 1 p. 92) that in 1862 Sturrock proposed to run trains from Kings Cross with one engine as far as Grantham ($105\frac{1}{2}$ miles) instead of changing engines at Peterborough ($76\frac{1}{2}$ miles) but as the existing tenders could not hold enough water for the longer journey, he said that a water crane would have to be provided at the stopping-point of northbound engines in Peterborough station and that in the same location there would need to be a pit between the rails "as the drivers will also need to prick their fires".

This last bit is inconsequential. What Sturrock probably meant was that the engines would need to have their ash-pans raked out and this could not be done, nor the ash put out of harm's way, without an inter-rail pit. When this facility had been provided, enginemen would no doubt take advantage of the opportunity of cleaning the fire a bit and disposing of such ash and clinker as could be poked down between the fire-bars. (The alternative possibility of using a rocking grate and a large ashpan with a bottom door had been recognised at the time but it was not effectively implemented in Britain for many years.)

The details of Sturrock's proposal suggest that even the main-line passenger train locomotives of the GN could be given dirty coal and that water-troughs as already in use on the London & North Western Railway might help in the running of GN locomotives over long distances.

The GN operating authorities may well have opposed Sturrock's proposal on the reasonable ground that taking water and "pricking" the fire might take more time than changing engines. Would Sturrock agree to a cut in the allowed running-time to balance extra time taken at the stop?

Sturrock's proposal was accepted in due course, but it was not until after water troughs had been laid down that any GN train ran from Kings Cross to Doncaster without changing engines either at Peterborough or Grantham. But before World War I, lightly loaded large Atlantics were regularly running non-stop between Kings Cross and Wakefield as part of a through working between London and Leeds.

Consequently one wonders why a special train of two coaches hastily commissioned to get from Kings Cross to York as fast as it could, should leave London behind a large Atlantic and then stop to change engines at Grantham. As it turned out, this procedure probably made little difference to the arrival time at York as a North Eastern train hindered the special over the last 25 miles. Perhaps it had been recognised that this would happen and therefore that the special train might just as well stop at Grantham, so that the big Atlantic could get back home as soon as possible, while a smaller engine took the train on to York.

This was a very special occasion, in the early part of World War I. Lord Kitchener and party had left Kings Cross by special train as the first step in a journey to Russia. About an hour later it was found that he had forgotten to take something that he would need and so someone followed him with it by a second special train to York, where his own train awaited its arrival before going on toward Scapa Flow.

The large Atlantic used was No 1442 "the Exhibition engine" and she reached Grantham in 101 min, equal to the best time made in the 1895 race.

From Grantham, Ivatt 4-4-0 No 57 (n22) reached Selby in 63 min. There it was held for 5 min, before continuing in the wake of a North Eastern train.

Kitchener's journey had a bad start but a very much worse finish as he was lost with the sinking of HMS *Hampshire*, presumably by torpedo. Two "specials" from Kings Cross to York in quick succession on a Sunday evening were bound to attract attention.

RACES TO THE NORTH (1888 AND 1895)

Every student of British railway history knows of the "Races to the North" and anyone who does not is likely to be surprised that any organisation so dignified as a British railway could indulge in anything so juvenile as racing. Nevertheless, in a sense, some of them did.

In running a railway in everyday fashion, it always seemed to be a feat to "keep time". One expected trains to arrive "behind time", perhaps not by very much, but punctuality was rather an occasion for comment. There were many circumstances that could help to make a train late, but only the engine and its crew could cause it to be early. So, without going into any detail, one may discern that the probability of lateness was always higher than that of any other possibility. Enginemen knew that there was no point in running certain trains before time because they would certainly be stopped by signal protecting trains ahead. Where traffic was light, running early was more readily possible but it was a nuisance rather than otherwise, to those concerned with controlling traffic.

How, then, can one possibly "race" with trains? Perhaps by laying down a schedule that the locomotive is unlikely to be able to maintain and even so, letting all concerned know that the train *may* be early and even if it is, it is not be be unnecessarily delayed.

But, in the interest of intending passengers, no train should be allowed to leave any station before the publicly booked time of departure. There may be good reasons why a train should arrive late, but none for leaving early. So on a run from London to Edinburgh with several intermediate stops the earliest time of arrival at Edinburgh is determined by what the engine can gain on schedule over the last part of the journey. A "Race to the North" between the trains of the West Coast route and those of the East Coast route was actually a race from Carlisle to Edinburgh (Princes Street) on the one hand, and from Newcastle to Edinburgh (Waverley) on the other.

As it ran trains from Kings Cross only so far as York, the GN had no competitive part in any such contest. This is made clear by the records of running of the 10 am from Kings Cross during the month of August 1888. The time to the first stop at Grantham (105½ miles) varied from 120 min with a 8-footer (n9) to 105 min with 2-2-2 No 238 (n8). The load was eight vehicles (120 tons) in the first case and seven vehicles (105 tons) in the other. The smaller engine just beat the magic mile-a-minute rate, but as that had been achieved on the GWR over 40 *years* earlier it did not suggest the "all-out" effort that one tends to associate with the adjective "racing".

On to York the GN ran even less risk of "burning up the rails". The route is distinctly downhill and like the one from Kings Cross has only one speed-restriction and yet on only one day did the "racing train" beat "even time". No 776 (n10) did this by covering the 82.7 miles in 81 min with seven vehicles. All the other times were between 84 and 93 min. These are "net" times, after subtracting estimates of time lost by delays. The actual times to the stop at York varied only from 88 to 93 min. This suggested an estimable aim to keep to booked time, but that is not what you can call "racing".

Things were different in the "race" in 1895, if only because the rival trains started at 8 pm and travelled for most of the time in darkness or in such approximation to it as one may expect in August. Perhaps the idea was that such passengers as remained awake would not so easily see how fast they were going as they could in daylight. The general aim was to get them as near to the extreme destination (Aberdeen, this time) before daybreak. The racing trains were lighter than those of 1888 and the booked departure times from intermediate stations were gradually made earlier. Insistence on "waiting for time" disappeared.

The New England (Peterborough) drivers responsible for the Kings Cross-Grantham part of the GN running were not amused by this kind of tomfoolery. It was all right trying to work to these fast timings (they said) but you can't expect us to make up for delays. What about our coal bonus? We get paid for saving coal not for burning it!

Stirling had gone off to Scarborough for a holiday (his last, poor chap!) and one of his assistants at Doncaster had to follow him to discuss this point. The head man at New England was then instructed to tell the men to get to Grantham on time or earlier and never mind about coal; that matter could be straightened out later. This may have had some effect as the Kings Cross-Grantham time was brought down to 101 min (Run 1/1, p. 197) by a New England driver whose normal gloom was deepened by orders to burn lovely coal that he would have preferred to save for tomorrow. Run 1/1 is not bad, but a lively young "passed fireman" could probably have knocked 5 min out of its time.

It is remarkable that whilst the race was in progress, high officials of the GN were shooting telegrams back and forth on the subject of tightening time-schedules, without bothering about whether the engines could comply with them or whether the drivers would allow them to try, in opposition to the existing attraction of a coal-saving bonus. What might have worked wonders south of Grantham would have been a promise that coal burned on the racing trips would not be counted and that driver and fireman would each be paid five shillings for every minute they arrived ahead of schedule. This last bit would need to be kept very quiet, but it might well have caused the Stirling singles to have been thrashed as heartily as was old *Hardwicke* in averaging 67 mph from Crewe to Carlisle on the North Western.

But even as it was, Grantham enginemen brought the Grantham-York time down to 76 min (65½ mph start to stop) which was good going, although surpassed by what the North Eastern did, when really stirred, from Newcastle to Edinburgh.

Many members of the public believed that this railway racing was risky and so it was on certain curved parts of the routes. Under emotional excitement, normally cautious people are apt to go to the other extreme and in this affair the wildest running was made by Scotsmen between Edinburgh and Aberdeen, and they were not hoarding coal either!

The GN took no unusual risk in any of their contributions to the racing runs. The only way in which risk-taking could have saved time south of York was by ignoring speed restrictions at Peterborough and Selby. The possible gain was only small and there is no hint that any GN driver of a racing train seriously misjudged his speed at these points. It is far more likely that drivers came right down to the nominal limit to emphasise their disapproval of the whole silly business.

They probably feared that the fastest running in the race might come to be demanded regularly and that might well have happened but in fact the long-term result was just the opposite. It was realised that the speeds attained with loads cut down to quite uneconomic levels were far higher than what was commercially practicable. So a truce was called and a time of $8\frac{1}{4}$ hr from London to Glasgow or Edinburgh was agreed upon. This agreement was not revised until 1932 and for many years the "Scotch expresses' were the least hurried top-rank trains on both routes.

FITTED FREIGHT

On all the Victorian railways of Britain, engines were apt to find great difficulty now and again in getting goods trains up steep gradients, but that was nothing compared with stopping them if they once got going down such grades. Our British goods trains were described as "loose-coupled" which is descriptive enough, but it also implied "unbrakable when going" and in many places it was this feature that set a limit to prudent speed. For quick delivery of long-distance goods, this simply would not do. An "express goods" train needed to have continuous brakes as on passenger trains. Used in this context the word "continuous" means "applicable at any time by the engine driver, regardless of speed".

The much younger term "fitted freight" means a train of vehicles designed to carry goods rather than passengers but fitted with the same kind of brake-apparatus as passenger trains and with screw-couplings, so that they could be "tight-coupled", well-braked and able to average 40 to 45 mph.

The GN started running such trains early in the 20th century from King's Cross to the North and during most of the elapsed part of that century a "fitted freight" left Kings Cross Goods station at about 3.30 pm for Edinburgh and Glasgow. Making good speed in the emptiness of the night, the train delivered its goods ready for distribution from the railway goods yards to all parts of Edinburgh and Glasgow "first thing" next morning, A similarly good service by GN "fitted freights" was from London to Manchester in the very heart of bigger competitors' territory.

ATLANTICS

For many years the GN small Atlantics were daily visitors to York and to Leeds (Central). At both places, Aspinall Atlantics of the L & Y were also to be seen everyday. Some purists used to insist that the type-name Atlantic was not properly applied to an inside-cylinder 4-4-2 because the original use of the name was to American 2/4-4-2s. Certainly it was a bit odd that such different-looking locomotives as a GN 990 and an L &Y 1400 should have a common type name.

The 990 with its original narrow smokebox was not very inspiring in appearance. The 1400 might impress with its apparent size, but it was not beautiful. How did they compare as train-pullers?

To some people it no doubt seemed miraculous that an engine with 7 ft 3 in driving wheels could run at all over the steep gradients of much of the L &Y railway. They could be convinced that the work of the 1400s with 280 ton trains from Manchester to Blackpool or to Southport proved them to be wonderful engines. But on getting down to figures one found that the best work they did was distinctly inferior to the best of the GN small Atlantics. One might give a hint of this by the difference between the maximum loads they regularly took into York and out of it.

There was never anything in the way of a comparative test between these designs, although there was a friendly relation between Ivatt and Aspinall and an L &Y 4-4-0 once made some experimental running on the GN main line. For this purpose a GN tender was substituted for the much smaller L &Y tender and rather dwarfed the engine (No 318).

The most spectacular running of the L &Y Atlantics was in their early days with light trains (many less than 100 tons) on the 40 min expresses over the 36 miles between Manchester (Victoria) and Liverpool (Exchange). They were said to touch 90 mph near Kirby (over the *second* set of water-troughs since Manchester!) and it was a long time before any 990 was observed to run at that rate.

For a time Great Central Atlantics worked Kings Cross-Sheffield trains between Grantham and Sheffield. These trains were not heavy and the running of the GC engines was as lively as that of any GN Atlantic on the stretch between Grantham and Retford.

Of all British Atlantics, those of the North Eastern Railway were perhaps the most closely comparable with the Ivatt large Atlantics in performance. This is suggested by the fact that it was common for East Coast main line trains to exchange GN and NE Atlantics at York and the best performances of large Atlantics and Class Zs before the 1923 grouping were at about the same high level. In later years the Doncaster engines showed up rather more noticeably.

Where the GN Atlantics really excelled was in numbers, so much so indeed that one wonders about their record for availability. By 1911 there were 94 of them. This means that (for imaginative example) if they were spaced equally over the GN line from London to Leeds there would be one for every two miles, whereas in making that journey one could not expect to see more than a couple of dozen at the most. Did this mean that apart from a half dozen that might have been seen between Doncaster and York, more than two thirds of them were not in active service during that period of four hours? It is certainly very remarkable that with this number of "big guns" the GN often provided 4-4-0s to work the heaviest passenger trains between Grantham and York.

It is true that the Atlantics did turn up in some surprising places. In October 1915, for example, the *Railway Magazine* published a "picturesque view" of No 1452 coming out of Crimple Tunnel on the North Eastern Railway near Harrogate. It was picturesque all right, but the enginemen may not have appreciated it. There were few British main line jobs that ended with $4\frac{1}{2}$ miles up at 1 in 90, but that's what they had in running London-Harrogate expresses from Doncaster by way of Church Fenton and Wetherby. Similarly, Harrogate to Spofforth was one of the few places where a pre-grouping train could be doing 70 before passing the first station after starting a regular journey.

MISHAPS

The GNR had only a few accidents that might be called "sensational", the double collision in Welwyn North Tunnel in 1866, that at Abbots Ripton in 1876 and the derailment at Grantham in 1906. The cause of the first was a signalling error, and of the second was freakish weather conditions that prevented signals from returning to the "stop" indication; something was done to make any repetition unlikely.

No explanation of the Grantham accident has ever been proved. A train ran through the station in defiance of signal and timetable and was derailed by excessive speed round a curve shortly afterwards. A probability is that the driver was taken ill and that the fireman omitted to apply the brake before going to his assistance. When he did, he was too late to save the situation and the guard was later still.

On August 6, 1921, a large Atlantic taking a train southwards through Selby station ran into a coach of a train that was wrongly running from the platform line onto the through line. The coach was derailed and pushed against the signal box, which suffered far more damage than anything else. The wrong movement of the starting train was the result of its driver's incorrect reading of badly-placed signals. The signal he accepted as his was actually "off" for the passage of the Atlantic and its train. This was not a GN accident; it is mentioned here only because a GN engine was involved.

SKEGNESS

The GN plentifully advertised Skegness as a holiday resort and as a destination for day excursionists. In 1908 for example, they advertised excursions from Kings Cross to run on Good Friday, Easter Sunday, Easter Monday and Sunday

April 26 at the fare of three shillings for a total distance of some 266 miles, and this at over seven miles a penny was not expensive even at a time when a penny could buy things. An average speed of 44 mph was not bad either.

Such excursions (wind and weather being propitious) were popular and up to ten trains might have to be run to take all the people. They were usually limited to Sundays and Bank Holidays because on other days few passengers were free to frolic and few London Suburban coaches could be spared from their real work.

Use was made of corridor stock for Skegness excursions but there was not enough for them all.

Sunday excursions to Skegness from non-Metropolitan parts of GN territory might have to be "covered" by London suburban stock run down during Saturday night and taken back where it really belonged during Sunday night.

Skegness excursions were commonly run by 0-6-0s or small 4-4-0s, but those out of Kings Cross might have main line passenger train engines, including the large Atlantics.

WHITE CITY

An extraordinary "train" left Doncaster for London on April 23, 1909. It consisted of five wagons, a passenger train brake van and GN locomotives Nos 1 and 1442, covered from smokebox to tender buffer-beam in sheets of snowy whiteness. They were going to the White City Exhibition (Shepherds Bush) and the special covering was to protect the gleaming "exhibition finish" that the engines had been given. The buffer-heads were concealed in giant "boxing-gloves".

The train remained at Hornsey till Sunday April 25 when it was taken by 0-6-0ST No 1201 (n60) from Hornsey by Finsbury Park to Kingsland on the North London Railway. That company took the train by Hampstead Heath and Willesden to Acton. Thence the GW completed the journey, by Old Oak Common to Uxbridge Road goods yard of the West London Railway. Moving the engines into the White City was a non-railway operation. After removal of the special coverings, addition of connecting rods and so on, the engines stood side by side to represent, very beautifully, some 30 years' progress in locomotive design on the GN. No 1 had been withdrawn from service in 1907 with a record of nearly 1½ m miles. All locomotive enthusiasts must be glad that No 1, No 990 and No 251 are all still on permanent public exhibition at York, not indeed in "exhibition finish", but available for examination at any time within prescribed limits.

LOCOMOTIVE EXCHANGE (GN AND LNW, JUNE 1909)

For four weeks in the middle of 1909, an Ivatt large Atlantic (n35) No 1449 worked main line trains of the LNWR between Euston and Crewe while North Western Precursor class 4-4-0 No 412 similarly worked on the GN main line between Kings Cross and Leeds. The object of this exchange was to try to learn something of the relative running costs of the two classes of locomotive in typical main line service. The only cost that could be usefully assessed in such a short period of operation was that of fuel.

On the North Western, No 1449 burned 4·6 lb of Welsh coal per drawbar horsepower hour, while the competing Precursor No 510 burned 5 lb for the same amount of useful work.

On the GN, large Atlantic No 1451 burned 5·2 lb of Yorkshire coal as against 5·6 lb by the Precursor.

The advantage of the Atlantic on the North Western was thus about 8 per cent and on the GN about 6 per cent.

The grate area of the Atlantic was nearly 40 per cent greater than that of the Precursor, and the consequently much lower combustion-rate could be expected to give the bigger engine an advantage. The relative coal consumptions were in the right order and it could be said that the two designs were about equally economical at equal combustion rates per square foot of grate area.

Loads averaged about 240 tons on the GN and 300 tons on the LNW. Booked average speeds ranged from about 50 mph to 55 mph.

It must be added that the duties of the engines in this comparison were unexacting. Mean drawbar horsepower of about 450 on the North Western and 350 on the Great Northern were trivial for the Atlantics and no more than ordinary for the smaller Precursors. Heavier loads would have produced lower coal consumptions per drawbar horsepower hour.

The only aspect of the work that might have daunted any of the enginemen was the start up the 1 in 70 of the Euston-Camden bank for No 1449 with 320 tons. The Atlantic had a nominal adhesion weight of 36 tons but with uncertainty associated with the loading of the rear axle. The Precursor had a minimum of 38 tons to which the backward pull of the drawbar might add a couple of tons when pulling hard. In normal conditions Precursors had no difficulty but there was reason to be a bit uneasy about an Atlantic before the first trial.

On one of the earliest runs of No 1449, her driver was encouraged by an assurance from the LNW pilotman that if he did not get up the bank he would not be the first to fail. But he did not ever fail and soon acquired such confidence on the West Coast main line as to justify a mild reprimand for running too gaily on the curved northbound approach to Stafford.

Ivatt is said to have promised the LNW driver of No 412 a new hat if he got from Kings Cross to Potters Bar in 18 min, but the prize was never claimed.

SIXTY YEARS ON

The Diamond Jubilee (1910) of the GNR was commemorated in the *Railway Magazine* of that year in articles including interesting statistics. During the summer of that year GN daily trains included 45 booked at or over 45 mph start to stop; of these, nine exceeded 56 mph.

The numbers of GN vehicles in the years 1850, 1866, 1896 and 1910 rather suggested that a zenith might be near. During the first and last intervals, the numbers of locomotives were multiplied by 4·8 and 1·3, those of coaches by 3·5 and 1·15, and those of wagons by 18 and 1·19.

It was remarked that a merger of the Great Northern with the Great Central and the Great Eastern was imminent, but the project was in fact abandoned. The wider merger of grouping occurred in 1923, when the railways had not entirely recovered from the effects of the 1914-1918 World War, and improvements on pre-1914 conditions were slow in coming. To quote a particular example, the GN in 1910 brought the Leeds "breakfast car" train into Kings Cross at 11.30 am, after a start at 7.50 am. It was not until 1932 that this train was accelerated; the arrival time was altered to 11.20 am. This gave a very useful ten minutes to any passenger who was going to Paddington to catch the down "Torbay Limited" at noon.

COAL, LESS COAL, SOME OIL, UNEASY END

Gresley's 2/2-8-0s (n76) introduced in 1913 were found to be useful engines for bringing coal trains into London from Peterborough. They were a good 10 per cent more powerful than Ivatt's "Long Toms" (n71) over 50 of which had been doing that job since 1906, and whenever fast running was possible, the pony-truck under the front of the bigger engines made for better riding.

Gresley's first 3/2-8-0 (n77) was the same sort of engine complicated by a third set of "motion" and by a conjugated valve gear that some people found unconvincing. Published comment about the engine had shown more doubt and criticism than anything else. Gresley may have thought that a bit of offsetting "build-up" in the Press would do no harm, but whether that thought was in his mind or not, Mr Charles S. Lake, a journalist with whom Gresley was very friendly, was allowed to ride on No 461 on a regular coal job from New England (Peterborough) to Ferme Park Sidings at Hornsey (London) and reported very favourably in a 10-page article in the *Railway Magazine* for March 1919.

Only a friend, one may surmise, would have made this trip, as a period of 6¾ hours in winter on a footplate hardly big enough for the enginemen themselves was probably no more comfortable than Mr Lake anticipated. A distance of 74 miles was covered in 4½ hr running time, and this is long enough for most people at one "go", but the additional 2¼ hr of standing on a stationary locomotive in strong cold wind must have tried men's patience, if not their souls.

The reporter was favourably impressed with the general running of the engine, but he did not mention any "beautifully even beat". (Too many people could hear the beat themselves without riding on the engine.) On the contrary a specific unevenness was ascribed to a "new piston valve on the inside cylinder".

Mr Lake remarked that the engine had no sand pipes in front of the leading coupled wheels. As the 2/2-8-0s had always been properly provided in this respect, one wonders whether some one had revived the obscure argument (if such there were) for keeping sand pipes away from where they could do most good on the Atlantics. However that may be, the omission was corrected in the later 3/2-8-0s.

The firing was light and frequent in conformity with needs anticipated from observation of the signals. The estimated coal consumption of 92 lb per mile seems reasonable enough for "stop and go" progress of a load of 1300 tons behind the tender. The pay-load was 800 tons of coal in 57 vehicles.

Water was taken at Huntingdon and at Hitchin and there were many other stops to await the opening of a "path" between up passenger trains. Consequently the run from Peterborough to Ferme Park took so long that the enginemen could not be scheduled to work back to Peterborough within any close approximation to the eight-hour day that became the accepted norm for enginemen after World War I. What happened after Mr Lake's trip was that the engine was taken over by a "disposal crew" at Ferme Park to prepare it for a return journey, while the men went down to Kings Cross to ride back home as passengers.

In 1920 Gresley introduced the Class K3 3/2-6-0 (n68) primarily as a mixed traffic engine. Ten or fifteen years later this class of engine was used between Peterborough and Ferme Park with goods trains limited in load to permit them to run fast enough to be slipped through the "bottle-necks" in shorter gaps between passenger trains than could be used by fully loaded 3/2-8-0s. With such trains, New England engine-crews could be scheduled to work to Ferme Park and back in a day.

Two and a half years after his rather slow journey on No 461, Mr Lake rode on two 3/2-6-0s in succession in a trip on the 10.58 am train from Doncaster to Kings Cross. This train was one of the heavy ones specially scheduled to run during the Coal Strike of 1921, to minimise coal consumption by making one engine do the work previously shared by two.

The two engines (Nos 1006 and 1007) were very new, the latest built of the Class K3 3/2-6-0s and they handled the job well. They had not only steam-chest pressure gauges but also superheat pyrometers and such profuse instrumentation would have delighted foot-plate riders in later years. Mr Lake contented himself with reporting that steam-chest pressure was usually 20 lb below boiler pressure and that the superheated steam was usually at about 700 deg F.

The 18-coach train was reported to have 850 passengers, thus showing a numerical near-coincidence with the tons of coal conveyed on Mr Lake's earlier journey from Peterborough to Ferme Park.

The average of 16 similar trips to this showed the K3s to have consumed 104 lb of coal per mile at 51 mph. This may be compared with the 92 lb of No 461 with her 1300 ton train averaging about 17 mph between numerous stops.

Down Essendine Bank No 1006 touched 76 mph which was about the usual maximum in those days for Atlantics in that neighbourhood, and so she did not fall behind schedule in getting down to Peterborough. There she was replaced by No 1007. This prompts the comment that coal could have been saved by allowing No 1006 to work right through to London. But reasons why anything should not have been done can always be imagined.

Here the emergency of the Coal Strike had induced one department to alter the train service very considerably, but to another department it was far less important than the fact that "we've always changed engines on this train at Peterborough."

The running of these heavy passenger trains by mixed traffic engines of dimensionally notable design was very interesting to students of the locomotive. It provided further evidence that big wheels were not essential for ordinary express train speeds, but there was nothing new about that. Every now and then over a century, some small-wheeled engine took on a fast job in emergency and did it quite well. The essential fact, however, is that regular hard running of small-wheeled engines at high speed is more expensive in wear and tear than that of big wheelers on the same work.

The coal strike of 1921 lasted long enough for many British railways to equip some locomotives for burning oil instead of coal. It must have been difficult to get anything so revolutionary going really well in a short time, specially as most people regarded it as only a temporary measure. On no railway were the conversions numerous enough to make any perceptible difference to the general picture. In no case was any converted locomotive reported to develop more power than it had done on coal.

The oil-burning system most widely used on British locomotives was that of the "Scarab" Company. GN locomotives thus provided included Class H3 2/2-6-0s (n67) Nos 1641, 1667, 1671, 1674; Class L1 0-8-2Ts (n75a) No 131 and two 0-6-0STs.

Oil firing obviously reduced very considerably the physical work demanded of firemen and they must have noticed the difference. It is believed, however, that until a fireman had been on the job long enough to have learned how to get oil firing to do just what he wanted, he might often wish he was back with the good old dusty coal that only needed putting on.

The long, hot summer of 1921 declined at last and before the cold weather came in, the miners were back at work. The consequent relief of industrial stress perhaps helped to persuade GN directors to let money flow more freely for the production of the first GN Pacific foreseen for so long, and by April 1922 she was on the road. Very nearly at the end of its history the GN had produced an engine named *Great Northern*.

By that time it also had plenty of large Atlantics, many of them superheated, smaller groups of small Atlantics, 4-4-0s and 2-6-0s and 60 lively 0-6-2Ts. Gresley had already given the locomotive stock an uplift and was all set to go on doing so.

What did GN railwaymen and GN railway enthusiasts think about as

December 31, 1922 wore on? On the following day there were to be some new railways, but no Great Northern. Standing at a platform end at Kings Cross in the evening rush-hour, one of the high spots of GN activity, could anyone imagine that all this would have disappeared by tomorrow? It was hard to think so. It had been vaguely suggested that near-miracles might result from the grouping of the railways, but it would take more than a miracle to displace the GN rolling stock overnight. The lettering was to be altered, true, and even that would take time, but would the daily Kings Cross picture ever be changed more than in the lettering?

Perhaps not. Tomorrow Gresley would still be in charge of GN locomotives and many others besides. Would he not develop locomotive design just as if he were still on the GN as he had been since 1911? Was it likely that the North Eastern Pacific, lately running trial trips, would turn out to be a better engine than the Gresley Pacifics? Had the LNE group any better locomotives than those produced for the GN by Gresley? Was, in fact, any other part of the LNER so good as the old GN? Time, perhaps, would tell.

Some Great Northern Running

To give some idea of what was good running by Great Northern locomotives, Tables 1, 2 and 3 contain details of trips over two sections of the main line by a variety of classes of locomotives with a variety of loads. Intermediate average speeds can be obtained by subtraction and division. Power developed in overcoming gravity may be estimated from the relevant heights of the timing points above datum. Power developed in overcoming train resistance can be estimated only with a wider range of uncertainty because it is impossible now to estimate the resistance of the particular trains concerned and because no information is obtainable now about the speed or direction of the natural wind at the relevant time. A reasonable estimate is that the number of horsepower absorbed by resistance per ton of train is the square of the number of miles per hour divided by 1900. For example, train resistance takes 2 hp per ton at 62 mph.

In Table 1, the stretches that really test the engine are Kings Cross–Potters Bar, and Essendine–Stoke. The "racing ground" is from Hitchin to Huntingdon and the speeds recorded over it are remarkably consistent especially in view of the fact that Run 1/1 was the first section of one of the fastest runs made by the GN during the Railway Race of 1895, and Run 1/8 was a special heavy-load test-run by the second GN Pacific soon after it was built.

Run 1/2 was made in ordinary service with a London–Sheffield–Manchester train. It matched the running of the racing train as far as Hitchin and after that the driver could take things easily although still remaining well ahead of every other run save the first.

Run 1/3 was typical of what the Stirling 2-2-2s continued to do with the light fast trains for ten years and more after the date of this run.

Run 1/4 brings us to much heavier loading and was a good effort by a small Atlantic with a train that stopped at Peterborough but not at Grantham.

Runs 1/5 and 1/6 compare a non-superheated big Atlantic with superheated engines of the same class. The times quoted in 1/6 refer to a run by No 1453 as far as Potters Bar; after that the times are those of a run by No 1442 which was in difficulties on the way out to Holloway because of greasy rails and reluctant sand and took 32 min to pass Potters Bar. After that, No 1442 made some lively running; from Hitchin to Huntingdon she averaged 75 mph and beat the 8-footer on the "racing run" by nearly a minute.

So, assuming that in normal circumstances No 1442 could have equalled No

1453's time to Potters Bar, a superheated Atlantic could beat No 287's time to Peterborough by 4 min. From passing Peterborough to stopping at Grantham, however, No 287 beat No 1442 by 3 min, although the latter was running late.

Finally comes No 1471, first in normal service with 525 tons and then on the test run, although not with a dynamometer-car.

Table 2 refers to an easy part of the main line as is shown by the trend in height figures. The efforts of the Stirling singles, Runs 2/1 and 2/2 were not very strenuous. That of the Ivatt single was better but not much so in view of the size of the engine. There is a jump in load at Run 2/4, but the small Atlantic ran at about the same average speed as that of Runs 2/1, 2/2 and 2/3.

Run 2/5 was a very creditable effort by one of the largest GN 4-4-0s, and so was 2/6, that of the non-superheated Class D2 4-4-0 with 425 tons which covered the ground inside the rather generous 97 min allowed at the time.

Run 2/7 should not really be included as it was made 13 years after the GNR ceased to exist, but the engine was not substantially different from the standard superheated big Atlantic of the GNR. This was an "emergency" run by a GN Atlantic, in this case handled (and pretty roughly) by men with no experience of the type. But after being last at Hougham, No 4404 bashed along with that enormous load to be ahead of the field at Doncaster, and led from there right into York.

Table 3 has an interesting point in that the first and last runs were made by engines with the common No 1007, but differing in every other significant respect. Note may be taken of the similarity of all the times at Hitchin for all loads between 200 and 500 tons and the similarity, 4 min slower, of the times there on Runs 3/7 and 3/8 which were made with specially heavy trains during the Coal Strike in 1921 by markedly different engines. The Atlantic was only slightly slower in getting away from Peterborough, was a minute down at Huntingdon, but picked up a half-minute to Hitchin. After that the 2-6-0 went ahead again and remained so right into the terminus.

Runs 3/1 and 3/2 show No 229 running distinctly faster than the 8-footer which had 35 per cent less load. In Run 3/3 another 2-2-2 did well with a heavy load of 275 tons to get past Potters Bar in less time than any of the bigger engines except No 1470. In Run 3/4, the K3 did not beat the more heavily-loaded Atlantic No 1452 to Hitchin and after that the driver relaxed, possibly because he was up to schedule.

Near the bottom of Table 3 are given estimated figures for drawbar horse-power per square foot of grate area for the Yaxley-Potters Bar length. The light loads on runs 3/1 and 3/2 give low figures, and Runs 3/3, 3/4 and 3/6 are fairly consistent at an average of 29. Because No 1470 was a much larger engine she did not have to exert herself to keep time with 455 tons on Run 3/5.

On Run 3/7, the big Atlantic No 290 with 600 tons was working at about the same intensity as Nos 231, 1001 and 1452.

On Run 3/8, the 3/2-6-0 left all the other engines well behind on the basi of useful power per unit of grate area and, so far as published figures can show, this was probably the best run made by a K3. The times were recorded by the late Mr Charles S. Lake who rode on the engine and were published in the *Railway Magazine* for September 1921. In some other references to this run, the engine-number was incorrectly given as 1001.

The last line in Table 3 "grades" the power output of the engine between Peterborough and Potters Bar in relation to the size of its grate on a basis described in the *Railway Magazine* for July 1956. Grade 20 represents a high class standard. Of the engines mentioned in Table 3, only the K3 No 1007 surpassed this standard, the two Atlantics came near to it and the Stirling 2-2-2 No 231 was close behind them.

A long time after the end of the GN, some of its large Atlantics showed that they could get into Grade 22. A demonstration by No 1404, renumbered 4404 by the LNE, is recorded as the last item in Table 2.

Notes on Tables 1 to 5

Any considerable amount of quantitative information is best presented in tabular form. It minimises time and trouble in finding items and it shows where there are gaps.

In this book, Tables 1, 2 and 3 show how fast certain GN engines could run, while Table 4 shows how slowly GN locomotives grew in size and number.

Table 4 is intended to present a general impression of the numerical strengths of the various classes and of numbers of locomotives produced during the different regimes. The figures are not guaranteed to the last digit.

Table 5 gives some dimensional details of most of the recognisable classes of GN locomotives. The decision as to the amount of detail to be shown in this table is arbitrary. A great deal more might have been given, or a great deal less. Grate area gives an idea of economic maximum sustained power, nominal tractive effort an idea of the economic speed range for any particular drawbar power, and adhesion weight sets an upper limit to the drawbar pull.

Where running numbers (Line 25) are quoted in a "block", eg 1400-1461, the meaning is that the class included a locomotive for each number in the block.

Where running numbers are quoted with an intervening × eg 157 × 168 the meaning is that the class included a locomotive for each of the numbers given and for some of the intervening numbers.

No attempt is made to present a complete list of running numbers of the locomotives of any class unless they happen to have been concentrated in one or two blocks.

The word "accuracy" is often bandied about in connection with anything expressed in figures. The first thing discovered by anyone who sets out to get down to minimum error in anything is that (in most cases) accuracy—meaning exactitude—is impossible. You may work hard to reduce errors to the practicable limit, but some will still remain. Every figure quoted to represent a dimension has a zone of uncertainty unavoidably associated with it.

Exceptions are associated with numbers of separate objects. For example, a locomotive quoted as a 4-4-0 is implied to have exactly 8 wheels—not 7.95 or 8.03, but exactly 8. Each wheel has an exact number of spokes, but nobody bothers to specify it, simply because nobody ever has bothered to do so, except on manufacturing drawings of wheels.

But the quoting of 18 inches as the diameter of the cylinders on a certain class of locomotive is quite different. It does not mean that any locomotive in the class ever had a cylinder of exactly that diameter. Even if a cylinder were exactly 18 in in diameter when standing cold on January 1, it would have a different diameter when hot and a different diameter, even if cold, at the end of March if the engine had done a good month's work in the intervening three months. Similarly it was most unlikely that the two cylinders of a mature engine were of equal diameter at any one time. In Stirling's practice, the diameters measured after general repair of a locomotive were sometimes recorded on the buffer beam, whether they were identical or not. Purist enthusiasts must have been horrified when they were not. Cylinder diameters could vary from the nominal figure by anything up to an inch, and wheel diameters by as much as 3 in. Weight-figures are just as impressionistic.

You may find this rather shocking, if you have been in the habit of thinking of accuracy, but the fact is that it is impossible to measure anything accurately even if it remains constant, and many dimensions of a locomotive did not.

Recognition of this has led me to "round off" nominal tractive effort figures to the first number of thousands of pounds above the calculated figure, to quote weights to the first ton above what may be discerned to be the "official" figure and to refrain from repeating any such things as "1450·1 sq ft".

So the figures in the tables are not guaranteed to be "accurate" even if that word be defined, very loosely and arbitrarily, to mean coincidence with what someone else has quoted.

Table 1

Miles from Kings Cross	Height (ft)	Run	1/1	1/2	1/3	1/4	1/5	1/6	1/7	1/8
		Engine No.	668	100	874	950†	287	1442†	1471†	1471†
		Wheel Arr'g't	2/4-2-2	4-2-2	2-2-2	2/4-4-2	2/4-4-2	2/4-4-2	3/4-6-2	3/4-6-2
		Reference	n9	n12A	n8A	n34	n35	n35	n69	n69
		Load (tons)	101	120	180	350	425	445	525	610
		Year of run	1895	1905	1895	1916	1916	1917	1922	1922
0	40	Kings Cross	0 0	0 0	0 0	0 0	0 0	0 0	0 0	0 0
2·5	120	Finsbury Park				7 30	7 30	6 56	7 30	7 30
12·7	315	Potters Bar	15 00	15 56	18 43	21 00	23 20	21 20	21 25	24 00
17·7	250	Hatfield	19 30	20 34	23 44	26 10	28 45	27 05	26 35	30 00
25·0	300	Knebworth	‡			33 20	36 25		34 30	38 30
31·9	205	Hitchin	33 00	33 12	37 10	39 35	43 00	41 25	41 10	46 00
37·0	125	Arlesey			41 22	43 35	47 05	45 25	45 15	
44·1	90	Sandy			47 36		53 15	50 55	51 15	56 00
51·7	75	St Neots	49 30		54 44	56 40	60 20	57 10	58 10	
58·9	50	Huntingdon	55 30	56 45	61 37	63 20	66 55	63 05	64 50	69 00
63·5	110	Abbots R.	60 05			68 30	72 05			74 00
69·4	20	Holme	65 30			73 30	77 20	73 25	75 15	79 00
76·4	45	Peterborough*	72 00	74 19	79 20	80 40	84 25	80 25	83 05	86 00
79·5	40	*Werrington Jc.*						85 45	6 25	
84·8	45	Tallington						91 45	12 10	
88·6	100	*Essendine Jc.*	84 30		93 07	15 50	99 15	95 55	16 15	101 00
92·2	165	Little Bytham				19 30		100 15	20 25	
97·1	260	Corby				25 35	110 15	107 55	27 15	112 00
100·1	350	*Stoke*	96 00	101 56		29 35	114 40	113 05	31 45	116 00
105·5	220	Grantham	101 00	106 24 pass	112 44	34 55 pass	121 05	120 10	38 05	122 00

† Engine with superheater. * Speed restriction. In practice to about 40 mph. ‡ Speed restricted for bridge repair. Time loss about 1¼ min.

Table 2

Miles from Grantham	Height (ft)	Run	2/1	2/2	2/3	2/4	2/5	2/6	2/7
		Engine No.	235	1008	266	258†	58†	41	4404†
		Wheel Arrangement	2-2-2	2/4-2-2	4-2-2	2/4-4-2	4-4-0	4-4-0	2/4-4-2
		Reference	n8	n11	n12	n34	n22	n21	n35
		Load (tons)	200	200	200	375	410	425	585
		Year of run	pre 1911	pre 1911	pre 1911	1915	1915	1915	1936
0·0	220	Grantham	0 0	0 0	0 0	0 0	0 0	0 0	0 0
4·2	165	Barkston		8 05	6 35				8 17
6·0	130	Hougham	9 20	9 50		9 15	9 30	9 40	10 03
9·9	95	Claypole		13 10	11 20				13 23
14·6	52	Newark	17 05	17 15	15 20	16 35	16 55	17 25	17 23
20·9	38	Carlton	23 20	23 15	20 50	22 10	22 35	23 20	23 22
26·4	140	Tuxford	29 30	29 20	26 20	28 20	28 45	30 10	
28·2	150	Markham							31 31
33·1	65	Retford	36 50	36 25	33 50	35 55	36 35	38 30	36 15
36·2	35	Sutton							38 49
38·4	35	Ranskill	42 20	41 40	39 15				40 37
42·2	50	Bawtry	46 05	45 05	43 00	44 10	45 30	47 45	43 43
44·0	85	Pipers Wood							45 22
45·8	30	Rossington							47 03
50·5	33	Doncaster	56 10	53 50	51 45	53 30	55 00	57 15	51 19
54·7	20	*Shaftholme Jc.*				57·55	pass	62 15	55 36
64·3	20	Templehirst		68 35	66 20				64 42
68·9	20	Selby*		73 35	71 25	72 35		78 35	69 17
73·0	35	Riccall							75 18
75·6	45	Escrick		82 55	80 40	81 15		87 25	78 04
78·5	55	Naburn							80 56
80·7	58	*Chaloner Whin Jc.*							83 09
82·7	58	York		92 25	89 40	90 00		96 50	87 40

† Engine with superheater. * Speed restriction. In practice to about 30 mph. On run 2/5 there were gross delays after Doncaster. On run 2/7 there was a signal check on the approach to York.

Table 3

Miles from Peterborough	Height (ft)	Run Engine No. Wheel Arr'g't Reference Load (Tons) Year of run	3/1 1007 2/4-2-2 n11 130 1909	3/2 229 2-2-2 n8 200 1909	3/3 231 2-2-2 n8 275 1904	3/4 1001† 3/2-6-0 n68 440 1921	3/5 1470† 3/4-6-2 n69 455 1922	3/6 1452† 2/4-4-2 n35 490 1922	3/7 290† 2/4-4-2 n35 600 1921	3/8 1007† 3/2-6-0 n68 605 1921
0	45	Peterborough	0*0	0*0	0 0	0 0	0 0	0 0	0 0	0 0
3·8	50	Yaxley			6 30	6 10	6 45	6 55	8 05	8 00
7·0	20	Holme		9 03	9 49	9 0	9 50	10 10	11 40	
12·9	110	Abbots Ripton	13 42	14 57	16 22	15 25	15 55	16 40	18 30	
14·4	130	Leys				17 25	17 35	18 35	20 45	
17·5	50	Huntingdon	19 08	19 43	21 39	20 40	20 35	21 45	24 05	23 00
20·4	38	Offord			24 17			24 20		
24·7	75	St Neots	25 44	25 43	28 30	28 30	27 25	28 25	31 00	
28·9	65	Tempsford						32 40		
32·3	90	Sandy			36 04	36 10	35 00	36 00	39 00	
35·3	105	Biggleswade			39 05			39 10		
39·4	125	Arlesey	40 14	38 52		43 30	42 30	43 45	47 00	
44·5	205	Hitchin	45 59	43 53	49 17	49 35	47 55	49 25	53 35	53 00
47·8	300	Stevenage	50 12	47 51		54 40	53 20	54 00	59 30	
51·4	300	Knebworth	54 09	51 39	58 03		57 40	58 10		
54·4	320	Woolmer Green				61 20			66 35	
58·7	250	Hatfield	61 00	58 54	65 21	67 05	64 45	65 35	72 25	69 00
63·7	315	Potters Bar	66 23	64 15	70 34	72 45	69 55	70 50	78 00	75 00
71·4	120	Wood Green					76 55	78 05		
73·9	120	Finsbury Park	76 00	74 20	79 57		79 25	80 35		
76·4	40	Kings Cross	80 17	78 15	84 10	87 00	83 40	84 40	92 35	90 00

* Passed at 30–40 mph.   † Engine with superheater.

	3/1	3/2	3/3	3/4	3/5	3/6	3/7	3/8
Speed (mph) from Yaxley to Potters Bar	59·5	61·7	56·1	54·0	57·0	56·2	51·3	53·7
Estimated dhp per ton	2·16	2·31	1·94	1·80	2·0	1·94	1·64	1·78
Estimated dhp	280	462	530	790	910	950	985	1080
Grate area (sq ft)	20	18·4	18·4	28·0	41·5	31·0	31·0	28·0
dhp/sq ft	14	25	29	28	22	30·5	31·8	38·5
Grade	8	14	16	16	12	17	18	22

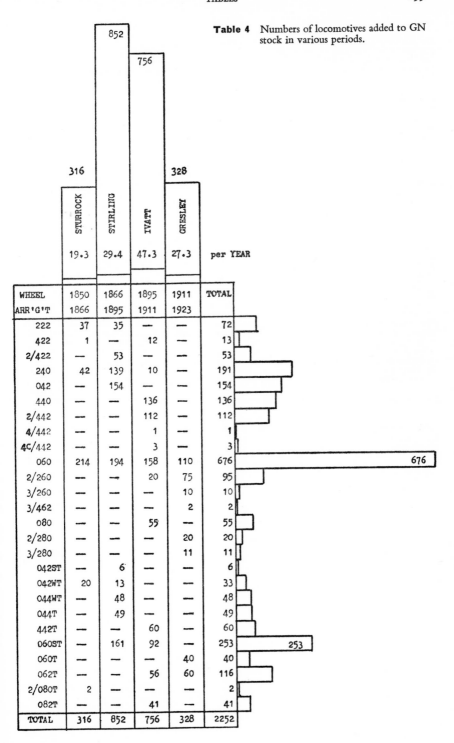

Table 4 Numbers of locomotives added to GN stock in various periods.

	STURROCK	STIRLING	IVATT	GRESLEY	
	316	852	756	328	
per YEAR	19.3	29.4	47.3	27.3	per YEAR
WHEEL ARR'G'T	1850 1866	1866 1895	1895 1911	1911 1923	TOTAL
222	37	35	—	—	72
422	1	—	12	—	13
2/422	—	53	—	—	53
240	42	139	10	—	191
042	—	154	—	—	154
440	—	—	136	—	136
2/442	—	—	112	—	112
4/442	—	—	1	—	1
4C/442	—	—	3	—	3
060	214	194	158	110	676
2/260	—	—	20	75	95
3/260	—	—	—	10	10
3/462	—	—	—	2	2
080	—	—	55	—	55
2/280	—	—	—	20	20
3/280	—	—	—	11	11
042ST	—	6	—	—	6
042WT	20	13	—	—	33
044WT	—	48	—	—	48
044T	—	49	—	—	49
442T	—	—	60	—	60
060ST	—	161	92	—	253
060T	—	—	—	40	40
062T	—	—	56	60	116
2/080T	2	—	—	—	2
082T	—	—	41	—	41
TOTAL	316	852	756	328	2252

Table 5

The following symbols are used throughout the tables on pp. 200–205.
Engineers: A—Sturrock, P—P. Stirling, I—Ivatt, G—Gresley.
Valve type and pos.: F—Flat, P—Piston (1—above cyl, 2—between cyl and 3—below cyl)
Valve gear: S—Stephenson, W—Walschaerts (R—with rocking levers or rocking shafts).

References	n1	n2	n3	n4	n5	n6	n7	n8	n8A
Engineer	A	A	A	A	A	P	P	P	P
Wheel arr'g't	222	222	222	422	222	222	222	222	222
GN Class	91	201	203	215	229	B F	Q	Q2	Q3
LNE class	—	—	—	—	—				
Number built	10	2	12	1	12	12	2	10	11
Date of first	1851	1850	1852	1853	1860	1868	1885	1885	1892
Date of last	1852	1851	1853	1853	1861	1870	1885	1888	1894
Grate area (sq ft)	13	15	13·6	20·3	20·5	16·3	17·3	18·4	18·4
Boiler barrel									
dia (in)	48	46	48	52	48	47	47	48	48
length (in)	120	130	120	144	120	126	126	137	137
Heat surf (sq ft)									
firebox	97	80	115	155	177	90	92	109	109
tubes	875	720	875	1565	883	922	876	1000	940
superheater	—	—	—	—	—	—	—	—	—
Nom TE (1000 lb)	7	8	8	9	10	10	13	14	14
Adhesion wt (tons)	12	10	11	13	13	15	17	17½	17½
Engine ,, ,,	29	24	28	38	35	34	40	40	41
Tender ,, ,,	20	20	20	32	33	27	39	39	42
Boiler pressure (lb/sq in)	120	120	120	130	150	130	150	160	160
Cyl dia (in)	15	16	16	17	17	17	18½	18½	18½
Piston stroke (in)	21	22	22	24	22	24	26	26	26
Wheel dia (in)	78	72	78	90	84	85	91	91	91
Valve type & pos.	F2	F2	F2	F2	F2	F2	F2	F2	F2
Valve gear	S	S	S	S	S	S	S	S	S
Description p.	38		38	36		39	39	39	39
Illustration p.						49			50/117
Running Nos	91–99	201/2	203–214	215	229–240	4×215	232/8	229–31 233–37 239–40	871–80 981

n1 "converted Crampton" n2 "Jenny Lind" n3 "Large Hawthorn"

References	n9	n10	n11	n12	n12A	n13	n14	n15	n16
Engineer	P	P	P	I	I	A	A	A	A
Wheel arr'g't	2/422	2/422	2/422	422	422	240	240	240	240
GN class	G	G2	G3	W	W2	71	223	251	264
LNE class	—	—	—	—	—	—	—	—	—
Number built	37	10	6	1	11	20	6	10	6
Date of first	1870	1884	1894	1898	1900	1851	1855	1866	1866
Date of last	1882	1893	1895	1898	1901	1851	1855	1866	1867
Grate area (sq ft)	17·8	17·8	20	23·2	23·2	14·5	15	21	20
Boiler barrel									
dia (in)	47	48	50	52	52	46	48	48	46
length (in)	137	137	133	136	136	120	120	120	120
Heat surf (sq ft)									
firebox	122	109	122	126	126	102	110	130	121
tubes	1043	940	910	1144	1144	904	872	900	907
superheater	—	—	—	—	—	—	—	—	—
Nom TE (1000 lbs)	12	13	16	14	16	9	9	11	—
Adhesion wt (tons)	15	17	20	18	18	19	23	25	11
Engine " "	39	45	50	48	49	28	33	37	27
Tender " "	27	34	42	41	41	20	25	26	38
Boiler pressure	140	160	170	170	175	130	130	150	150
(lb/sq in)									
Cyl dia (in)	18	18	19½	18	19	16	16½	16½	17
Piston stroke (in)	28	28	28	26	26	22	22	22	24
Wheel dia (in)	97	97	97	91	91	72	78	72	84
Valve type & pos.	F2	F2	F2	F2	F1	F2	F2	F2	F2
Valve gear	S	S	S	S	SR	S	S	S	S
Description p.	40	40	41	42	43	46	46	46	46
Illustration p.	49/123		124		50	46	46	51/123	46
Running Nos	1×671	771–8 1001/2	1003–8	266	92–100 261–5 267–70	71–90	223–8	251–60	264–9

References	n17	n18	n19	n20	n21	n22	n23	n24	n25
Engineer	P	P	I	I	I	I	P	P	P
Wheel arr'g't	240	240	240	440	440	440	042	042	042
GN class	280 H	H2–H5	H6	S–S3	V–V3	D1	A A2	A3–4	Reb.
LNE class	—	—	—	D3	D2	D1	—	—	—
Number built	22	117	10	11	110	15	121	33	2
Date of first	1867	1874	1897	1896	1898	1911	1867	1882	1874
Date of last	1871	1895	1897	1899	1909	1911	1879	1895	1874
Grate area (sq ft)	16·3	16·3	17·8	17·3	20·8	19·0	16·3	16·3	14
Boiler barrel									
dia (in)	47	49	52	52	56	56	47	49	48
length (in)	120	122	121	121	121	121	120	120	120
Heat surf (sq ft)									
firebox	94	92	103	103	120	120	95	92	85
tubes	992	837	1020	1020	1130	852	743	824	820
superheater	—	—	—	—	—	258	—	—	—
Nom TE (1000 lb)	12	14	16	15	15	16	13	15	13
Adhesion wt (tons)	26	28	29	28	31	36	26	27	26
Engine " "	37	39	42	45	48	53	32	36	34
Tender " "	27	41	38	38	41	43	27	35	27
Boiler pressure	150	160	170	170	170	160	140	160	140
(lb/sq in)									
Cyl dia (in)	17	17½	18	17½	17½	18½	17½	17½	18
Piston stroke (in)	24	26	26	26	26	26	24	24	24
Wheel dia (in)	79	79	79	79	79	80	67	67	72
Valve type & pos.	F2	F2	F2	F2	F2	P1	F2	F2	F2
Valve gear	S	S	S	S	S	SR	S	S	S
Description p.	46	46	46	46	47	47	44	45	45
Illustration p.		51	52	55	56		53	119	
Running Nos	54–63 725–34 261/2	51×1000	1061 –1070	400 1071 –1080	41–50 1180 1301–99	51–65	9×600	10×960	67 70

References	n26	n27	n28	n29	n30	n31	n32	n33
Engineer	A	P	P	P	P	P	P	I
Wheel arrangement	042WT	042WT	042ST	044WT	044T	044T	044T	442T
GN class	241	D	N N2	K K2	O	R	R2	TXX2
LNE class	—	—	—	—	—	—	—	C12
Number built	20	13	6	48	16	29	4	60
Date of first	1865	1868	1876	1872	1881	1889	1895	1898
Date of last	1866	1871	1878	1881	1885	1895	1895	1907
Grate area (sq ft)	12·5	14	12·8	12·8	16·3	16·3	16·3	17·8
Boiler barrel								
dia (in)	48	47	47	46	49	49	49	52
length (in)	120	120	111	118	121	121	121	121
Heat surf (sq ft)								
firebox	80	100	74	81	100	100	100	103
tubes	790	820	689	806	830	830	830	1020
superheater	—	—	—	—	—	—	—	—
Nom TE (1000 lbs)	12	12	16	13	16	17	17	18
Adhesion wt (tons)	27	27	27	27	31	35	33	35
Engine ,, ,,	41	42	38	41	50	54	52	62
Tender ,, ,,	—	—	—	—	—	—	—	—
Boiler pressure (lb/sq in)	150	130	140	140	150	160	160	170
Cyl dia (in)	16¼	17½	17½	17½	17½	18	18	17½
Piston stroke (in)	22	24	26	24	24	26	26	26
Wheel dia (in)	66	67	61	67	61	67	67	67
Valve type & pos.	F2	F2	F2	F2	F2	F2	F2	F2
Valve gear	S	S	S	S	S	S	S	S
Description p.	47	48	48	48	48	48	48	65
Illustration p.				54		54	54	119
Running Nos	241–50 270–9	116 ×132	501 ×632	93 ×657	658 ×765	766 ×940	941–4	1009 ×1020 1501–50

References	n34	n35	n36	n37	n38	n39	n40	n41	n42
Engineer	I	I	I	I	I	I	I	G	G
Wheel arr'g't	2/442	2/442	4/442	4C/442	4C/442	4C/442	442	4/442	2/442
GN class	U	LU	Z	ZZ	—	ZZ2	Z reb	279	n38 reb
LNE class	C2	C1	—	—	—	—	C2	C1	C1
Number built	21	91	1	1	1	1	1	1	1
Date of first	1898	1902	1902	1905	1905	1907	1911	1915	1917
Date of last	1903	1911	1902	1905	1905	1907	1911	1915	1917
Grate area (sq ft)	24·5	31	24·5	31	31	31	24·5	31	31
Boiler barrel									
dia (in)	56	66	55	66	62	66	55	66	62
length (in)	156	196	168	196	143	174	168	186	143
Heat surf (sq ft)									
firebox	140	141	140	141	170	144	140	138	167
tubes	1300	2360	1163	2360	2344	2208	1080	1882	1367
superheater	—	—	—	—	—	—	310	427	280
Nom TE (1000 lb)	17	17	17	15	30	18	16	22	19
Adhesion wt (tons)	31	36	33	37	37	37	33	40	38
Engine ,, ,,	58	69	59	70	71	70	58	74	71
Tender ,, ,,	41	41	39	41	41	41	39	43	43
Boiler pressure (lb/sq in)	175	175	175	200	200	200	170	170	170
Cyl dia (in)	19	19	15	13 16	14 23	13 18	18½	15	20
Piston stroke	24	24	20	20 26	26 26	20 26	26	26	26
Wheel dia (in)	79	80	80	80	80	80	80	80	80
Valve type & pos.	F2	F2	P1*	F1 F2	P1 F1	F1 F1	P1	P1 P3	P1
Valve gear	S	S	SR†	W S	W W	W W	SR	WR	W

References	n34	n35	n36	n37	n38	n39	n40	n41	n42
Description p.	66	67	101	103	'104	104	102	102	104
Illustration p.	57/124	59/60	58	61	61	62	59	62	61
Running Nos	250 ×260 949‡ ×990	251 272–301 1400–61 except 292–1421	271	292 Comp.	1300 Vulcan Comp.	1421 Comp.	271	279	1300

* In the first rebuild this item was P1 F1
† In the first rebuild this item was W SP1
‡ No 990 was named "Henry Oakley"

References	n43	n44	n45	n46	n47	n48	n49	n50	n51
Engineer	A	A	A	A	A	P	P	P	I
Wheel arr'g't	060	060	060	060	060*	060	060	060	060
GN class	—	—	—	—	—	474 E	I	—	—
LNE class	—	—	—	—	—	—	—	J3 J7	J1 J5
Number built	31	30	20	63	70	37	6	151	113
Date of first	1850	1851	1851	1853	1865	1867	1871	1874	1898
Date of last	1851	1853	1853	1866	1866	1873	1874	1896	1899
Grate area (sq ft)	13	14·5	15	15	23·6	17·8	18·4	16·3	17·8
Boiler barrel									
dia (in)	46	50	52	51	50	47	51	49	52
length (in)	120	129	127	127	118	120	136	121	121
Heat surf (sq ft)									
firebox	78	100	116	123	113	94	112	92	103
tubes	815	900	994	1176	970	986	1240	830	1020
superheater	—	—	—	—	—	—	—	—	—
Nom TE (1000 lb)	10	12	12	11	19*	13	20	18–21	19
Adhesion wt (tons)	28	30	31	34	64*	33	40	37	41
Engine „ „	28	30	31	34	35	33	40	37	41
Tender „ „	20	21	21	25	29	27	30	35	41
Boiler pressure (lb/sq in)	120	130	130	130	140	130	140	140–170	170
Cyl dia (in)	16	16	16½	16	16 12	17	19	17½	17½
Piston stroke (in)	22	24	24	24	24 17	24	28	26	26
Wheel dia (in)	60	60	63	63	60 49	61	61	55 61	61
Valve type & pos.	F2	F2	F2	F2	F2 F2	F2	F3	F2	F2
Valve gear	S	S	S	S	S	S	SR	S	S
Description p.	31	31	31	31	31/9	31	32	31	31
Illustration p.					63 –			64	
Running Nos	116 ×167	168–97	308–27	328–90	400–69	4×380	145 ×376	101 ×1090	315 ×1173

* With steam tender.

References	n52	n53	n54	n55	n56	n57	n58	n59	n60
Engineer	I	I/G	I	P	P	P	P	P	I
Wheel arr'g't	060	060	060	060ST	060ST	060ST	060ST	060ST	060ST
GN class	EE	J22	J21	C	J J2	M M2	J3 J4	M3–5	M6 M7
LNE class	J1 J5	J6	J2	—	—	J54–6	J57	J53	J52
Number built	15 20	110	10	8	2 6	35 43	8	57	92
Date of first	1908	1911	1912	1868	1872	1874	1882	1891	1894
Date of last	1910	1922	1912	1873	1874	1891	1892	1897	1909
Grate area (sq ft)	19	19	19	12·7	11·5	16	16	16	17·8
Boiler barrel									
dia (in)	56	56	56	45	47	47	47	47	52
length (in)	121	121	121	122	120	121	120	121	121
Heat surf (sq ft)									
firebox	120	120	120	80	73	83	83	83	103
tubes	1130	852	852	480	500	715	715	715	1020
superheater	—	258	258	—	—	—	—	—	—
Nom TE (1000 lb)	18 20	21	20	13	13	16	22	22	22
Adhesion wt (tons)	47	53	53	30	27	41 43	41	43	52
Engine ,, ,,	47	53	53	30	27	41 43	41	43	52
Tender ,, ,,	43	43	43	—	—	—	—	—	—
Boiler pressure (lb/sq in)	170	170	170	130	130	130	170	170	170
Cyl dia (in)	18	19	19	17	16	17½	17½	18	18
Piston stroke (in)	26	26	26	24	22	26	24	26	26
Wheel dia (in)	68 62	62	68	61	49	55	49	55	55
Valve type & pos.	F1	P1	P1	F2	F2	F2	F2	F2	F2
Valve gear	SR	SR	SR	S	S	S	S	S	S
Description p.	31	31	31	33	33	33	33	33	33
Illustration p.			64			113			
Running Nos	1–15 21–40	521–610 621–40	71–81	124 ×398	470–1 136 ×604	139 ×853	134 ×687	854 ×980	111 155 1201–90

References	n61	n62	n63	n64	n65	n66	n67	n68	n69‡
Engineer	I	G	G	G	I	G	G	G	G
Wheel arr'g't	062T	062T	060T	060T	2/260	2/260	2/260	3/260	3/462
GN class	MM	N2	J23	J23	—	H2	H3	H4	A1
LNE class	N1	N2	J51	J50	—	K1	K2	K3	A1
Number built	56	60	30	10	20	10	65	10	2
Date of first	1906	1920	1913	1922	1899	1912	1914	1920	1922
Date of last	1912	1921	1919	1922	1900	1913	1921	1921	1922
Grate area (sq ft)	18·4	19	17·8	16·3	16·7	24·5	24·5	28	41·5
Boiler barrel									
dia (in)	56	56	48	46½	55	56	66	72	77
length (in)	121	121	121	126	120	140	138	138	228
Heat surf (sq ft)									
firebox	120	118	112	112	120	137	144	182	215
tubes	1130	880	650	870	1260	980	1520	1720	2715
superheater	—	207	230	—	—	303	403	407	525
Nom TE (1000 lb)	17	20	24	24	19	22	22	30	30
Adhesion wt (tons)	52	53	57	57	38	52	54	60	60
Engine ,, ,,	66	70	57	57	45	62	64	72	93
Tender ,, ,,	—	—	—	—	38	43	43	43	56
Boiler pressure (lb/sq in)	170	170	175	175	175	170	170	180	180
Cyl dia (in)	17½	19	18½	18½	18	20	20	18½	20
Piston stroke (in)	26	26	26	26	24	26	26	26	26
Wheel dia (in)	68	68	56	56	61	68	68	68	80
Valve type & pos.	F1	P1	F1	F1	F1	P1	P1	P1†	P1†
Valve gear	SR	SR	SR	SR	SR	W	W	W*	W*

References	n61	n62	n63	n64	n65	n66	n67	n68	n69‡
Description p.	34	34	33	33	75	76	76	78	81
Illustration p.	114	114	113		115	116	116	116	128
Running Nos	190	1606–15	157	221–30	1181	1630–9	1640	1000–9	1470–1‡
	1551–99	1721–70	×168		–1200		–1704		
	1600–5		211–20		Baldwin				

* Holcroft-Gresley conjugating mechanism for "inside" valve
† "Inside" valve alongside inside cylinder.
‡ No. 1470 was named "Great Northern".
 No. 1471 was named "Sir Frederick Banbury".

References	n70	n71	n72	n73	n74	n75	n75A	n76	n77
Engineer	A	I	I	I/G	I	I	I/G	G	G
Wheel arr'g't	2/080T	080	080	080	082T	082T	082T	2/280	3/280
GN class	—	Y	K1	K2	YT	L1	L1 reb	O1	O2
LNE class	—	Q1	Q2	Q3	—	—	R1	O1	O2
Number built	2	45	10	1	1	40	41	20	11
Date of first	1866	1901	1909	1918	1903	1904	1918	1913	1918
Date of last	1866	1906	1909	1918	1903	1906	1926	1919	1921
Grate area (sq ft)	20	24·5	24·5	24·5	24·5	17·8	24·5	27·5	27·5
Boiler barrel									
dia (in)	52	55	55	66	55	49	55	66	66
length (in)	164	153	153	138	153	141	153	186	186
Heat surf (sq ft)									
firebox	100	137	137	144	137	108	135	162	164
tubes	1450	1300	1027	1520	1300	936	1027	1922	1870
superheater	—	—	343	403	—	—	254	570	431
Nom TE (1000 lb)	19	28	31	28	28	23	28	32	37
Adhesion wt (tons)	56	55	58	62	66	59	61	68	67
Engine „ „	56	55	58	62	79	71	73	77	76
Tender „ „	—	41	43	43	—	—	—	43	43
Boiler pressure (lb/ sq in)	140	175	175	175	170	170	170	170	180
Cyl dia (in)	18¼	20	21	20	20	18	20	21	18¼
Piston stroke (in)	24	26	26	26	26	26	26	28	26
Wheel dia (in)	54	55	55	55	55	55	55	56	56
Valve type & pos.	F2	F1	P1	P1	F1	F1	F1	P1	P1†
Valve gear	S	SR	SR	SR	SR	SR	SR	W	W*
Description p.	89	89	89	90	90	90	90	92	93
Illustration p.	122	120		120	122		122	120	121
Running Nos	472–3	401–45	446–55	420 (reb.)	116	117–56	116–56	456–60 462–76	461 477–86

* Holcroft-Gresley conjugating mechanism for "inside" valve (except on No. 461).
† "Inside" valve alongside inside cylinder (except on No 461).

CONCLUSION

In this book we have looked back at the steam locomotive as employed on a particular British railway. We have touched only the "high spots" of the story, and it may therefore have appeared to us to be more glamorous than it really was. The railways, even well back in Victoria's reign, were struggling always against rising costs just as we are all struggling a century later. In spite of that, the Great Northern produced strong engines to get its top-rank passenger trains to their destinations faster than the competing trains ran, and those were the engines that attracted the keenest attention from enthusiastic admirers. Those were the engines that provided the most striking and varied highlights of history examined in this book. But the dividend-earning goods engines tended to remain unsung. They did not go fast and they did not pull the public except on Bank Holidays. There was neither inducement nor opportunity for enthusiasts to study their details or performance. So any book of this kind is unbalanced and it must be so. Enthusiasm for the steam locomotive and its history is an emotional interest in particular examples of an elemental type of machine that was just one item in the complex assembly of fixed and moving material and men that constituted a railway.

Students of Great Northern steam were numerous and wide spread. Some saw it at work in the fens, some in London, some in the West Riding, some at York, some even at Stafford. For half a century at least the last GN word in locomotives was renowned throughout Britain. Stirling's 8-footers held the stage for nearly thirty years, the small Atlantics for four, the large Atlantics for twenty and the Gresley Pacifics for two years as GN engines, and very much longer under later ownership.

These periods draw attention to the low rate of change of conditions on railways after about 1850. By then the pattern of the large British railways had been set, and the whole railway system had set the pattern of transport in Britain. After fifty years, the immortality of that pattern could be doubted as the combination of the pneumatic tyre and the light and compact internal-combustion engine had shown that very lively speeds could be reached on public roads. From then on, railway managers became apprehensive but this was not at all obvious to every student of the steam locomotive. There were at least fifty years of steam locomotive development to come, fifty years over which the interest of amateurs in locomotives and railways grew stronger, and as yet the afterglow of historical interest is hardly less intense than was the climax.

Right down to the last of them, GN engines were noisy workers. Steam blasted from most of their chimneys with a metallic clatter and brought plenty of sparks and bright cinders with it, as anyone could easily see unless the sun were shining on the engine.

Along the GN main line after dark, the trains were gleaming snakes each blowing red lights up into the sky and chattering invective after them. Small boys—and big ones—were bound to think that it was all magnificent, but it was not unique. The North Western engines were almost as brilliantly bad on the steeper gradients of their main line but the GN engines could also show fiery fury on the down-grades.

Development of design under Gresley gradually reduced coal-consumption, rockets and line-side fires in the days of the LNER; the visual drama diminished. When, many years later, the end of good coal was specifically promised by the National Coal Board, oil moved in, all drama moved out, and British Railways began to seek solvency without steam.

The author of any such book as this has to carry out dismal chores scarcely imaginable by the average reader and he can endure them only because in doing so he may be reminded of some of the most interesting bits of his past. Writing the book brings some of what was dead to life again in the mind of the writer. He hopes that reading it may do as much for the reader.

But can anyone hope to convey in words the difference between a polished locomotive standing cold and dead in a museum or elsewhere and the same engine, oily and a bit grimy, with white-hot fire, bumping, lurching and quivering along at 75 mph with a dozen coaches? Will future readers credit that firemen commonly shovelled half a hundredweight of coal a minute for hours on end in dust and heat competing with rain-water and cold draughts? But they did!

In 1912 A. Rosling Bennett foresaw a time when it would be hard to believe that every locomotive had a fire. It was a fire, moreover, hot enough to keep one at a distance, but it warmed the body hardly more than recollection of live locomotives may warm the heart.

On British rails, fires are now found only in goods guards' vans. The hardest work any engineman does is to climb into his cushioned seat. His most anxious moment is when he finds, too late to stop, that some honest, God-fearing num-skull has left an odd hundred tons of hardware on the main line just for a minute or two. On the railway now we have greater power, higher speed, greater risk and higher cost than ever before.

At still higher cost and far greater risk one may join the rabble on the road and endure—choice product of mechanisation—the crude drudgery of steering by hand. Or one may, with the support of flat, paper-thin tin boxes full of fire-fluid over red-hot engines, fly through the air, serene in certainty that the thing will get back to earth (or sea) eventually, one way or another.

The supreme travellers (so far) leave the air altogether and seek a better world on some more heavenly body than this.

Never look back, the wise wits warn us, but which way offers more?

BIBLIOGRAPHY

1. *Great Northern Locomotive Engineers Vol. I* F. A. S. Brown (Allen & Unwin)
2. *The Great Northern Railway* O. S. Nock (Ian Allan)
3. *Master Builders of Steam.* H. A. V. Bulleid. (Ian Allan)
4. *The Stirling Singles* K. H. Leech & M. G. Boddy (David & Charles)
5. *The Locomotives of the Great Northern Railway (1847–1910)* G. F. Bird (Locomotive Publishing Co.)